EDUCATIONAL ADMINISTRATION

IN CANADA

SECOND EDITION

T. E. Giles
University of Calgary

Detselig Enterprises Limited
Calgary, Alberta

T. E. GILES
Professor, Educational Administration
The University of Calgary

Other books by T. E. Giles

Educational Accountability, 1972
Educational Administration, 1972
Educational Administration for the Beginning Teacher, 1973
Educational Administration in Canada, First Edition, 1974
Strategies for Instruction and Organization (with C. Braun), 1976

© 1978, 1974 by Detselig Enterprises Limited
6147 Dalmarnock Dr. N.W.
Calgary, Alberta T3A 1H3

Printed in Canada   ISBN 0-920490-08-5

PREFACE

This text is designed for those education students who will soon be entering the classrooms of the nation as newly certified teachers —those men and women who are preparing themselves for service as professional teachers. The primary purpose is to examine the school and the role of the teacher within the legal and structural setting as provided by the neighborhood, municipal, provincial, national and professional communities. Sufficient historical perspective and current examples have been added to provide depth and make the present legal and structural setting more understandable.

Many expectations are held for the teacher. Some of these are structured and comprehendable, others although very real, are somewhat elusive and difficult to describe. Frequently, these expectations appear to stand in contradiction to each other, and to the expectations which the teacher himself holds for the task of teaching in modern society.

The teacher has many publics to serve—the students, professional colleagues, central office staff, department of education officials, and parents to name but a few. The teacher lives and works educationally in a number of communities. The neighborhood and its school; the various levels of municipal government, especially the school board and central office staff; the department of education and the various activities, services, laws and regulations to be found at that level;the national scene including the aspirations and desires of the Canadian people; and the community of professional teachers all of which places its own set of expectations upon the classroom teacher. It is not possible for the teacher to disregard these forces. However, by understanding the structure within which he operates, the teacher will be better able to cope—or at least, be better able to avoid some of the sanctions which can be brought to bear by different referent groups.

The first part of the text deals with the development of the Canadian design for education; the second part with the structure and financing of Canadian education; the third with teacher relationships, emphasizing the direct contacts of the teacher with his publics; the last part with teaching as a profession.

Much of the information contained in this book will be useful to the school administrator but the main emphasis is on providing the classroom teacher with information on the structure within which he operates.

Second Edition

Although some of the material in the second edition remains the same as in the first edition, some chapters were completely rewritten and all others up-dated, with sections added. The author wishes to acknowledge with thanks the assistance given by Dr. A. J. Proudfoot in writing the first part of chapter thirteen, relating to merit rating and merit pay, and to other members of the Department of Educational Administration for their thoughtful suggestions. The provincial teachers' associations were helpful in up-dating information relative to their associations, an assistance which was appreciated.

TABLE OF CONTENTS

LIST OF FIGURES

DEVELOPMENT OF THE CANADIAN DESIGN OF EDUCATION

PART ONE

1

Education in Early Canada

Introduction

The Canadian educational plan, or organization, developed over a period of time, and is still developing. At no time was there produced a master document, or model, for education in Canada. True, the basic act establishing Canada as a country containing four provinces and other territories did include education in its constitutional concerns, but this inclusion was hardly more than the acceptance of what had already developed on the educational scene from as far back as the middle of the eighteenth century. To a certain extent the educational provisions of the 1867 B.N.A. Act set the stage for the Acts establishing the next six provinces and will no doubt be influential in the Act establishing the next two provinces (Yukon and Northwest Territories). The B.N.A. Act essentially put into writing two already accepted principles, first, that education was a provincial, rather than a federal, right; secondly, under certain conditions, the two religious groups, Protestants and Roman Catholics could establish public school systems based on one or the other religions, such systems to be known as either dissentient or separate. This statement of separate schools being public schools will be explained more fully later in this, and the next, chapters.

The B.N.A. Act, however, is an important bench mark and provides a constitutional basis for education. An understanding of the B.N.A. Act requires an understanding of the historical background from the middle of the 18th century up to 1867. The emphasis of the discussion here will be on education even though it is somewhat difficult to isolate education from the rest of life's activities.

3

Three main groups of people influenced the Canadian Design of Education before 1867. A fourth main group of people, the Canadian Indians, were for the most part ignored, other than being the occasional recipient of education from the developed systems of the other three groups. The three groups were the French, the English and the United Empire Loyalists (these terms to be used in a relatively broad sense). Now to place these groups in perspective.

The French Prior to 1763

Until such time as the "Americans" rebelled against rule from England and formed the United States of America in the last part of the 18th century, the countries of Canada and the U.S.A. did not exist as separate entities. Rather, there were colonies of settlement in various locations. The discussion here focuses primarily on the area which we know today as Canada. Although the use of the word "Canada" may not be technically correct in all cases, it is descriptive of the part of North America that we now recognize as Canada.

Other than the native indians, the first major group of people to settle in Canada was the fur-traders from France. Their major interest, as they settled along the banks of the St. Lawrence River and down into the Annapolis Valley of Nova Scotia (as it is now known), was the procurement of furs, particularly the beaver pelts sought after by the European market. Permanent settlement was slow, with education initially being of little concern. Gradually, however, as the permanent population grew (by 1666 this population was reported to be 3418, with the main centres being Montreal, Trois Rivières and Quebec), more interest in developing schools was evident.

It is interesting to note that even though often ignored in the early development of the Canadian Design of Education, the earlier schools were for Indian children. This facet was not influential in the main educational planning which was to come.

The settlers and fur-traders came from France and therefore the pattern of early Canadian education naturally followed that of the homeland, France (up until 1760, when French immigration ceased). The French immigrants were primarily Roman Catholic, but included some Huguenots (French Calvanists). This latter group was not influential in the earlier education development of Canada, or New France as it was called at that time.

In this 1600 to 1760 period there developed a system of parish schools, controlled and dominated by the Roman Catholic church, through the direction of the bishops. By 1760, there were approximately 90 parish schools, the teachers being primarily clergy and members of religious orders, supplemented by a few devoted lay people. The church was as generous with its funds for schools in Canada as it was in France, even though by today's standards this financial assistance was minimal. The King of France did make cash grants of support to these schools, which may have assisted in the later recognition of government financial support to education, a principle not generally recognized in England and some other countries at that time. Taxes, particularly land and property taxes, as we know them today, were not used to support education.

Three of the religious orders appeared to be most influential in the educational scene, these being the Jesuit priests, the Ursuline and Notre-Dame Sisters. Even in the early 1600's the Jesuit priests were teaching Indian boys, teaching being one of the important aspects of missionary work. The work of the Ursuline and Notre-Dame sisters in the schooling of young ladies was widely recognized as being superior. The first "elementary" school, in Trois Rivières, was established in 1616. The first secondary school, College de Quebec, was established in 1633 and remained the only secondary school in Canada prior to 1760. The prime function of this school was to prepare boys for entrance into a religious life. The Seminary of Laval, later to become Canada's first university, was established in 1665.

A brief note is needed of the type of colonists who settled in Canada in the period prior to 1760. Of the 10,000 immigrants, nearly 4000 were tradesmen, 3500 military recruits, over a thousand marriageable girls and a thousand exiles (England was not the only country to get rid of convicts through forced emigration). Through a very high birth rate (up to 65 per thousand), these original 10,000 expanded to approximately 85,000 (depending upon the definition of Canada) by the cessation of French immigration in 1760. The colonization of the Canadian part of the North American continent proceeded at a much slower pace than did the areas to the south. The 85,000 figure is small by comparison to 1,200,000 for the colonies to the south of Canada.

During this French immigration period a particularly significant event happened. This was the Treaty of Utrecht in 1713, a result more of the European Wars but significant to Canada. Under the terms of this treaty, the French lost control of the lands around the Hudson's Bay, Newfoundland and an indeterminate area of Acadia. The French inhabitants of these areas were permitted to return to France if they wished. For those who stayed (most of the population), guarantees were given for the free exercise of their Roman Catholic religion, and essentially their way of life. Historians have indicated little effort by the English to interfere with the religion, language and social traditions of the newly-conquered peoples. This has not been interpreted as genuine understanding but rather a way to minimize potential conflict.

The guarantee of the free exercise of religion at this stage was reflected again in the 1763 Treaty of Paris and subsequent enactments such that the formation of dissentient and separate schools can be traced back to the foundation established in the 1713 Treaty of Utrecht.

The English

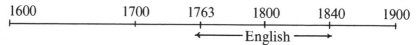

By definition, the English in this section will be taken to mean these people who settled in what is now Canada after the English victory of 1760, but not to include the United Empire Loyalists. This latter group was not entirely distinguishable from the English but their influences on the educational scene were different. In this section the English were made up of the Irish (by Confederation the second largest racial group in Canada), the Scottish, the English direct from England, and some English who moved from the thirteen colonies of the south to this new (after 1760) "fourteenth" colony.

During this period of colonization (1760–1840) the educational system in England emphasized the class structure prevalent at that time and the non-interference of government in educational matters. This non-interference also meant non-government financial support through grants and tax monies. The control over education by the Anglican church was fairly complete. Education for the masses was possible through a monitorial organization (described in educational literature as having been started by Bell (1753–1832) or Lancaster (1778–1838) but really already had approximately 300 years of use). At any rate, even though education was more important for the upper classes, it was available for many others as well. The religious base for education was quite evident.

The history of education in Scotland prior to, and during, the 1760–1840 period involved a heavy dependency upon the church, more noticeably the Church of Scotland. By 1745 the acceptance of the highlands and lowlands of Scotland being in essence the same country brought a degree of peace and stability to the country. Conditions of overpopulation and poverty convinced large numbers of Scottish people to emigrate to "Canada".

Ireland, then as now, was beset with religious strife and the Irish Protestant-Roman Catholic conflict was reflected in the Canadian separate school question. The conflict at Ulster in 1795 brought forth the Orange Order which pledged "to maintain the laws and peace of the country and the Protestant constitution, and to defend the King and his heirs so long as they shall maintain the Protestant ascendancy." The Orange Order was one of several forces which helped to mold the separate schools in Canada. The Irish have perhaps been, unfortunately, stereotyped as indicated in the following quotation, "In the field of Canadian education Irish influence has been mainly exhibited by the projection of an attitude, sometimes positive, at other times negative, but always rigid and determined."

In these years of English immigration into Canada, and the non-immigration of the French, there developed two major educational systems, one French and Roman Catholic and the other English Protestant. The factors of religion and language then, as now, were both important.

Consider first the French, located primarily in what became to be known as Lower Canada. With their defeat in 1760 came the end of continual contact with France. The clergy (the educational leaders) that chose to stay in Canada were, of course, abandoned by France, as Voltaire indicated in his writings, "with no regret". No new French clergy came to Canada. No grants were forthcoming from the King of France. In England, Educational grants from the government were not yet an accepted practice and so no government grants to education from the new Canadian government could be expected. A war had just ended, and wars are notable for placing education in a less favorable situation. In general, the education in Lower Canada deteriorated considerably in both quantity and quality, this situation lasting for at least two generations.

The 1763 Treaty of Paris basically imposed the English system of government and education on the French with minimal success. This situation was considerably improved with the 1774 Quebec Act, which granted the French a return to French civil law, the right to tithe, and the retention of the seigneurial land-holding system. Through the Treaty of Paris and the Quebec Act, like the Treaty of Utrecht, the guarantee of free exercise of the Roman Catholic religion helped to mold the dissentient and separate schools which exist in Canada to this day. When the American expeditionary force invaded Canada in 1775, the French did not support the Americans and thus the English Canadians readily repelled the invaders. Perhaps the English were generous in their provisions in the Quebec Act, but more likely they believed they would eventually assimilate the French, an idea that floundered through the very high birth rate of the French.

As the English settled into Canada, requests were made, and approval given, for Protestant schools, mainly in Montreal and Quebec. Lower Canada remained primarily French Roman Catholic, but the beginnings of an English Protestant school system was established. In other areas of Canada, the English Protestant schools were the domineering force.

The United Empire Loyalists

During, and after, the American War of Independence, thousands of United Empire Loyalists moved to Canada, particularly in the area of what is now New Brunswick, Nova Scotia and Prince Edward Island, as well as the Niagara peninsula, with others settling in Montreal and Quebec. "Late Loyalists" as they were sometimes called, were still coming in the 1800's (post-Loyalists being a more appropriate name).

Early American education had a very firm base in religion, as had Canada. However, the educational system in the "United States" had nearly one hundred years more to mature and change. Also, in addition to the Roman Catholics and Anglicans, there were a number of religions, resulting in many groups not trusting other groups, educationally, with the result of a movement toward state direction of education, with the development of locally elected school boards, and the elimination of sectarianism within the school systems. These influences were brought into Canada and obviously were somewhat at variance with the system being developed here. Most of these Loyalists had the same background as the English direct from England, Scotland and Ireland, but the additional one hundred years in the States had modified and changed some of the older traditions in regards to education.

There had developed in the States a system of compulsory education enforced and supported by the state. Education had become a very important matter, not to be entrusted to the various denominational churches but rather through local democratically elected school boards. The overall school system, with extensions into the college and university levels, was far more developed and extensive than it was in the parish schools operated by the churches in Canada. This is not to downgrade the Canadian system at that time. Progress was being made in Canada but the quite limited population, coupled with the efforts needed to survive in this wilderness in a war situation, was not conducive to educational development.

Amalgamation of Three Influences

The Quebec Act of 1774, acceptable by the French at that time, and grudgingly acceptable by the minority English, was not a suitable framework to accommodate the extensive emigration of the English and the United Empire Loyalists. The British government therefore passed the Constitutional Act of 1791 which divided the Quebec colony into two parts. Lower Canada (which is now southern Quebec), primarily French Roman Catholic, was to be governed by a Lieutenant Governor, an appointed Council and an elected assembly. French civil law and Roman Catholic religious privileges were confirmed. Upper Canada (now southern Ontario) was to have a similar governance, but otherwise a very British system.

At the time of this Constitutional Act, there were approximately 10,000 English people, almost all of whom were Protestant, in Lower Canada. Even before 1791 these people were beginning to apply pressure for what they would consider a suitable educational system. Earlier, in 1789, a committee appointed by the governing Council had recommended free parish schools, county grammar schools and a liberal arts college (with no theology to be taught). As this would have effectively removed education from the control of the Roman Catholic church, the opposition was sufficiently extensive to force the shelving of the report.

The next attempt by the English minority in Lower Canada resulted in the 1801 Act for "the Establishment of Free Schools and the Advancement of Learning in this Province." The Royal Institution for the Advancement of Learning, a public corporation, was organized to administer nondenominational common schools in the parishes or townships where the majority of the inhabitants petitioned for such schools. The teachers were appointed by the Governor and his administrators. Confiscated Jesuit estates were transferred to this Royal Institute to assist in financing the schools. The fact that only 37 of these schools were established in the next 37 years attests to the non-acceptance of the Royal Institute by the French population. Efforts were made to organize a dual system with the Royal Institute, one for the Roman Catholics and another for the Protestants, but again little success was achieved.

During this period, in 1824, the Fabrique Act was passed which permitted common schools to be established under the lay board of the parish (fabriques). They could hire the teachers and set the curriculum for their local schools. Sixty of these schools were operational in the next five years.

Also during this period, in 1829, the bill for "the Encouragement of Elementary Education" was passed which provided for elected boards of trustees to govern the parish and township schools, with some government financial assistance. Although not labelled as such, these resulted essentially in denominational schools.

By 1835, in Lower Canada, there were 1372 "trustee schools," and over 100 schools which were private, Royal Institution, and those operated by religious orders. The 1839 Lord Durham report to the British government indicated the low level of education in Lower Canada, even though the education for the French children tended to be of a higher quality than for the English.

Lord Durham was not impressed with education in Upper Canada either during this same period. Only about one-half of the children attended school, and of these many for only brief periods of time. The 651 common schools in operation in Upper Canada at that time were the results of two acts in particular. The 1807 Act, "to Establish Public Schools in Each and Every District of This Province" made provision for the establishment of eight school districts, managed by boards of elected trustees, and introduced the concept of government grants for education.

While the 1807 Act directed schools toward the English tradition of public schools, the 1816 Common School Act was decidedly the American pattern of public schools. This Act provided local option for the election of a three man board of trustees and the building of a school when twenty or more school age children were available.

This board would hire the teacher, set the curriculum and in general, regulate the school. The War of 1812 no doubt was in the minds of the legislators when they insisted upon the teachers being British subjects, complete with the corresponding oath of allegiance.

One of the results of the 1839 Lord Durham's report was the Act of Union of 1841 which brought Upper and Lower Canada from being legislative entities into merely administrative divisions of one united colony of Canada. On paper, Upper and Lower Canada became Canada East and Canada West, but most of the populace continued to use the old familiar titles. Out of the Act of Union of 1841 arose the Common School Act of the same year. Basically it was an act designed to give both Canada East and Canada West a uniform school system (ignoring for the moment the New Brunswick, Prince Edward Island and Nova Scotia areas). Initially there was one Superintendent of Education with one assistant for Canada East and another for Canada West. This was soon changed to have a Superintendent of Education for each of these two "provinces." This Act gave municipal councils (appointed members) the right to construct schools and levy taxes to pay for same. Government grants supplemented local tax levies. Trustees, called commissioners, were elected within the local school districts to operate the schools.

This Common School Act of 1841 also provided that "any number of persons of a different faith from the majority" could establish minority schools distinct from the majority schools but nevertheless eligible for government grants. This clause was another milestone in the establishment of dissentient schools in Quebec and separate schools in Quebec and Ontario. Subsequent school acts strengthened the stand of dissentient schools for the cities of Montreal and Quebec and separate schools for the remaining parts of the "Provinces" of Quebec and Ontario.

A very influential educational leader in the mid 1800's was Edgerton Ryerson who stressed a unified system of education, rather than the dual system which was developing in Lower Canada. He believed in control by a "Department of Education" in each "province" which would control one system of textbooks and curriculum, and for Roman Catholic parents to support either the "public" or "separate" systems with both systems to share government grants on an equitable basis. The Roman Catholic church worked towards a dual, rather than separate, system.

During this period the other areas of Canada, namely New Brunswick, Nova Scotia and Prince Edward Island (ignoring Newfoundland for the moment) were also having their problems relative to religions and the schools. The Caraquet Riots of 1875 (see Appendix A), eight years after confederation indicated the intensity of feelings between the Roman Catholics and Protestants over educational matters, even to the extent of killing members of the opposing groups. Basically, however, the people of these Atlantic provinces were able to work out their differences within the established framework rather than developing separate school systems.

The B.N.A. Act of 1867

With the B.N.A. Act of 1867, the four provinces of Quebec, Ontario, Nova Scotia and New Brunswick were united into one country called Canada. This union was difficult to achieve and major differences had to be by appeasement basis agreements, a situation very similar to the United States about a hundred years previous. In the United States education was one of a number of controversial issues and therefore was not even mentioned in the constitution of 1789. It was not until the tenth amendment that education was even mentioned in the constitution, with the result that education became a state right and responsibility (in the United States Constitution all the areas not designated as federal areas automatically became state rights and responsibilities, the opposite situation to that of the Canadian British North American Act).

Therefore the B.N.A. Act became a description of generally accepted practices existent at that time. It was not really a tremendous blueprint for the future but rather a codifying of already accepted principles. A number of sections of the B.N.A. Act have relevance to education, but section 93 was, and is, of particular importance.

93. In and for each Province the Legislature may exclusively make Laws in relation to Education, subject and according to the following Provisions: —

(1) Nothing in any such Law shall prejudicially affect any Right or Privilege with respect to Denominational Schools which any Class of Persons have by Law in the Province at the Union:

(2) All the Powers, Privileges, and Duties at the Union by Law conferred and imposed in Upper Canada on the Separate Schools and the School Trustees of the Queen's Roman Catholic Subjects shall be and the same are hereby extended to the Dissentient Schools of the Queen's Protestant and Roman Catholic Subjects in Quebec:

(3) Where in any Province a System of Separate or Dissentient Schools exists by Law at the Union or is thereafter established by the Legislature of the Province, an Appeal shall lie to the Governor General in Council from any Act or Decision of any Provincial Authority affecting any Right or Privilege of the Protestant or Roman Catholic Minority of the Queen's Subjects in relation to Education:

(4) In case any such Provincial Law as from Time to Time seems to the Governor General in Council requisite for the due Execution of the Provisions of this Section is not made, or in case any Decision of the Governor General in Council on any Appeal under this Section is not duly executed by the proper Provincial Authority in that Behalf, then and in every such Case, and as far only as the Circumstances of each Case require, the Parliament of Canada may make remedial Laws for the due Execution of the Provisions of this Section and of any Decision of the Governor General in Council under this Section.

REFERENCES

Chaiton, A. and N. McDonald. *Canadian Schools and Canadian Identity.* Toronto: W. J. Gage, 1977.
Gillette, M. *Readings in the History of Education.* Toronto: McGraw-Hill, 1969.
Johnson, F. H. *A Brief History of Canadian Education.* Toronto: McGraw-Hill, 1968.
MacNaughton, K. F. *The Development of the Theory and Practice of Education in New Brunswick 1784–1900.* Fredericton: University of New Brunswick, 1947.
Munroe, D. *The Organization and Administration of Education in Canada.* Ottawa: Secretary of State, Government of Canada, 1974.
Phillips, C. E. *The Development of Education in Canada.* Toronto: W. J. Gage, 1957.
Printice, A. L. and S. E. Houston. *Family, School and Society in Nineteenth-Century Canada.* Toronto: Oxford University Press, 1975.
Wilson, J. D., R. M. Stamp and L. P. Audet. *Canadian Education: A History.* Scarborough: Prentice-Hall, 1970.

Questions for Discussion

1. To what extent did the concessions given in the B.N.A. Act in Section 93 contribute to Canadian Confederation?

2. Has a real mixture of the early British, French and American influences been achieved, as reflected in Canadian education today?

3. What is the difference between a Roman Catholic public school, a Roman Catholic separate school and a Roman Catholic private school?

4. Were the guarantees given the Quebec people in Section 93 of the B.N.A. Act different than the guarantees given to other Canadians?

5. Why were the powers relative to education granted to the individual provinces instead of being retained by the federal government?

6. Are publicly supported separate schools desirable?

7. Will Canada ever have a fully bilingual (English and French) educational system?

8. Which had the greatest influence on the development of the Canadian educational system—the British, French or Americans?

9. Explain why neither the school as in the United Kingdom nor the district as in the United States but rather the province in Canada has become the basic decision making unit.

10. To what extent is there separation of church and state in Canada?

11. Compare the population of each of the four Canadian provinces in 1867 and today as to religion and language.

2

Interpretations of the B.N.A. Act

Introduction

Although other sections of the B.N.A. Act could have a bearing, indirectly, on education with the various provinces, section 93 dealt directly, if somewhat generally, with education. The preamble stated very definitely that education was a provincial responsibility, subject only to the four subsections following the preamble. It should be remembered that section 93, in 1867, referred only to the provinces of Quebec, Ontario, Nova Scotia and New Brunswick. As other provinces joined confederation (Manitoba in 1870, Prince Edward Island in 1873, British Columbia in 1871, Alberta and Saskatchewan in 1905, and Newfoundland in 1949), section 93 applied only to the extent the agreed upon act incorporating the province stipulated that section 93 was to apply. The B.C. Act of 1871, for example, stated,

> The Provisions of the B.N.A. Act, 1867 shall...be applicable to B.C. in the same way and to the like extent as they apply to any other provinces of the Dominion, and as if the Colony of B.C. had been one of the Provinces originally united by the said Act.

This section was not as clear as it might be because the original section 93 referred, directly and indirectly, to three different situations—that of Quebec, of Ontario, and of Nova Scotia and New Brunswick. The situation referred to B.C. was really that of Nova Scotia and New Brunswick, that is, no public separate schools at the time of joining confederation. Before referring to the other provinces, however, it might be profitable to consider the section 93 provisions.

Section one refers to denominational schools. Of the four provinces, only Quebec had denominational schools, and therefore section one stated that Quebec entering confederation did not affect the denominational schools that in the future would be established. The denominations were, then as now, Roman Catholic and Protestant.

To oversimplify, section two states that whatever "rights" (powers, privileges and duties) the Roman Catholics had in Ontario in regards to education, the Dissentient (minority) group in Quebec (whether Roman Catholic or Protestant) also had. Some question has been raised as to whether Quebec ever has had Dissentient (Separate) schools because the province operated on the basis of two educational systems, one Roman Catholic and the other, Protestant, rather than one educational system combining the majority (public) and the minorities within particular areas (separate).

However, section 93, subsections 1 and 2, appears to have been interpreted to mean that any denominational and dissentient (separate) schools that were lawfully existent in Quebec, Ontario, New Brunswick, and Nova Scotia in 1867 were to have continued protection as to existence in the future. Nova Scotia and New Brunswick, not having separate schools by 1867, did not therefore have any protection for separate schools in the future, except however, if separate schools were established in the future, they would enjoy the same protection as had they been in existence in 1867. Subsections 3 and 4 provide for appeal to the Governor-General and the right for the federal government to make any necessary remedial laws to enforce compliance with subsections 1 and 2.

As events following the 1867 confederation and subsequent enactments were made, the general provisions of section 93 needed further clarification. The remainder of this chapter describes some of the many situations which resulted in decisions as to what was really meant by the four subsections of section 93.

New Brunswick Common Schools Act

As stated in the previous chapter, compromises between the Protestants and Roman Catholics in New Brunswick and Nova Scotia resulted in a school system devoid of the legally established separate schools similar to Ontario or the two denominational school systems in Quebec. This should not be interpreted as meaning mutual satisfaction but rather a tenuous peace between the two sides. Schools did exist which loosely, but not legally, could be considered separate, or at least denominational in nature. In 1871, four years after New Brunswick entered confederation, the New Brunswick legislature passed "The Common Schools Act" providing for a free, tax-supported school system which was definitively non-sectarian in nature.

This was followed, in 1872, by regulations which educators across Canada today would find familiar. They provided for the recitation of the Lord's Prayer, a reading from the Bible, and the omission of emblems and symbols of any society (and presumably of any religious faith, but this latter provision was not common throughout Canada).

Obviously, the minority were not pleased with the act and its subsequent regulations and therefore petitioned the federal government in accordance with section 93. Sir John A. Macdonald ruled the act was within the power of the New Brunswick legislature (intra vires). An appeal was also made to the New Brunswick Supreme Court which stated, in essence, there were no legally established separate schools in New Brunswick at confederation and therefore any subsequent establishment of a separate school system would rest entirely with the provincial legislature (if however, then and at any future time, if publicly supported separate schools were established, provision of section 93 would then apply). The following provincial election provided five of the forty-one members of the legislative assembly as separate school supporters, and thus while some modifications to the regulations existed, the basic tenet continued of no publicly supported separate schools.

Religious disagreements have a tendency to continue beyond the legal framework within which they are decided and such was the case in New Brunswick. In 1875 The Caraquet Riots demonstrated the intensity of feelings. A document relative to these riots is included in Appendix A.

The Manitoba School Question

Manitoba, with an approximate population of ten thousand, the majority of whom were Roman Catholic, entered confederation in 1870. Section 22 of the Manitoba Act of 1870 stated,

> In and for the Province, the said Legislature may exclusively make Laws in relation to Education, subject and according to the following provisions:—
>
> (1) Nothing in any such Law shall prejudicially affect any right or privilege with respect to Denominational Schools which any class of persons have by Law or practice in the Province at the Union:
>
> (2) An appeal shall lie to the Governor General in Council from any Act or decision of the Legislature of the Province, or of any Provincial Authority, affecting any right or privilege of the Protestant or Roman Catholic minority of the Queen's subjects in relation to Education:
>
> (3) In case any such Provincial Law; as from time to time seems to the Governor General in Council requisite for the due execution of the provisions of this section,

is not made, or in case any decision of the Governor General in Council or any appeal under this section is not duly executed by the proper Provincial Authority in that behalf, then and in every such case, and as far only as the circumstances of each case require, the Parliament of Canada may make remedial Laws for the due execution of the provisions of this section, and of any decision of the Governor General in Council under this section.

The school system in Manitoba at that time parallelled the Quebec system, basically a two denominational system. This guaranteed the continuation of the parish schools in existence under the Riel provisional government prior to the 1870 entry of Manitoba into Canadian confederation.

As early as two years after The Manitoba Act concerns were being expressed about the impracticality of two systems. By 1875, provincial educational grants were changed from equal division to a population proportionate division, the protestants now being in the majority. The new liberal government in Manitoba in 1888 reflected the large protestant majority which now could out-vote the Roman Catholics by a four to one margin. In 1890 the Protestant dominated legislature abolished the dual school arrangement and declared provincial support would be given to only the public school system, other schools becoming private schools and left to find their own financial support.

An appeal was launched through the courts, with the Manitoba courts upholding the new provincial act, the Supreme Court of Canada declaring the Act ultra vires, and finally the British Judicial Committee of the Privy Council declaring the Act not discriminatory. This Privy Council ruling stated that, as there were no laws governing education in Manitoba at the time of joining confederation in 1870, it was not possible for there to be any violation attributed to the 1890 Act. Secondly, the practice in 1870 was for the Roman Catholics to maintain their schools at their own expense, and the new Education Act, by placing these schools basically into a private school situation, really did not change the practice which was in effect in 1870. The fact that the minority groups would now not only have to finance their own schools as well as tax assessments to the public system (and thereby effectively eliminating most of the separate schools) was not a question for consideration by the judicial body.

The minority appealed, as provided in subsections 3 and 4 of section 93, and restated in subsections 2 and 3 of The Manitoba Act, effectively placing the problem into the political realm. Conservative Thompson, successor to Sir John A. Macdonald upon his death in 1891, requested a ruling from the Supreme Court as to whether the federal government must hear the appeal from the minority. The Supreme Court, in a close decision, said no, but in the subsequent hearing at the Privy Council level the decision was yes, the federal government must hear the appeal. This higher judicial body said that, although the 1890 Act was intra vires, it did prejudicially affect the minority, thus placing the matter in the hands of the federal government.

Thompson was replaced by Bowell as prime minister, who was then replaced by Tupper, certainly an insecure political base from which to decide a highly emotional issue. Before a federal decision was made rectifying any prejudicial effects upon the minority groups, a federal election was held, with the controversial education problem as a major issue. The liberals, headed by Roman Catholic Laurier, won—mainly upon the strong Quebec support. In 1896 the Laurier-Greenway agreement, a compromise, was accepted. This agreement still denied provincial financial support to separate schools, but did make specific arrangements for religious instruction and the hiring of Roman Catholic teachers where warranted by the number of Roman Catholic students.

There the matter rests to this day, basically unsettled and still liable to legal and political manoeuvering in the future. Rumblings from within the successive governments of Manitoba would indicate this matter of public supported separate schools in Manitoba will again become a live issue.

Provincial versus Federal Rights

Section 93 of the B.N.A. Act states quite clearly that educational concerns are matters for provincial governments. Chapter three will discuss the federal involvement in educational matters, while recognizing this provincial right. However, there have been direct challenges which have resulted in the courts clarifying to a much greater degree this basic provincial right.

In 1873, a time for the encouragement of immigrants, the federal government, by an Order-in-Council, stated,

> The fullest privilege of exercising their religious principles is by law afforded to the Mennonites, without any kind of molestation or restriction whatever, and the same privilege extends to the education of their children in schools.

Some of the Mennonites settling in Manitoba did so believing this Order-in-Council promised them exclusion from provincial education requirements. Hildebrand,[1] in contravention of Manitoba's compulsory attendance laws, refused to send his children to school. The court ruled that the Order-in-Council, as it applied to educational matters, was ultra vires, and thus Hildebrand was forced to have his children attend school. This court case was in 1919, but even in 1962 in magistrate's court in Fort Vermilion, Alberta, reference was made to the 1873 Order-in-Council as a defense against compulsory attendance, with the same result as in the Hildebrand case. This matter was raised again in 1978 in the discussions relating to the legal maneuvering resulting from some of the Holdeman Mennonites in Alberta refusing to send their children to the public schools.

Another landmark case involved the Christian Brothers,[2] a religious order founded in France in 1684. The Supreme Court of Canada ruled that a bill to incorporate the Christian Brothers as "a Company of Teachers for the Dominion" in 1876 as being unconstitutional. The basis again was section 93 of the B.N.A. Act.

Defining Minority Rights

The Chabot Case.[3] In this case, the Chabot children were Jehovah's Witnesses, attending the only school provided in the area, that school being a public school in a predominately Roman Catholic area. By regulation of the Quebec Council of Public Instruction, all students were compelled to attend the religious instruction which was considered part of the curriculum. Refusal to do so by the Chabot children resulted in expulsion from the school. As a result of the ensuing court case, it was established that the non Roman Catholic Chabot children had a right to attend the Roman Catholic school in the area (there being no separate Protestant school) and that the Chabot children did not have to attend the religious instruction part of the school curriculum. While the province has the right to make laws and regulations in regards to education, there are other rights, such as freedom of religion, which cannot be transcended by educational laws and regulations.

The Bartz Case.[4] In this 1917 Saskatchewan case, Bartz, a Roman Catholic living in a Separate School District, wished to have his

---

[1]R. vs Hildebrand, (1919) 3 W.W.R. 286.

[2]*Canada Supreme Court Cases 1875–1906* (Christian Brothers Case), p. 1–2, April, 1876.

[3]Chabot v Les Commissaires d'Ecoles de Lamorandière (1957) Que. Q.B. 707 (C.A.).

[4]McCarthy v City of Regina and the Regina Board of Public School Trustees 32 D.L.R. 741 (1918).

school taxes paid to the public school district. The ensuing litigation confirmed that his taxes must be paid to the Separate School district. Justice Newlands stated,

> Can it, then, be argued that such a district is established only by those voting in favour of it? There being no individual right to form such a district, how can it be said that the individuals voting for the formation of the district are the ones who established it? The minority voting are bound by those in the majority, if they decide not to form such a district, and are they not equally bound where the majority vote is in favour of forming the district? Otherwise what is the object of taking a vote? Surely it is to decide whether the religious minority as a class will establish a separate school district, and surely when that vote is favourable, that the whole class is bound, as it would be bound if the vote was unfavourable.

The Renaud Case.[5] In this 1934 Ontario case, the Renauds, who were both Roman Catholics, decided to have Mr. Renaud's taxes paid to the public school district and Mrs. Renaud's taxes (on a different parcel of land) to the separate school district, and the children to attend the separate school. Justice Kerwin of the High Court of Justice decided, in reversing a lower court ruling, that this arrangement was legally acceptable. This case confirmed that, in Ontario, ratepayers could pay their taxes to whichever school system they wished (public or separate), but having made that choice, the children would go to the school of that same system.

In 1962, another case (LeBlanc v Hamilton Board of Education)[6] furthered the Renaud case decision by confirming that, in Ontario, a Roman Catholic can withdraw his support from the separate school.

The Schmidt Case.[7] Since the earlier cases indicated that (in Saskatchewan) the formation of a separate school by the minority group obligated all members of that minority group, and in Ontario where the children were to attend the school of the system to which the parents decided to pay their taxes, a more recent basis developed for challenging earlier rulings. This basis was in the area of human rights, a factor in the Schmidt case which started in Calgary in 1974.

Mr. and Mrs. Schmidt, both Roman Catholics, moved to Calgary from Willowdale, Ontario, where their taxes and children went to the public school district even though they resided in a separate

---

[5]Renaud v Board of Trustees of R.C. Separate School Section 11 in the Township of Tilbury North (1934) OWN 218 (1933) 3 D.L.R. 172 (1933) O.R. 565.

[6]Leblanc and Leblanc v Board of Education for City of Hamilton 35 D.L.R. (2d) 548.

[7]Schmidt v Calgary Board of Education and Alberta Human Rights Commission (1975) 6 WWR 279 (1975) 57 D.L.R. (3d) 746 (1976) 6 WWR 717.

school district. In Calgary (where there is both a public school district and a Roman Catholic separate school district) the Schmidts decided to send their children to the public school. As there was sufficient accommodation, the children were accepted, but Mr. Schmidt was charged tuition fees at the rate of twenty-two dollars per month per child. Mr. Schmidt filed a complaint of discrimination with the Alberta Human Rights Commission under a section of the 1972 Individual Rights Protection Act. The Commission agreed with the interpretation of Mr. Schmidt but was not able to reach agreement with the Calgary Board of Education. Therefore, Mr. Schmidt appealed to the Minister, who ordered a Board of Inquiry (still within the provisions of the same act). This Board ruled the Individual Rights Protection Act did not supercede the pertinent sections of the School Act, and further, if it did, the school was not a place of public accommodation, and therefore the pertinent sections of the Individual Rights Protection Act would not apply.

Mr. Schmidt's subsequent appeal to the Supreme Court of Alberta was successful, with the court saying that charging tuition fees on the basis of religion was discrimination. Calgary Public School Board was ordered to repay the fees.

Calgary School Board then appealed to the Appellate Division of the Alberta Supreme Court, effecting a reversal of the earlier court decision. Mr. Schmidt's subsequent appeal to the Supreme Court of Canada resulted in a refusal by that court to hear the appeal.

This case appears to have confirmed the supremacy of the provisions in section 93 of the B.N.A. Act, as worded in the 1905 Alberta Act, over subsequent Alberta "Human Rights" legislation. This case also helps to establish the extent to which "public schools" provide "public accommodation." However, many areas of Human Rights, as they relate to the educational scene, will require further definition.

The Ottawa Separate School Board Case.[8] In 1915 the Ottawa Separate School Board, representing Roman Catholics who were primarily French, decided the language of instruction in the schools under its control would be French. This was not permitted by the Ontario Department of Education, with the result qualified teachers were not hired and the schools remained closed. This action, in turn, resulted in an Order-in-Council abolishing the separate school

---

[8]Ottawa Separate School Trustees v City of Ottawa (1917) A.C. 76, 32 D.L.R. 10, 30 D.L.R. 770, (1916) 24 D.L.R. 497.

board. The authority for this action rested in a provincial statute passed by the legislature that same year.

The question of whether a separate school board could be abolished by the province was negated by the Privy Council. They indicated the right, in Ontario, was protected by section 93 of the B.N.A. Act. Therefore the province could not abolish a separate school board through action based in a provincial statute. The court ruled further that even though the right to maintain a separate school board was inviolate by the province, the right did not extend to separation from the Ontario educational system as such. That is, the province was quite within its rights to pass laws and regulations governing the conduct of schools, both public and separate.

The Ottawa separate schools operated as private schools until 1927 and during this period no provincial grants were paid. In 1927 arrangements were made which settled the controversy and grants were reinstated.

Non Roman Catholic, non Protestant

The provisions of the B.N.A. Act clearly recognized Protestants and Roman Catholics, the two groups which included nearly every person in Canada in 1867. The Newfoundland Act of 1949 distinguished among Roman Catholics, United Church, Anglican Church, Salvation Army, Seventh Day Adventists and Pentecostal Assemblies. Problems have arisen in the provinces which have separate schools when determination is needed as which school system should be attended by the Jewish, and the other groups of children who are non Roman Catholic and non Protestant. While there is no doubt about their right to attend the "public" school, because that is the school for all those except the minority (Protestant or Roman Catholic), problems sometimes arise when the "public" school is primarily Roman Catholic and the separate school is Protestant. Basically, this dilemma has been solved by agreement and negotiation, usually resulting in agreement with the Protestant "public" or separate schools. This problem does not arise in the provinces which do not have separate schools, namely, British Columbia, Manitoba, Prince Edward Island, Nova Scotia and New Brunswick.

REFERENCES

Bargen, P. F. *The Legal Status of the Canadian Public School Pupil.* Toronto: The Macmillan Company, 1961.

Child, A. H., "The Board of Education, Joseph Martin, and the Origins of the Manitoba School Question: A Footnote," *Canadian Journal of Education,* Vol. 2, No. 3, 1974.

Davis, M. and J. F. Krauter. *The Other Canadians.* Toronto: Methuen Publishing, 1971.

Friesen, J. W. *People, Culture and Learning.* Calgary: Detselig Enterprises, 1977.

Jaenen, C. J., "Ruthenian Schools in Western Canada," *Paedagogica Historica,* 1970.

Johnson, F. H. *A Brief History of Canadian Education.* Toronto: McGraw-Hill, 1968.

Norris, J. Strangers Ente ained: *A History of Ethnic Groups in British Columbia.* Evergreen Press, 1971.

Phillips, C. E. *The Development of Education in Canada.* Toronto: W. J. Gage, 1957.

Wilson, J. D., R. M. Stamp and L. P. Audet. *Canadian Education: A History.* Scarborough: Prentice-Hall, 1970.

Questions for Discussion

1. Were any references made in the B.N.A. Act regarding usage of languages in Canadian schools?

2. What effect today has the Common Schools Act of 1850 (Ontario) granting to the colored people the right to establish their own separate schools?

3. Once a separate school district is formed, what is the procedure for dissolving the district?

4. There are separate school districts in Alberta and Saskatchewan. Why not separate school divisions, counties and units?

5. What provisions are made to assist other minority groups (Ukrainian, German, Italian, Chinese, for example) in the preservation of their language and cultural heritage?

6. Publicly supported separate schools have been considered by some as "inefficient, archaic appendages". Is this true?

7. Does the quality of education in a separate school equal that of a public school?

8. How has each of the following cases helped to define constitutional issues relative to Canadian education?

    Shannon v Les Syndics d'Ecoles Dissidents de St. Romuald (1930) S.C.R. 599, 4 D.L.R. 190.

    McCarthy v City of Regina and the Regina Public School Trustees (Neida case) (1917) 32 D.L.R. 755.

    Tiny Separate School Trustees v The King (1928) 3 D.L.R. 753, (1927) 4 D.L.R. 857, S.C.R. 637, (1927) 1 D.L.R. 913, 60 O.L.R. 15, 59 O.L.R. 96.

    Perron v School Trustees of Rouyn (1956) 1 D.L.R. 414, Que.Q.B. 841.

    Hirsch v Protestant Board of School Commissioners (1928) 1 D.L.R. 1041.

    Re Hutchinson and the Board of School Trustees of St. Catharines (1871) 31 U.C.Q.B. 274.

    Leblanc and Leblanc v Board of Education for City of Hamilton (1962) 35 D.L.R. (2d) 548.

    Gallagher v Winnipeg School Division No. 1 (1963) 42 D.L.R. (2d) 370.

    Bintner v Regina Public School Board District No. 4 (1965) 55 D.L.R. (2d) 646.

    Re Fardella and the Queen (1974) 47 D.L.R. (3d) 690.

3

Federal Involvement in Education

Delineation of Responsibility

The responsibility for education in Canada rests with the provincial governments, a responsibility clearly stated in Section 93 of the B.N.A. Act. Other sections are very explicit as to the powers and responsibilities of the federal government—national defense, postal services, excise tax, tariffs, to mention a few. The residual areas, those not specified as being provincial or federal, are to be considered within the federal umbrella. This may have appeared very neat and definite at the time of Confederation but events since that time have shown a considerable area of jurisdictional greyness. At the time of Confederation universities were nearly foreign to the Canadian populace, vocational and technical schools non-existent, Indian and Eskimo education in a relatively primitive stage of development. Education was just not a high priority item in the minds of the pioneering populace—important, yes, but food, shelter and clothing certainly were far more important and immediate.

There were areas which were not thought of in 1867, or at least not considered as being either in or out of the education package. If the label "education" is applied to these areas then they are within provincial jurisdiction. But there are some areas which may or may not be "education"—if they are not, then they become federal responsibilities (assuming these areas were not specifically mentioned in other parts of the B.N.A. Act). An example of this is the use of the word "training" instead of "education" in the federal government vocational training acts described later. Teaching arithmetic to grade three students is definitely "education", whereas drilling soldiers on the parade square is generally accepted as "training", but which word best describes the program of academic subjects plus apprenticeship training and vocational education which is now a relatively common route for many students?

Even in the more specified areas there can be conflict. Defense is specifically federal, education specifically provincial. Then what happens when the defense of the country is endangered by the poor quality of education which prevents Canada from developing a defense force which can readily understand and manipulate the latest technological and scientific attributes of the defense system? In such conflicts between jurisdictional responsibilities, the country as a whole must come first, that is, national interests. There is a reference to this type of conflict of interests in the B.N.A. Act. In fact, the section goes much further than merely indicating priorities of legislation. The Governor-General-in-Council was given the power to disallow any provincial act within one year of its acceptance. Although this power has been rarely used, the power is still there and no doubt will be used in the future as circumstances warrant.

Our neighboring country to the south has attempted to delineate more specifically the responsibilities of the state versus federal by way of successive amendments to the Constitution. Canadians have chosen instead to depend upon negotiation, discussion, and even referral to the courts. Perhaps Canadians are still not sure in their own minds the distinction between federal and provincial responsibilities and thus would prefer to retain certain grey areas, including certain aspects of "education".

Therefore, right or wrong, the federal government is quite involved in education in Canada. The next part of this chapter describes some of this involvement.

Areas of Federal Involvement

1. Non-provincial parts of Canada. The northern parts of Canada, the Yukon and Northwest Territories, are not included in provinces and therefore the education for people in these areas becomes a direct responsibility of the federal government. Until recently these educational affairs were handled directly from Ottawa. In recent years, Departments of Education for the Yukon and the Northwest Territories have been formed, located at Yellowknife and Whitehorse. The relationship of the federal government to these Departments of Education tends to parallel the relationships with the provincial Departments of Education, even though jurisdictionally the northern departments are ultimately responsible directly to the

federal government. Financially, the education in these territories is supported by the federal government, offset to a small degree by local property taxes and other miscellaneous revenues.

2. Education of Native Peoples. In accordance with formal treaties and other agreements, the federal government has retained the responsibility for the education of the Indians and Eskimos in Canada. While there never has been a federal office or Department of Education, various departments in the government over the years have supplied that function for the education of Canadian native peoples. During the last decade and a half, there has been an accelerating movement to have the respective provinces provide educational services for the Indians, with complete reimbursement of costs by the federal government. In effect, the federal government retains its responsibilities, shown by its complete cost coverage, through contracts for educational services with school boards in the various provinces. Such contracts are always subject to the approval of the native peoples involved.

3. Education of Armed Forces Children. The Department of National Defense provides schooling for the children of servicemen. Since the families of servicemen are normally provided housing adjacent to the military bases, the Department provides for a school within the confines of the base community. Buildings, teachers and supervision are supplied by the Department. The program of studies follows the program for the province in which the base is located, and generally follows the Ontario curriculum for overseas bases. In a number of instances, especially at the high school level, servicemen's children are educated in nearby public or separate schools through a tuition-fee arrangement. In some instances the public school jurisdiction has accepted complete responsibility for the operation of the school and has charged the Department of Defense for the actual costs involved.

4. Vocational and Technical Education (Training). The history of the interest and involvement of the federal government in vocational and technical education dates from 1901 when representatives of Boards of Trade and the Dominion Trades and Labour Council met with Prime Minister Laurier. From then until the present there have been a number of incursions into this area by the federal governments. For example, there was the Royal Commission on Industrial and Technical Education of 1910; the Agricultural Aid Act of 1912; the Agricultural Instruction Act of 1913; the Technical Education Act of 1919; the Youth Training Act of 1940; the Vocational Training Coordination Act of 1942, to mention a few. One of the most recent

was the Technical and Vocational Assistance Act of 1960, under which dozens of schools were built which included vocational education areas, training programs developed for vocational teachers and job re-training for older and unemployed people, all on a cost-sharing basis with provincial governments. Partly because of the pressure for provincial autonomy in education, this act was phased out and replaced by an agreement whereby the federal government would pay one half of the operating costs of all post-secondary institutions in Canada (and including grade twelve students) and a re-shuffling of grants so that monies formerly paid direct to provinces for technical education would be paid into provincial coffers with no specified educational strings attached.

5. Department of External Affairs. The federal government, through the department of external affairs, is involved in several programs which include educational components. This department maintains links with the United Nations Educational, Scientific and Cultural Organization (UNESCO), the Organization for Economic Cooperation and Development (OECD), the International Bureau of Education, and the Commonwealth Education Liaison Committee.

Education is one facet of the Canadian International Development Agency (CIDA) which provides for the administration of educational and technical assistance to other countries. Through this plan students and trainees from developing countries study in Canada, and Canadian teachers teach and assist in program development in developing countries.

Canada finances an International Development Research Centre at Ottawa, the emphasis of this centre being research into the problems encountered by developing countries throughout the world.

6. Research Support Programs. Research in physical and natural sciences, in social sciences and in humanities, is assisted by grants from the National Research Council, Canada Council and Medical Research Council as well as other agencies and departments (Atomic Energy of Canada, Central Mortgage and Housing Corporation, the National Research Board, as examples).

7.   Other areas of Federal Involvement:
   a.   Canadian Broadcasting Corporation. Production of radio and television programs at public school, university and adult education levels.
   b.   Department of Veterans' Affairs. Academic and vocational correspondence courses for public servants, armed forces members, and others.

c.   Statistics Canada. Collects, coordinates and publishes statistics and information on all levels of education.
d.   Department of Justice. Educational and training programs among inmates of penitentiaries.
e.   Public Service Commission of Canada. Training and education of public service staff members, including intensive courses in French.
f.   National Film Board. Production of educational slides, films and filmstrips.
g.   Department of Agriculture. Prepares publications, motion pictures and displays for educational purposes.
h.   Historic Sites and Monuments Board of Canada. Advising on the marking and commemoration of national historic sites of interest and significance in Canada.
i.   Department of National Health and Welfare. Promotion and preservation of the health, social security and social welfare of the people of Canada. Issues Family and Youth Allowances.
j.   Public Archives. Assembles and makes available to the public a comprehensive collection of source material relating to the history of Canada.
k.   Department of National Defense. Military Colleges at Kingston, Royal Roads and Saint-Jean; Regular Officer Training Program; other service training programs; Cadet Corps for Youth.

The Case for Federal Involvement in Education

The previous section of this chapter showed that the federal government is involved in education to a considerable extent. The question here is whether they should become more involved, less involved, or retain the present level of involvement. The following illustrates some of the difficulties encountered in ever expecting an entirely satisfactory solution.

1. On a constitutional basis the provinces were provided with the responsibility for education and, on that basis, incursions into the area by the federal government are unconstitutional. However, the Constitution also made some direct references to federal involvement in education (Indian education, separate school protection, as examples) and therefore, even on a constitutional basis federal involvement can be justified. Some claim that Section 93 related

only to the kind of education in vogue in Canada in 1867 and therefore the extensions to the educational program (university, vocational, adult education, as examples) properly are within federal jurisdiction.

It becomes fairly obvious the Constitution is not a clear statement of jurisdictional rights today. Also, the Constitution and the laws of the country should reflect the wishes of the people (assuming that the wishes of the people can be determined), and it should be amended, even though this would be difficult. As was mentioned earlier in this chapter, there also appears a willingness on the part of the general public to retain some undefined area between federal and provincial educational jurisdiction. To legislate definitively can mean future rigidity and Canadians are not ready at this time to rigidify educational control.

2. Canadians are very mobile; they move from place to place within their provinces and from province to province. This mobility creates certain hardships for the children attending school—stories are told of children being in one grade in one province and then being placed either a grade ahead or a grade behind upon moving to another province. Also material studied in one grade may appear in another grade in another province, thus forcing either a repetition or omission of certain topics—and frequently they find the necessity for purchase and rental of different textbooks and workbooks. The proponents of greater federal involvement in education state that greater uniformity can be achieved through such devices as a national curriculum, thereby relieving the mobile population of many hardships.

While some of these hardships suggested must be accepted as being hardships, perhaps a more accurate description of some of the difficulties would be termed inconveniences. Also, mobility happens within a province, often with very similar disruptions, other than grade dislocations. That is, the school systems within a province, practising some local autonomy, differ as to when various topics are taught, and often use different textbooks and reference books. This can happen even within a school system, and even within a school itself. The uniformity that can be achieved on a national level perhaps is more mythical than real.

On the other hand, it is wrong to assume the materials and curriculum are vastly different from province to province. There is a great deal of borrowing of ideas and consulting among the provinces, expedited by the recent formation of the Council of Ministers of

Education. Also, publishing houses, through their interests in gaining national rather than provincial markets, influence the purchasing practices of educators, thus assisting in greater national uniformity.

3. The development of curriculum is usually very expensive. Resources of school boards, and even provincial departments of education, are often insufficient to finance the constantly changing curriculum desired. Therefore, the federal government, if it was permitted, could provide financing on a national basis, thus eliminating much of the need for area curriculum development. Further, much of the present planning could be termed wasteful because of so many groups going through the same planning procedures. However, this reasoning tends to ignore regional differences which are difficult to incorporate in national planning. Moreover, perhaps cooperation among provinces could achieve sufficient national aspects without having national control. Financing could also be on a pooled basis. National curriculum to overcome the problems of mobility would of necessity be more rigid thus violating the presently accepted premise for the need for flexibility in curriculum development. Another point which should not be overlooked is the value in the planning process itself, that is, the reinventing of the wheel does not add to the overall scientific knowledge, but the education obtained by the people who are reinventing the wheel can be a valuable education which can be used to strengthen other planning and development.

4. The equalization of educational opportunity and costs across Canada can best be achieved on a federal basis. Federal aid to education can assist the poorer provinces. The matter of equalization and its consequences will be discussed further in the chapter on financing education in Canada.

5. Uniformity of curriculum may lead to standardization of university students, making it easier for students to enter a university of his choice. Although this possibility exists, the trend appears to be in the other direction, with entrance requirements being different even for the universities within a province. Teacher training and teacher certification could perhaps be made more uniform as well, facilitating the transfer of teachers from province to province, but again different requirements and preferences seem to be as important as uniformity in standards.

6. Throughout the previous five points runs the theme of the importance and desirability of national unity. Canada is one country, not ten, eleven or twelve countries. Regional differences, as reflected

through provincial structures, are important, but a unified Canada is even more important. The children who are now in school are the ones who will decide the extent of future unity of Canada. Recognition of the importance of education for the strengthening of Canada as a country necessarily involves a degree of federal involvement in education, or for those who do not like the word "involvement", at least a deep, real concern of the federal government for education in Canada.

In summary, the strength of the Canadian educational system may be achieved by determining the optimal balance between the needs of conformity and flexibility, as they are reflected in national and provincial interests. It appears at this time that federal involvement in education is necessary and desirable but the optimal extent of this involvement remains questionable. Any changes in the present federal-provincial balance of necessity involves political action and politicians have learned that one way to deal with a hot potato is to not touch it.

REFERENCES

Bergen, J. J., "Council of Ministers of Education in Canada: At a Political Juncture?", *The Politics of Canadian Education.* Canadian Society for the Study of Education, 1977.

Brown, W. J. *The Impact of Federal Financial Support on Elementary and Secondary Education in Canada.* Ottawa: The Canadian Teachers' Federation, 1975.

Bryce, R. C. The Technical and Vocational Training Assistance Act of 1961–67: An Historical Survey and Documentary Analysis. Unpublished doctoral dissertation, University of Alberta, 1970.

Cheal, J. E., H. C. Melsness and A. W. Reeves. *Educational Administration: The Role of the Teacher.* Toronto: Macmillan Company, 1962.

Corry, J. A., "Higher Education in Federal-Provincial Relations," *University Affairs,* December, 1966.

Daniels, E. R. The Legal Context of Indian Education in Canada. Unpublished doctoral dissertation, University of Alberta, 1973.

Downey, L. W., "Trends in Canadian Studies," *Education Canada,* Winter, 1976.

Glendenning, D. *A Review of Federal Legislation Relating to Technical and Vocational Education in Canada.* Ottawa: Department of Manpower and Immigration, 1968.

Hodgson, E. D. *Federal Intervention in Public Education.* Toronto: The Canadian Education Association, 1976.

Lloyd, W. S. *The Role of the Government in Canadian Education.* Toronto: W. J. Gage, 1959.

Lucas, B. G., "Participation and Accommodation in Educational Policy Development at the National Level," *The Politics of Canadian Education.* Canadian Society for the Study of Education, 1977.

Peitchinis, S. F., "Is There a Federal Role in Education?" Paper presented to the Western Canada Education Finance Conference, Banff, April, 1974.

Review of Educational Policies in Canada. Ottawa: Submission of the Secretary of State to the OECD Study of Canadian Education, 1975.

Stager, D. A. *Financing Post Secondary Education in Canada.* Calgary: The Council of Ministers of Education of Canada, 1971.

Statistics Canada. *Education in Canada.* Ottawa: Information Canada, 1973.

Tomkins, G. S., "The Canada Studies Foundation: A Canadian Approach to Curriculum Intervention," *Canadian Journal of Education,* Vol. 1, No. 1, 1977.

Questions for Discussion

1. Do the provinces in Canada wish constitutional reform of education? If so, in what ways? If not, why not?

2. Should the responsibility for the education of Indians in Canada be given to the respective provinces?

3. How effective have the federal incursions been into the vocational and technical areas of education?

4. After weighing the pros and cons as to federal involvement in education, indicate the optimum level of federal involvement.

5. How successful have the educational programs been for inmates of federal penitentiaries?

6. Should there be national certification of teachers?

7. Does a student acquire a better level of education by attending schools within the same system for twelve years or having attended a variety of educational systems?

8. Considering the mobility of the present Canadian population, why should localized preferences be considered in the development of a satisfactory educational program?

9. Would the adherents of separate and private schools in Canada be in favor of more, or less, federal involvement in education?

10. Should the training of the severely handicapped children be the responsibility of the federal government or the provincial governments?

11. To what extent should the federal immigration personnel control admittance of non Canadians to Canadian schools?

STRUCTURE OF CANADIAN EDUCATION

PART TWO

4

Departments of Education and Centralized Control

The Canadian Design

As was indicated in the first chapter, and elaborated upon in the second, each province is responsible for education within its borders. True, there are limitations, but these deal mainly with national security, national interest, protection of guarantees of certain religious minorities, and provision of education for native peoples. Within these bounds, the provincial governments have latitude in providing education for their constituents. Such provincial autonomy would lead one to expect great differences among the provinces but surprisingly, the educational structures of the provinces are more obvious for their similarities than their differences. This chapter considers provincial centralized control of education and the organizational structure of Departments of Education.

Considering the historical development of education in Canada, the local school district or the local school would be expected to be the main decision-making unit, with the larger units and the provincial Department of Education as being secondary in importance. The emphasis of the supremacy of the local school has been indigenous to the English school system and, considering the emigration from England to Canada in the formative years, the "local authority" principle would be expected to become established. Secondly, early education in what is now Quebec was based on the idea of the parish school—a close educational tie to the local parish church. Thirdly, the United Empire Loyalists brought into Canada a strong tradition of the supremacy of the local school district. However, in spite of these three major influences, there developed in Canada a structure in each province in which the provincial Department of

Education (or its equivalent) become the central authority, followed by school board control, and lastly by the community surrounding the local school. Various writers have tried to explain this strange phenomena, suggesting three main reasons. First, Edgerton Ryerson, Superintendent of Education in Ontario (Upper Canada) from 1844 to 1867, was very influential in determining the direction education was to take in this fledgling country—and he was a strong advocate of centralized control. Secondly, the inability of either the Protestants or the Catholics to gain complete domination over the other tended to push the control of education a little further away and thus on to more neutral and less emotional ground, the central (provincial) government. Thirdly, Canada has been an agricultural nation, particularly in its formative years. The local areas did not have the population and resources upon which to develop a sound educational program. Whatever the real reasons, today we have a highly centralized form of educational direction and control, followed by area control, and lastly by local control.

Thus, in each province the Department of Education of the government is the central authority, a position which none of the provincial governments appears willing to vacate. Any other authority is delegated by the Department of Education, through its minister and various provincial legislative acts and regulations (mainly the School Acts). This authority delegation can be recalled at the whim of the provincial government, subject of course to the electors at the next provincial election. That is, the various types of local or regional organizations (districts, divisions, units, counties) and their respective governing bodies exist at the pleasure of the provincial legislatures. By law, the responsibility for education in each province rests with the provincial government, a position which cannot be overlooked. School districts and school boards then become creatures of the provincial government. In the event the school board neglects its responsibility, this must then be recaptured by the provincial Department of Education. School boards, publicly elected or appointed, can and have been, dismissed by the provincial government.

The Canadian design for education is a strong centralized authority located at the provincial government level, supplemented by elected and/or appointed school boards with limited authority, and ineffective vestigal bodies associated with the local school. Provincial politicians, in response to pressure from school boards and constituents, have in the last few years attempted to give the impression of local autonomy for school boards and, to a lesser degree, the individual schools. For example, the departmental examinations for the senior grades are gradually being eliminated; departmental curriculum guides for individual subjects are becoming less prescriptive; local advisory councils to advise school boards are becoming more fashionable; departmental inspectors and superintendents are less in evidence. However, these are mainly surface trends—there has been very little real change in the control departments of education have over education. Inspectoral bodies are becoming advisory bodies but the monitoring functions are still there; the leadership services are often mantles of "suggestive" prescription.

Often in the business world the statement is made that whoever controls the purse strings wields the greatest power. This is also true in education. The provincial governments need not dictate that a particular program be initiated or furthered because provision of sufficient financial incentive will achieve the same purpose.

This discussion on centralized authority is not meant either as a support for centralized authority nor as a criticism. Rather, this discussion has focussed on the importance of education as perceived by the provincial governments and the determined efforts to fulfill their responsibilities in this regard.

The Department of Education

In each province the senior position in the Department of Education is the Minister of Education. He is an elected member of the legislative assembly, granted the portfolio of education from the lieutenant-governor on the recommendation of the premier. All other members of the Department of Education are hired, non-elected, employees of the government. The structure and organization of the Department of Education varies from province to province, as illustrated in figures 4–1 to 4–9. In general, there tends to be a deputy minister responsible directly to the minister, and two, three or four associate or assistant deputy ministers each in charge of a particular part of the responsibilities of the department. For example, one associate deputy minister may be concerned with instruction and curriculum development, another with research and development, another with finances, grants and taxation. The next level of operations becomes more specific. The person in charge, normally called a Director, has a much more specific area of concern, and heads a staff to fulfill that function. The total number of Department of Education employees can therefore be quite extensive. Alberta, for example, has over seven hundred employees in the Department of Education.

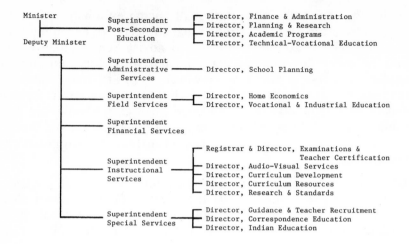

Figure 4-1
British Columbia Department of Education

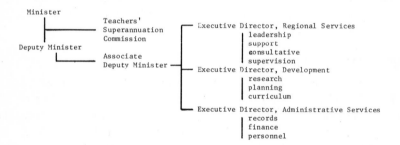

Figure 4-2
Saskatchewan Department of Education

Figure 4-3
Manitoba Department of Education

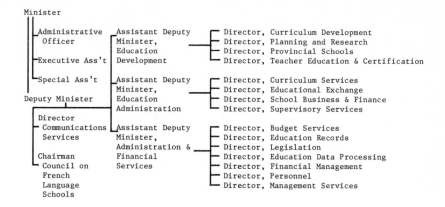

Figure 4-4
Ontario Ministry of Education

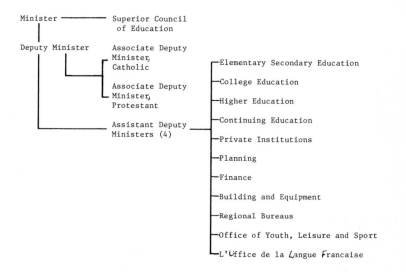

Figure 4-5
Quebec Department of Education

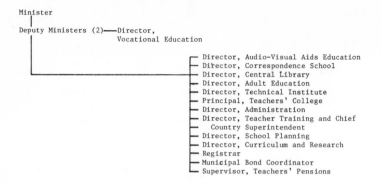

Figure 4-6
New Brunswick Department of Education

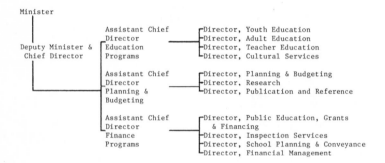

Figure 4-7
Nova Scotia Department of Education

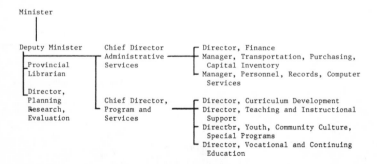

Figure 4-8
Prince Edward Island Department of Education

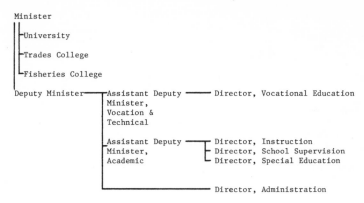

Figure 4–9
Newfoundland Department of Education

In addition to a Department of Education, four provinces have a department responsible for post-secondary education. Ontario has a Department of Colleges and Universities, Manitoba has a Department of Colleges and Universities Affairs, Saskatchewan has a Department of Continuing Education, and Alberta has a Department of Advanced Education.

The organization of the Departments of Education in Quebec and Newfoundland have the added complication of denominational considerations. In Quebec the dual aspect (Roman Catholic and Protestant) is represented by two Associate Deputy Ministers, one Roman Catholic and the other Protestant, and through them two confessional committees of the Superior Council of Education. In Newfoundland the problem of departmental organization is complicated by the existence of five denominational systems—Roman Catholic, Anglican, United, Salvation Army and Pentecostal Assemblies. Each has an Assistant Superintendent but it is the Council of Education, consisting of the Minister and Deputy Minister meeting with the Assistant Superintendents, that achieves unity in standards and curriculum, in vocational training, teacher education, adult and higher education. Amalgamation of denominational schools in Newfoundland in recent years has considerably reduced the denominational emphasis. No special provision is made in the organizational structures of the Departments of Education in Ontario, Saskatchewan and Alberta where publicly supported separate schools exist.

A more extensive description of one Department of Education, that of Alberta, is illustrated in figure 4-10. Although the following

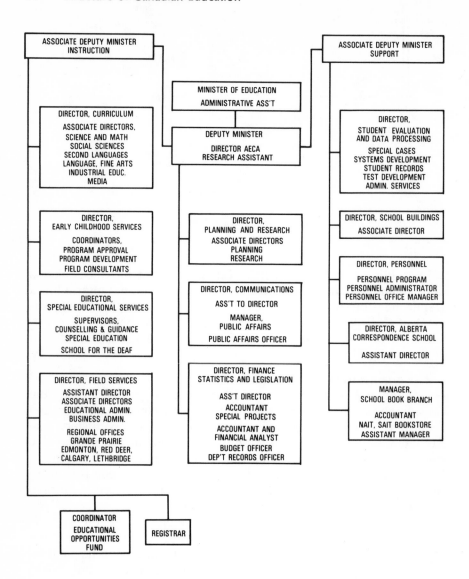

Figure 4-10
Alberta Department of Education

discussion pertains to that department, many aspects are typical for corresponding departments across Canada. The two main divisions according to function are instruction and support, with a third division appearing to develop which would be research and development. The two main divisions are headed by Associate Deputy Ministers while the third division (which currently is not labelled a division) is responsible directly to the Deputy Minister.

The Division of Instruction includes four branches plus the Educational Opportunities Fund and the Registrar. Even though considerable curriculum planning work is done at the school and district levels, the Curriculum Branch is involved deeply with course and program development, assistance and monitoring services. Much of this is done through provincial curriculum committees, usually headed by departmental officials but including various educators throughout the province, most of whom are referred to the curriculum committees by the professional teachers' association. Organizations such as the Home and School Association also have representatives on these committees. The prescriptive nature of school subject offerings are outlined in Programs of Study and in Handbooks; the suggestive and supportive functions are found in Curriculum Guides. The use of particular textbooks and reference books are subject to the approval of the Minister of Education, who normally relies on the judgment of the respective Curriculum Committee.

The Early Childhood Services Branch, while structurally part of the Department of Education, functions in close association with other government departments, such as Social Services and Community Health. The branch coordinates the services provided by various agencies in helping to meet the needs of young children and their families. Early Childhood Services are operated at the local level by both school boards and community groups. The Early Childhood Services Branch assists these groups, considers and approves applications from local organizations, approves programs, special teacher certification, evaluation of programs and funding through government grants.

The Special Educational Services Branch supervises all aspects of special education, including administration of the Learning Disabilities Fund, regulation of private schools, the activities of the supervisor of counseling and guidance, operation of the Alberta School for the Deaf, and regulation of summer and extension programs in basic education operated by school boards.

The Field Services Branch provides guidance and advice to schools and school boards throughout the province, mainly through the five regional offices located in Grande Prairie, Edmonton, Red Deer, Calgary and Lethbridge. Among the many activities of this branch are included consultative and inspectoral services for the instructional and related areas of education, program development, cooperative evaluation of school systems, programs, agreements, budgets and financial statements.

The Educational Opportunities Fund provides funding for projects which are planned and operated by school boards for the purpose of upgrading services of direct benefit to students and their teachers. The main objective is to increase the proportion of students acquiring mastery of basic and auxiliary skills. The funds provided are supplemental to other grants provided to school boards by the provincial government.

The office of the Registrar examines credentials and recommends to the Minister of Education teachers for certification. This Branch also evaluates documents of foreign secondary students as a service to the schools. Through the Board of Teacher Education and Certification, teacher training programs are examined and monitored. Disputes, usually between teachers and their employers, are dealt with through the Board of Reference, the secretary of which is the Registrar.

The Division of Support Services has three branches, each headed by a director, plus two services, headed by a director and a manager respectively. The Student Evaluation and Data Processing Branch provides data processing services, maintenance of student and teacher records, distribution and analysis of surveys and studies, development of examinations, statistical analysis of student and teacher populations, and scoring and analysis of standardized tests for schools.

The School Buildings Branch administers the School Buildings Act and the Regulations of this Act. The director and associate director act as chairman and member of the School Buildings Board, a five member interdepartmental board of the provincial government. The funding for school construction is reimbursed to school boards if the construction is in accordance with the approved location, size and cost as indicated by the School Buildings Board, as administered through the School Buildings Branch.

The Personnel Branch assists in recruitment, selection, classification and staff development of employees of the Department of Education.

The Correspondence School Branch provides courses for school credit and general interest to residents of Alberta and Northwest Territories. These are provided at low cost to over 18,000 registrants each year. Some students supplement their regular high school program with correspondence courses while other students are unable to attend regular school for various reasons, location and physical handicaps being two of these reasons.

The School Book Branch provides, on a non-profit basis, educational books and tests to school boards in the province. Where the school boards utilize a textbook rental plan for its students (nearly every board in the province does this), a subsidy of forty percent is provided by the Department of Education. The School Book Branch also operates the bookstores at the two technical institutes, NAIT and SAIT.

The branches which are responsible directly to the Deputy Minister are Planning and Research, Communications, and Finance, Statistics and Legislation. The Planning and Research Branch selects research and projects for study. Those that are approved are conducted mainly through contract with universities or other research groups. The Communications Branch develops and maintains an exchange of information from and to the public, interest groups and individuals.

The title of the Finance, Statistics and Legislation Branch explains the purpose of the Branch. Much of the centralized control of the Department of Education is exercised through manipulation of financing and thus this Branch assumes a very important role in the Department. The accounting of the foundation program and school grants is processed through this Branch as well as the checking and filing of budgets and annual statements from the school boards. Changes in legislation may be instigated from any part of the Department, and even from "outside" organizations such as The Alberta Teachers' Association and The Alberta School Trustees' Association, but all are organized and examined through this Branch.

The powers and responsibilities of the Departments of Education are enumerated mainly in the Department of Education Act and the School Act. Typical of references to centralized control is the following section in the Alberta School Act.[1]

12.   (1)   In addition to his other powers specified in this Act the Minister may make regulations

(a) governing the use of English as a language of instruction,

(b) governing the use of French as a language of instruction,

(b1) governing the use of any language other than English or French as a language of instruction,

---

[1]*The School Act, 1970.* Chapter 297 Revised Statutes of Alberta.

(c) respecting the inspection of pupils, teachers, schools, pupil programs and courses of study,

(d) respecting the inspection of schools for the purpose of insuring that a proper educational program is carried on and that the Act, regulations, courses of study and pupil programs are complied with,

(e) governing
   (i) the examination of pupils,
   (ii) the remuneration of examiners and markers,
   (iii) the fees for taking examinations and in connection with re-reading examinations, remission and refund of fees,
   (iv) appeals from examinations, and
   (v) hourly fee rates for temporary staff, and granting certificates to school graduates,

(f) respecting the matters concerning which boards, teachers and other employees of boards must supply information, including the times and dates by which the matters must be reported on and information supplied,

(g) prescribing notices and forms whether or not specifically required by this Act,

(h) governing the insurance of a board, its teachers and other employees,

(i) respecting the winding up and dissolution of boards and districts or divisions including the procedure to be followed and the rules for paying assets and liabilities,

(j) governing the employment of superintendents employed by a board with respect to his qualifications and experience,

(k) respecting the payment of grants of money in lieu of transport,

(l) respecting maintenance grants for pupils,

(m) respecting the form, content, confidentiality, use, maintenance and and disposition of student records, and

(n) respecting the manner in which and the persons to whom a board shall give notice of its intention to and the conditions under which it may
   (i) dispose of land, or
   (ii) dispose or discontinue use or accommodation of a school building or other improvement or part thereof used for the instruction or accommodation of pupils.

(2) The Minister may

(a) prescribe
   (i) courses of study or pupil programs or both, and
   (ii) instructional materials, and

(b) approve any course of study or pupil program submitted to him by a board, but instruction in the course of study or pupil program shall not commence without the prior approval of the Minister in writing,

and The Regulations Act does not apply to anything done by the Minister or a board under this subsection.

Throughout the School Act are phrases such as "subject to the approval of the Minister," and "shall submit to the Minister," which are constant reminders that the Minister of Education has many other powers additional to those listed in Section 12. The next section in the School Act reads as follows:

13. (1)   The Minister may delegate all or any of his powers or duties under Section 12 to a board, with or without restrictions.

     (2)   The Minister may delegate all or any of his powers or duties under section 65, 93, 95, 96, 115, 116 or 144 to any person designated by him in writing.

This tempers the centralized control somewhat, but the word "may" becomes quite important.

Attempting to summarize the functions of the various branches of a Department of Education and the Minister of Education leads to over-simplification of an organization which really is much more complex. The Department of Education has a political base and operates on political expertise as well as directives and regulations. This is not to say that the Departments of Education operate "not legally" or entirely according to pressure but rather, within the overall framework within which they operate, the manner of operation must be a result of sensitivity to the general public.

REFERENCES

Annual Reports of the Departments of Education of the Governments of the Provinces in Canada.

Chalmers, J. W. *Schools of the Foothills Province.* Edmonton: The Alberta Teachers' Association, 1967.

Cheal, J. E., H. C. Melsness and A. W. Reeves. *Educational Administration: The Role of the Teacher.* Toronto: Macmillan Company, 1962.

Johnson, F. H. *A Brief History of Canadian Education.* Toronto: McGraw-Hill, 1968.

Munroe, D. *The Organization and Administration of Education in Canada.* Ottawa: Secretary of State, Government of Canada, 1974.

Phillips, C. E. *The Development of Education in Canada.* Toronto: W. J. Gage, 1957.

The School Act 1970. Chapter 297 Revised Statutes of Alberta.

Stapleton, J. J., "The Department of Education as a Policy-Maker: The Case of the Credit System in Ontario," *The Politics of Canadian Education.* Canadian Society for the Study of Education, 1977.

Stewart, B. C. *Supervision in Local School Districts—Canada.* Toronto: Canadian Education Association, 1972.

Questions for Discussion

1. How will the provincial departments of education monitor educational standards without the use of the traditional external examinations?

2. How do the provinces determine and influence education for teachers when such education is provided through the university setting?

3. How effective will "control by finances" be in maintaining provincial control over education?

4. What evidence is available which would indicate greater or less provincial control over education in the future?

5. Should ministers of education be selected from only those MLA's who have had previous teaching experience?

6. Are administrative assistants to ministers and deputy ministers of education a means of making the department more sensitive, politically, to the electorate?

7. How effective was Edgerton Ryerson in determining future directions for education in Canada?

8. Are regional offices of the departments of education effective in decentralizing control of education?

9. How can additional flexibility and greater local autonomy be built into the educational structure, at the same time ensure the provincial government does not abrogate their responsibilities?

5

School Boards and District Organization

School Districts and Early Consolidation

The basic unit of organization for the operation of schools in Canada is the school district. These vary in size and shape and in the organization of the controlling board but the common element of all is the delegated authority from the Department of Education. The historical Canadian school district was organized to serve the population, usually rural, within reasonable walking distance of a central point which in some parts of Canada was the local church.

Thus there developed thousands of small districts (sometimes called four by fours because of their size). The purpose of the school district was to provide schooling for the children of the area and therefore each school district built a school, usually one room. In this small school, under the direction of an ill-paid and often inadequately trained teacher, students of many different grades received a rudimentary education.

Financing these schools was difficult and the provision of education beyond grade nine or ten often became impossible. These hardships resulted in cooperative efforts among districts, that is, a consolidation of efforts and finances. The first consolidated school districts in Canada were formed in Prince Edward Island and Nova Scotia in 1900 and 1903, in Newfoundland in 1903, and in British Columbia in 1905, but the main swing to consolidated school districts corresponded with the improvement of roads and the beginning of the motor age in the 1920's. Saving of money was supposed to occur with consolidation because there would be one building instead of several to equip and maintain and fewer teachers would be required due to the increased pupil-teacher ratio. This cost saving, however, was rarely achieved. Transportation became an added cost. Also, a greater range of subjects was offered at the senior levels and thus additional costs for space, teachers and equipment. Offices for administrators were required, as well as released time from teaching for administrative tasks, thus increasing the expenditures.

Instead of one board of trustees for each district, one board was required for the enlarged district, with trustees representing areas which formerly were represented by a number of trustees. The purpose of the board remained the same, however. The board became the buffer between the general public and the professional staff, the policy setting body, as well as the administrative body which hired the teachers, hired a local farmer to cut the grass on the school yard and dig the well, and a host of other administrative details. The larger the consolidated school district, the more these administrative details were left to the hired staff.

Larger School Jurisdictions

Roads continued to improve and increasing demands were being placed on the educational provisions of Canadian schools. Thus in the middle 1930's another reorganization began—that of the enlarged local units. The reasoning paralleled that of the change to consolidated school units from the individual one-room schools. There would be, the proponents of enlarged units would say, a real cost saving. This was not to occur. However, other advantages were achieved—larger centralized schools which could be better equipped, staffed and able to provide a much wider range of subject offerings, including non-academic courses such as home economics and shop. Also, specialists could be hired to travel among the schools in these larger units to teach French, band, shop, home economics, and other subjects, as well as the provision of services of counseling, library and testing. The model for this expanded local unit was the school division developed in Alberta in 1936, the principle features of which were:

1. The district organization remained but the duties and responsibilities of the district school boards were drastically reduced. The boards of the districts within the division were left with authority to determine whether religious instruction and French instruction would be provided, to nominate a teacher, and to do those things specifically requested by the divisional board.

2. Initially, school divisions consisted of rural districts only, later modified to include villages and towns.

3. The school divisions were to be governed by an elected board of trustees consisting of from three to five trustees (plus elected trustees from larger towns within the division) on a three-year revolving basis. The school division was divided into wards called subdivisions with one trustee representing one subdivision.

4. There would be a central office with a full-time staff, supplemented by a provincially-appointed superintendent of schools assigned to that particular school division to act as advisor to the divisional board of trustees.

5. The school divisions varied in size but averaged about seventy-five districts per division.

6. The school division was an organization which encouraged the closing of many of the small schools and the consequent building of larger centralized schools.

The formation of school divisions and the subsequent centralization of schools was not without repercussions however. The closing of a smaller, local school was viewed as a threat to the local merchants, local school board members lost authority and prestige, and students had to spend longer hours on a school bus over roads which had not yet developed to satisfactory standards. In all, there were 55 school divisions formed in Alberta from 1937 to 1959, almost completely blanketing rural Alberta, including nearly all of the villages and towns. Thirty of these divisions are still in operation today, most of the remainder being reorganized into counties.

At the present time Alberta has 60 larger jurisdictions (30 counties and 30 school divisions), two urban counties, 19 city school districts (9 public and 10 separate), 40 town school districts (9 public and 31 separate), 7 village school districts (2 public and 5 separate), 3 consolidated school districts, 58 rural school districts (16 public and 42 separate), and 4 regional school districts.

In British Columbia, three experimental large units, the first one in the Peace River area in 1934, were started. The success of these and the influence of the 1945 Cameron Commission report encouraged the provincial government to the extent that the large units were put into effect in 1946 on a permanent basis. The Cameron Commission report recommended the reorganization of the 800 school districts into 74 large units, the successful basis of which would be, "...large enough to provide adequate schooling from grades one to twelve, that it should comprise a comprehensible geographic and economic community and be large enough to employ at least forty, though preferably one hundred teachers." British Columbia now has 74 large school districts which include various combinations of villages, cities, district municipalities, rural school districts, consolidated school districts and those areas which were previously unorganized. Consideration is being given to further amalgamation of large school districts to reduce the number even further.

The Larger Units Act was passed in Saskatchewan in 1944 which permitted, and forced, the organization of school districts into Units, comparable in purpose and extent to the school divisions in Alberta. Saskatchewan now has 60 school units, 32 Roman Catholic and 4 Protestant separate school districts, 178 consolidated districts, 29 urban districts, 150 town districts, 351 village districts and 16 high school districts.

The reorganization into larger units in Manitoba developed in two stages. The first stage was the development of larger units (school divisions) for the purpose of consolidating and improving the high schools. The second stage was to include elementary schools in these school divisions (called unitary divisions). Manitoba now has 46 unitary school divisions, 1 multi-district division, 15 remote school districts, 7 special revenue school districts (Department of National Defense schools and company town schools), and 3 special schools in sparsely populated communities.

In Ontario the 3465 rural school districts were reorganized into township units by 1950. In 1969 these township units were further reorganized into approximately 100 counties. At the present time Ontario has 76 boards of education, 36 public school boards (remote areas), 31 other public school boards (crown lands, hospitals, etc.), 2 Protestant separate school boards, 49 Roman Catholic combined separate school boards, 12 Roman Catholic separate school boards (remote areas), and 1 Metropolitan Toronto school organization.

In Quebec the one-room parish school districts gradually were enlarged so that by 1960 the average parish school system comprised seven schools. In 1964 the province started the reorganization of the province into 55 school regions, later extended to 63 to accommodate Protestant school regions. Quebec now has 168 Roman Catholic and 21 Protestant school commissions which are members of 54 Roman Catholic and 9 Protestant regional school boards. In addition, Montreal has 5 Roman Catholic and 2 Protestant school commissions which cooperate under one School Council of the Island of Montreal for financing and developmental planning.

New Brunswick has 33 school districts, grouped into 7 regions. Nova Scotia has 20 municipal school units, 34 town school sections, 3 city sections, 3 amalgamation areas, and 15 regional units each with its own school board. Prince Edward Island has 5 large administration units. Newfoundland has 19 consolidated integrated districts, 12 consolidated Roman Catholic districts, 1 Pentecostal district, 1 Seventh Day Adventist district, and 2 other districts.

School-Municipal Amalgamation

Throughout Canadian educational history there has been, in general, a separation of school and municipal governance. There have been many examples of overlapping between the governing bodies but, even today, education and municipal affairs are distinct entities in most of Canada. The main common element is, and has been, property taxation as a source of revenue. Financing education will be discussed in greater detail in the next chapter but it is an important consideration in school-municipal relations.

Where school districts pre-dated municipal organization, as was the case in the early 1900's in Alberta, the school districts obviously had to collect their own taxes from property owners. With the formation of municipal districts the duplication of costs and efforts were unnecessary and costly and thus one body, the municipal district, became the collector of taxes. The feeling of municipal councillors has generally tended to the assumption that school boards were extravagant and not as responsible as the municipal council, a position that was abetted by corresponding provincial leglslation. Municipal councillors, generally forced to collect whatever levy the school boards stated, felt that if only they could control education, everything would operate much better.

Another factor of commonality was the duplication of central offices. Protaganists for amalgamation of school and municipal affairs argued that one central office could serve both purposes. Also, if there was one board, fewer meeting days and thus less mileage and expense for trustees and councillors. Municipal districts were quite cooperative in snowplowing school driveways and bus routes, and in the maintenance of roads—this cooperation, plus maintenance of buildings and equipment, would be improved by one organization rather than two. These, and other reasons were advanced by the "pro-amalgamators". Underneath, however, one of the prime justifications was for the municipal authority to gain control over the education authority. Thus, in 1950, the County Act was passed in Alberta permitting the formation of counties (municipal-educational combinations). The first attempts were to include hospital organization as well but this idea was soon dropped as being not feasible. In 1951, the first counties were formed in the Grande Prairie and Vulcan areas, and others through the years so that by 1969 thirty-one counties in all were formed (one was subsequently dissolved). Therefore, in 1978, approximately half of rural, settled, Alberta was organized into counties and the other half in school divisions. The type of county organization in Alberta is somewhat unique and bears further discussion.

The county organization in Alberta brings together in one administration two rural oriented governments—the municipal and education aspects. The county is formed by the Lieutenant-Governor-in-Council, that is, by recommendation of the provincial cabinet. The initiation for the formation of counties has invariably come from the municipal interests rather than the educational. The towns, villages and improvement districts within the area can be included in a county but this is subject to a plebiscite if requested by those concerned. The pattern has been for the towns and villages not to be included for municipal purposes, but if they were already included in the school division for educational purposes, they would then be included in a county for educational purposes only. After a county is organized, provision is made for a plebiscite, if requested, four years later. From 1950 there have been 31 counties formed, the last one in January, 1969 (one has been dissolved as a result of a negative vote four years after establishment).

The size of the counties vary but compare favorably in size to the school divisions which they replaced. The order establishing a county indicates the number of divisions (meaning is analagous to wards or electoral divisions, and does not refer to school divisions), up to eleven in number, into which the county is divided. Normally, one councillor is elected per division for a three-year term. The councillors so elected select one of their members to be reeve—the chief executive officer who has all the rights, duties, privileges and powers of the reeve of a municipality and the chairman of the board of trustees of a school division.

At the organizational meeting of the county council (reeve and councillors) two major committees are formed—a municipal committee and a board of education (prior to 1977 called a school committee). Each of these committees must have at least three members of the county council, and each committee appoints a chairman. In practice all of the councillors become members of the municipal committee (with the reeve as chairman) and all of the councillors also become members of the board of education. Each committee establishes a budget and submits this to the county council for approval. When passed, the budget forms the operational authority for the committees. There is one county office which houses the administrative officers and staff for both municipal and school affairs.

The main complicating factor arises when there are towns and villages within the county which are part of the county for educational purposes but not for municipal purposes. There have been several changes in the County Act since 1950 to provide educational representation for these towns and villages, but currently the legislation permits elected school representatives from these educational units (towns, villages, hamlets, summer villages and other areas which are in the county for educational purposes only) to sit on the board of education as full-fledged members, but up to a maximum equal to the number of (electoral) divisions within the county. Towns with a population of 2000 to 4000 have two school representatives and towns with a population of over 4000 have three representatives, and educational units of less than 2000 population having one representative. Where the number of school representatives exceeds the number of divisions, a rotation system is established, first guaranteeing the educational units with populations of under 1000 at least one school representative to be on the board of education, this one person to represent all the units under 1000 population. A second rotation system is established to equate the number of remaining places on the board of education with the number of school representatives from population areas of greater than 2000.

The board of education does not have the power to borrow money, collect taxes for educational purposes or to pass the final budget. Other than these limitations, the board of education operates in exactly the same way as does a board of trustees for a school division. The amalgamation of municipal and educational services is more imaginary than real in that both committees operate independently of each other (keeping in mind there are members who sit on both committees) and the financial and bookkeeping aspects are kept separate even though housed in the same building.

Figure 5-1, the County of Mountain View, is a representation of an Alberta County. The governing body of the county is the county council comprising seven councillors (one from each of the divi-

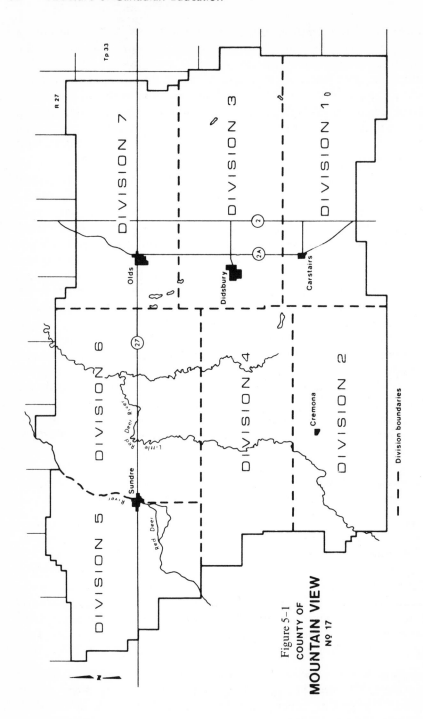

Figure 5–1
COUNTY OF
MOUNTAIN VIEW
№ 17

sions). The county council forms a municipal committee which, in this case, consists of all seven councillors. The other main committee, the board of education, consists of fourteen members—the seven councillors plus two representatives from Olds, two from Didsbury, one from Carstairs, one from Sundre and one from Cremona. These five towns and villages are in the county of Mountain View for school purposes but not for municipal purposes.

REFERENCES

Annual Reports of the Departments of Education of the Governments of the Provinces in Canada.

Bargen, P. F., "The Local School Board: What Flexibility Does It Have?" *Education Canada*, Winter, 1977.

Brown, A. *Changing School Districts in Canada*. Toronto: The Ontario Institute for Studies in Education, 1968.

Chalmers, J. W. *Schools of the Foothills Province*. Edmonton: The Alberta Teachers' Association, 1967.

Cheal, J. E., H. C. Melsness and A. W. Reeves. *Educational Administration: The Role of the Teacher*. Toronto: Macmillan Company, 1962.

Coleman, P., "Power Diffusion in Educational Governance: Redefining the Roles of Trustees and Administrators in Canadian Education," *The Politics of Canadian Education*. Canadian Society for the Study of Education, 1977.

The County Act. Chapter 71 Revised Statutes of Alberta, 1970, with amendments to 1977.

Educational Leadership: The Organizational Framework. Toronto: The Canadian Education Association, 1974.

Enns, F. *The Legal Status of the Canadian School Board*. Toronto: Macmillan Company, 1963.

Flower, G. E. *How Big is Too Big?* Toronto: W. J. Gage, 1964.

Friesen, D. and C. S. Bumbarger (eds.) *Board/Administrator Relationships*. Report of Banff Regional Invitational Conference for School Administrators. Edmonton: Department of Educational Administration, University of Alberta, 1970.

Greenhill, C. J., "Central Office Officials in the Politics of Education," *The Politics of Education*. Canadian Society for the Study of Education, 1977.

Hickox, E. and G. Burston, "The Question of Size," *Education Canada*, September, 1973.

Humphreys, E. H., "What It Takes to Develop a Good School Board Planning Unit," *Education Canada*, Fall, 1975.

Plenderleith, W. A. *The Role of the District Superintendent in Public School Administration in British Columbia*. Toronto: The Ryerson Press, 1961.

Stewart, B. C. *Supervision in Local School Districts—Canada*. Toronto: Canadian Education Association, 1972.

Taylor, Anson S., "Reorganization of School Board Administration Structures," *Education Canada*, December, 1973.

Questions for Discussion

1. Should the larger city school districts elect trustees on a ward basis?

2. How does the quality of school board members in school divisions, units and counties compare with the trustees of the larger city districts?

3. State the pros and cons of having trustees elected (appointed) for staggered terms as compared to electing the entire board each three (or specified number) years.

4. Should superintendents of schools be appointed by the provincial government or by the local school board?

5. Should both the secretary-treasurer and superintendent of schools be chief executive officers of the school board?

6. Explain the organization of school jurisdictions in the northern parts of Alberta, Saskatchewan and Manitoba (Northland School Division, Northern School Board, Frontier School Division).

7. Does the administration of school affairs through the Board of Education of a county effectively place education within the Department of Municipal Affairs?

8. Compare the Alberta counties with counties in England and the United States.

9. The movement towards county formation in rural Alberta appears to have stopped. Why?

10. Why are the boundaries of school jurisdictions so irregular?

11. Compare the advantages and disadvantages of electing. versus appointing school board members.

6

Financing Canadian Education

This chapter discusses the principles of equalization, foundation, lighthouse, incentive and flat grants, as they apply to financing Canadian education. The principles are then illustrated through the explanation of financing education, using one province as an example.

Equalization Principle

The basic reasoning to the equalization principle is that all children deserve an equality in educational opportunities, at least as far as this can be measured in dollars and cents. Whether a child comes from a poor area or a rich area should not be sufficient grounds for varying educational opportunities. Children are victims of their environments, they have no choice, usually, as to where they will receive their education. Therefore the financial resources for education must be distributed on an equitable basis. Equalizing the financial basis does not necessarily mean an adequate education for all but rather an equal educational opportunity for all—whether this is a poor opportunity or a good opportunity.

To illustrate the equalization principle, consider three areas with the following abilities to pay for education:

Area A—$250. per student per annum
Area B—$650. per student per annum
Area C—$950. per student per annum

The average ability to pay would be $617. per student (assuming equal numbers of students in the three areas). To equalize these three areas, Area A would need $367. per student assistance ($617.–

61

$250.). Area B would contribute $33. ($650.-$617) per Area A student and Area C would contribute $333. ($950.-$617.) per Area A student. This is illustrated graphically in figure 6-1.

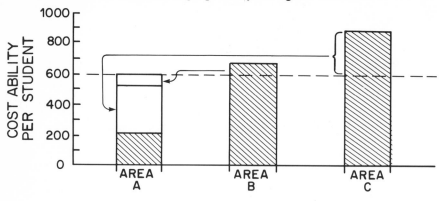

Figure 6-1
Illustration of Equalization Principle

This explanation is a vast oversimplification of the equalization principle, as becomes obvious when one attempts to work out details for such a system. For example, consider the possibility of Area C in our illustration as being an area in which the cost of living, services, etc., is much higher than in Area A. After re-distribution, both Areas A and C will have $617. per student, but because the cost of living is higher in Area C, the general wage scale is higher and therefore Area C will have to hire teachers with lower qualifications than Area A to compensate for this wage differential. Likewise with supplies, buildings, and equipment. Therefore the quality of education in Area C could very well be less than in Area A because each dollar in Area C would purchase less than each dollar in Area A. Therefore a device would be required to compensate for dollar value in each area.

Further, it may be that in Area A the people have decided that roads and hospitals are priority items before education. That is, after the other priorities are considered, they have left $250. per student as ability to pay for education. But Areas B and C may have placed education as a high priority. If so, it would not be fair to penalize Areas B and C to compensate another area which has different priorities. Therefore a factor must be included in the equalization which compensates for priorities.

An analysis of nearly any financial statement will show that senior high education is more expensive than elementary education. If one area has a different ratio of senior high to elementary as compared to another area, a compensating factor would need to be included in the equalization formula.

It may be that Area B is a rural area, requiring extensive busing of students. A factor in the equalization formula would be needed if Area A was urban and therefore required no busing. Further, what is meant by an area? Should the equalization take place province by province, with the "have" provinces of British Columbia, Alberta and Ontario equalizing the "have not" provinces; should the equalization be on a major regional basis; should it be on a school district basis; or perhaps compare school against school? As education is a provincial responsibility, the federal government cannot equalize for educational purposes per se, but through the federal government the "have" provinces do assist the "have not" provinces, thus directly affecting the equalization principle for education on a province by province basis. In each province the areas which have better paying abilities assist the less fortunate areas. Even within a school jurisdiction (district, division, unit, county) the equalization principle is at work.

Another difficulty in establishing a fair equalization formula is establishing ability to pay. In a very general way it is easy enough to say that Area C is richer than Area A, for example. But putting this feeling down in a formula expressed in exact numbers is a more difficult problem. Does one consider as evidence of wealth, the number of cars per house, the size of the house, to which clubs the people belong, or should the basis be the market value of the property? Should the evidence be the average income of the people as determined from the amount of income tax paid or perhaps the size of their bank accounts? One area may be rural, another suburban, another inner city, thus complicating comparisons. One area may be older and thus have fewer children in school, and thus inflate figures based on a per student basis. It is becoming more common to live in one area, say on an acreage or in an adjoining town and work in the city. The problem then arises as to which area has the responsibility for the education of the children—the area from which the income is derived or the area in which the children live.

The foregoing illustrates the difficulty of obtaining a workable equalization formula after accepting the desirability of equalization. The purpose of equalization is to force areas with a more substantial financial base to help areas with a less substantial financial base. However, if this was the only base for determining educational financing it could mean that instead of having "good" educational programs and "poor" educational programs, the net result would be an entire system of mediocre educational programs.

The Foundation Program

A modification of the equalization principle is the principle of the foundation program. There is determined a base program, a minimum acceptable educational program below which no area would be permitted to fall. For the purposes of illustration, consider the same three areas as in the illustration for the equalization principle. Suppose the provincial department of education determined that an expense of $750. per student was necessary to maintain an acceptable minimum program. The provincial government would therefore be required to assist Area A by $500. per student. Area B would require $100. per student and Area C would not require grants to bring it to the foundation level as it was already above this level. The amount this Area was above $750. probably would be retained by Area C, but the possibility is to have the amount above $750. from Area C redistributed to Areas A and B, with the provincial government contributing the remaining amount needed.

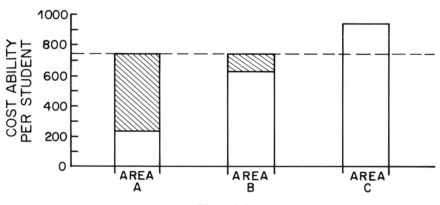

Figure 6-2
Illustration of Foundation Program

The foundation program, then, is basically not a redistribution of monies among areas but rather the subsidizing of an area by the provincial government (directly or indirectly) to bring the area up to an acceptable minimum. There is not true equalization but there is equalization to a minimum standard.

Incentive Grants

If the provincial government wishes the school jurisdictions to implement a particular program, the department of education could demand that such be done. As agents of the department of education, the boards of trustees would be forced to comply. That is, whether reading is taught in the schools is not an optional matter for school boards—they must ensure that reading is taught. However, there are other programs which the departments of education wish included in the school program but are not prepared to demand that it be done (too much visibility of central authority being one reason). In such cases the carrot and the donkey approach is used—if you want the donkey to move, dangle a carrot in front of his nose. For example, if the department of education wishes school systems to hire teacher librarians for school libraries, the department could offer a grant of a few thousand dollars per year if such was done. That way the school board wouldn't be forced to hire teacher-librarians, but if they didn't there would be a "loss" of the grant, something that local pressure probably wouldn't permit.

Often the departments of education will use the incentive grant to initiate a course of action which has not yet been established. When the course of desired action is firmly implanted, the department may withdraw that incentive grant, realizing that local pressure would ensure the retention of the idea.

An example of an incentive grant is the following:

A grant of $9500. is paid for each special education teaching position approved by the Deputy Minister in which a teacher is employed full time exclusively for teaching students who require special instruction because of sub-normal mentality, defective hearing or eyesight or for other reason determined by the Minister.

School boards are prone to use the incentive principle when they make offers such as "for equipment which is desirable in a school but is not normally supplied by the school board, the school board will match the community-raised money on a dollar-for-dollar basis". Many a projector has been purchased for schools on this basis.

Incentive grants usually involve some spending on behalf of the school board and therefore the poorer the district the more likelihood of the district not "taking advantage" of some of the incentive grants of the department of education.

Flat Grants

Flat grants are grants paid on a specific basis regardless of other factors such as ability to pay. For example, a grant may be paid on the basis of a specified number of dollars per elementary student, or per teacher. It is sometimes difficult to determine the difference between an incentive grant and a flat grant because of the overlap between the two. Let us say the department of education pays $9500. per year for each special education teacher hired by the board. If the grant is the same as for other classroom teachers, then the $9500. is probably a flat grant. But if the grant for other teachers is $7500., then the $2000. difference may be an incentive grant. Or it may be that the $2000. is recognition of reduced enrolment in special education classes, and therefore the $2000. difference is only a flat grant.

Flat grants and foundation program grants are not mutually exclusive categories of grants even though the principles involved are distinguishable from each other. For example, a department of education may pay $5000. per teacher hired by the school board plus $1000. per student enrolled, these two grants then becoming flat grants. However, if the department of education determined these payments would enable all school jurisdictions within the province to maintain a certain minimum acceptable level of education, the grants are also foundation program grants.

Lighthouse Principle

Some specific areas may wish to provide for education above and beyond any foundation or average levels. Providing they do so from additional revenue raised in their own area, the area invariably is permitted to do so. That school, or that area, then becomes a lighthouse, educationally speaking. While equality of educational opportunity is an important principle, lowering the standards of the above-average schools in order to achieve equality is not an acceptable procedure. Where areas wish to finance beyond the capabilities of other areas, it must be their prerogative to do so. In the example used previously in this chapter, Area C would be a lighthouse area if they used the revenue raising ability to provide $950. or more per student.

From time to time various terms become "in words" which are used in ways which make meaning quite difficult. A current example is, "block grants for generic services", the meaning of which is not aided by use of a dictionary. Another difficulty in understanding grant structure is the mixing of types of grants. Quite often it is not possible to say with assurance whether a grant is equalization, foundation, incentive or flat because it may contain elements of several of these factors, previous examples illustrating this difficulty. Sometimes a grant is labelled "foundation" when it really is a "flat" grant, that is, the basic terms are not always properly used. In spite of the difficulties of improper terminology and the use of terms which are not effectively descriptive, a basic understanding of the principles of equalization, incentive, flat, foundation and lighthouse should improve understanding of financing education in Canada.

The remaining part of this chapter discusses educational finance in one province, that of Alberta. Although the amounts vary from province to province and there are varying emphases according to the needs and interests of people living in different parts of Canada, the basic ideas and the direction of financing is, for the most part, typical of other Canadian provinces.

Financing Education in Alberta

A school jurisdiction, whether it is a school district, school division, or board of education of a county, receives financing for education from the following sources:

1. Foundation program grants from the Department of Education.

2. Other grants from the Department of Education.

3. Local supplementary requisitions.

4. Miscellaneous sources.

Ideally a school board, in developing a budget, would list the programs desired, then determine the cost of satisfactorily staffing, housing and maintaining these programs. The next step would be to determine the financing available from the foundation program and other grants from the Department of Education, plus any miscellaneous sources. This amount would be subtracted from the total cost previously determined, leaving a balance which would have to be paid from additional local property taxation. In practice, this balance remaining would result in excessive local supplementary taxation (requisition). Therefore the board reexamines the programs, eliminating some, changing others, examines staffing and maintenance patterns until this extra amount to be levied against the local property taxpayer is reasonable and politically acceptable. Changing programs and staffing patterns effects departmental grants and other sources of financing and therefore there is a continual reshuffling at each stage of the budgeting process until the final budget is approved. The approved budget is then the direction and control of the approved educational plan for that school jurisdiction for the fiscal year.

The discussion following focuses on each of these categories in turn. But first, a reminder that the proportions in each of the categories vary from jurisdiction to jurisdiction. That is, for the fiscal year 1976 the sources of revenue for the total of all jurisdictions in Alberta was as follows:

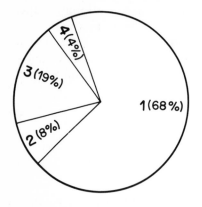

1.	Foundation Program	$468,678,120.
2.	Other Prov. Grants	57,200,586.
3.	Supplementary Req.	130,325,222.
4.	Miscellaneous	29,602,392.
	Total	685,806,320.

Figure 6–3
Total 1976 Revenues for
School Jurisdictions in Alberta

To illustrate the differences in revenue among jurisdictions, two examples are illustrated in figure 6–4. These are the Rocky View School Division and the Fort Vermilion School Division. The numbers 1 to 4 correspond to the categories Foundation Program, Other Provincial Grants, Supplementary Requisitions, and Miscellaneous respectively.

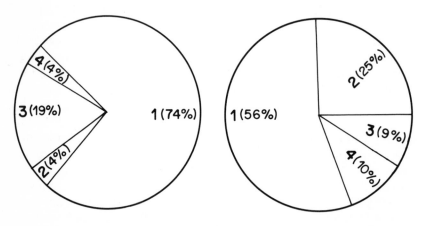

Rocky View School Division   Fort Vermilion School Division

Figure 6–4
Revenues for Two School Divisions for 1976

1. Foundation program grants from the Department of Education.

The basis for the school foundation program is found in section 129 of *The School Act*. The parts of this section which are relevant to this discussion are as follows:

129.(1) The School Foundation Program Fund heretofore established is continued.

(2) The Lieutenant Governor in Council shall by February 15 in each year, or as soon thereafter as possible, establish a rate expressed in mills, not exceeding 30 mills.

(3) Each municipality shall pay into the School Foundation Program Fund annually a sum equal to the amount which results from applying the mill rate established pursuant to subsection (2) to the equalized assessment of the municipality as established for the year by the Alberta Assessment Equalization Board under *The Municipalities Assessment and Equalization Act*.

(7) The Lieutenant Governor in Council may make regulations

(a) authorizing the Minister to pay from the School Foundation Program Fund such sums as are required to be paid by the regulations;

(b) prescribing the amounts to be paid each year from the School Foundation Program Fund to each board and county either specifically or in accordance with a formula;

(c) authorizing the Minister to make any calculation or perform any function or duty that is required to determine a sum to be paid to a board or a county from the School Foundation Program Fund;

(d) empowering the Minister to determine the entitlement of any board or county or make any calculation, perform any function or do any act for the purpose of determining the entitlement of any board or county to any sum from the School Foundation Program Fund.

(9) Nothing in this section restricts or prohibits or limits the power of a board to requisition a municipality for such further revenue as it may require for its operations but the requisition shall be subject to section 119.

(11) Notwithstanding anything contained in this section

(a) property assessed for separate school purposes shall not be included in the equalized assessment referred to in subsection (3), and

(b) no payment shall be made out of the Fund to any separate school district, unless the board of the district certifies to the Minister under the seal of the district, pursuant to a resolution passed by the board, that this section is to apply to it.

(14) Notwithstanding subsections (3) to (8), the Lieutenant Governor in Council may by order suspend or defer in whole or in part the payment of any sum required to be paid under subsection (3) for such period of time and on such terms and conditions as he prescribes.

In 1976 the equalized assessment of taxable property in school jurisdictions in Alberta was as follows (all figures rounded off to the nearest million):

School Division and Counties	$1,459,940,000.
City School Districts	3,220,131,000.
Town School Districts	207,991,000.
Village School Districts	5,090,000.
Consolidated School Districts	4,268,000.
Rural School Districts	41,614,000.
Total	$4,901,584,000.

There was an additional $350,000,000. (approximately) of equalized assessment to which the school foundation program mill rate applied, but was not within the school jurisdictions indicated above. That is, there was a total equalized assessment of approximately $5,300,000,000. which served as the basis for the school foundation program.

Equalized assessment differs from the ordinary (actual) assessment. It is based on the principle that a standard mill rate applied to property across Alberta would not yield comparative revenues if the properties were assessed on different bases. For example, if a house in Calgary is assessed (for taxation purposes) at $10,000., the maximum levy of 30 mills would yield $300. But if the exact same house in Edmonton, with other factors being equal, is assessed for $8,000., the yield would be $240. Therefore, equalized assessment is an attempt to ensure when a standard mill rate is applied, the taxes paid would be equitable.

All property in Alberta (and other provinces) is not necessarily assessed and/or taxed. There are three general categories of such property. First, there is property which is not taxed but for which an equivalent amount is paid. The best example is property (land and buildings) owned by the federal government. Usually the federal government pays the local municipality a grant which would be nearly the same as if the property had been assessed and taxed. Secondly, there is property which is not taxed but for which some compensation is afforded the municipality. An example of this is property under railway land grants which date back many years. Usually the municipality receives some revenue from this property but proportionately little in comparison to other taxed property. Thirdly, there is property which is not taxed and for which no compensation is afforded the municipality. Churches generally fall within this category.

Another special category involves residential property which is occupied by the owners. The foundation program levy is not applied to the residences which are occupied by the owners and thus are not revenue-producing. Perhaps more correct, technically, would be to say this property is assessed and taxed for the foundation program but this amount is then rebated. Renters are also given some assistance towards their rental costs, but there is no direct connection between renters and the school foundation program.

The mill rate established in 1976 according to section 129(2) of *The School Act* was 26 mills. Thus a sum of $137,800,000. was payable by the owners of the properties into the provincial school foundation program fund ($80,305,000. of which was attributable to homes and therefore not collected). This was supplemented by $411,183,000., from other provincial revenues. The total of these two amounts, $468,678,000., was distributed back to the school jurisdictions in Alberta, according to the formulas set out in the school foundation program fund regulations.

The following is a summary of the pertinent parts of the school foundation program fund regulations.

The annual grant (1978) is the sum of parts (a), (b), (c) and (d).

(a) Instruction. The grant is based on $1049. for each elementary student, $1100. for each junior high student, and $1260. for each senior high student. The grant for students who reside in a school district established for the purpose of educating the children of employees of the Government of Canada is 50 percent of the regular grant.

(b) Transportation. For other than city school boards the basic transportation grant is $28.00 to $41.50 per school bus per day operated, depending upon the size of the school bus. To this is added a grant which is the product of A and B, where A is $0.46 and B is the sum of the route eligible mileage during the transportation year for all the school buses of the board minus the product of the number of days in the transportation year and 50. Several other factors also influence the size of the transportation grant, for example, a weighting factor for junior and senior high students, non-operating day allowances and special education student allowance. Where it is necessary for the parent instead of the school board to provide transportation and the board pays for such transportation, the board is reimbursed by grants of 23 cents per kilometer or $3.25 per day (whichever is less), or where the student is necessarily maintained away from home, a maximum rate of $5.00 per day. Where city school boards necessarily provide transportation, the grant is the lesser of the actual cost of the transportation and $100. per year per student.

(c) Administration. The administration grant is three percent of the total of parts (a) and (b), that is, three percent of the grant paid on the basis of Instruction and Transportation.

(d) Debt Retirement and Capital Expenditure. The grant is equal to the cost of repayment of debentures as they become due provided the debenture borrowing was for area sizes within the limitations set by the School Buildings Board and within an approved cost per square foot limit.

The approved area for a school building is decided by the School Buildings Board of the Department of Education and is based on a Statement of Building Needs completed by the school district. The maximum supported cost limits range from a maximum of $20. per square foot for portable buildings to a maximum of $35.50 per square foot for permanent type construction, plus an allowance of up to $5.00 per sq. ft. where the distance to the nearest city is over 225 miles and an allowance of up to $2.00 per sq. ft. for water and sewage systems. School boards may build beyond the approved areas and pay beyond the maximum support limits providing such additional costs are paid for by the school district's finances other than those with this part (d). Additional allowances are provided for quality restoration programs.

2. Other Grants from the Department of Education. The basis for payment of other grants for education is found in *The Department of Education Act,* which states, in part:

> 7.1 (1) The Minister may make grants if
>> (a) he is authorized to do so by regulations under this section, and
>> (b) moneys are appropriated by the Legislature for that purpose of the grant is authorized to be paid pursuant to a special warrant.
>
>   (2) The Lieutenant Governor in Council may make regulations
>> (a) authorizing the Minister to make grants;
>> (b) prescribing the purposes for which grants may be made;
>> (c) governing applications for grants;
>> (d) prescribing the persons or organizations or classes of persons or organizations eligible for grants;
>> (e) specifying the conditions required to be met by any

applicant for a grant to render that person eligible for the grant;...

(h) limiting the amount of any grant or class of grant that may be made;

The following is a summary of the pertinent parts of the regulations referred to above (details will be found in the *Alberta Education Grants Order, 1978*). It should be remembered these grants are in addition to those from the School Foundation Program Fund. For example, the students who are counted in these regulations for a special classroom for subnormal mentality are also counted towards the instruction grant of the School Foundation Program Fund.

1. A grant is paid, "...for each full time special education teaching position approved by the Deputy Minister and in which a teacher is employed by a board exclusively for teaching special education extension students or pupils requiring special education, ..." These grants range from $10,050. to $19,875. per position per year. The specialty of positions are: educable mentally retarded, learning disabled, socially maladjusted, resource room, language deficit, trainable mentally retarded, institutional, homebound, severely learning disabled, hard of hearing, low vision, speech disorders, specified special school, braille, deafness, deafness (total communication program).

2. A grant not to exceed $250. per year, or $5. per day (whichever is less) is paid with respect to any intern teacher employed in a classroom.

3. Where a board pays a grant to another approved organization or agency for special education services for individuals who are trainable mentally retarded, severely learning disabled, or socially maladjusted to the extent that he cannot be educated in a school of the board, a reimbursing grant is paid to the board on a sliding scale ranging from $1300. for trainable mentally retarded over 24 years of age, to $3240. for severely learning disabled from 15 to 24 years of age. To obtain maximum grant, the board contribution would need to be $180.

4. Where a board pays a grant, for capital purposes, to an approved organization or agency to provide instruction for persons who are trainable mentally retarded or severely learning disabled, a reimbursing grant is paid to the board for the lesser of 90 percent of the actual cost or 90 percent of the support for which the project

would be eligible if it was a project of the board under The School Buildings Regulations.

5. Where a board provides day school instruction in a trade or other occupational subject in a vocational program, the grant is either (a) or (b).

(a) $2330. per shop facility, plus $300. for each student enrolled in a vocational program carrying a total credit of at least 15, plus $270. per each student enrolled whose education is the responsibility of another board.

(b) $24.25 per credit enrolment unit in a vocational course included in a vocational program, plus $8.75 per credit enrolment unit for such students who are the responsibility of another board.

6. Where a board provides extension programs for day, evening or summer students, a grant is paid on the basis of:

(a) $50.30 per credit enrolment unit for students receiving at least 21 hours of instruction per credit, to a maximum of $1260. per student.

(b) $7.00 per hour for instruction of extension students at the elementary or junior high levels (minimum of 12 students per class).

(c) $1172. less any amount paid under (a) and (b), per school year, in respect of any special education extension student.

7. A grant may be paid to a board to enable it to continue the operation of its school, and to augment an approved special program.

8. A grant may be paid to a new, rural school district to enable the board to provide a school building. The normal grant is $5000. but this may be extended to $10,000. under special circumstances.

9. Grants may be paid to boards and other agencies providing education for students from unorganized territory. Generally, these would not exceed the tuition fee to the board providing the education and up to $2200. per annum to a temporary community in unorganized territory for provision of transportation to an organized school district, or up to $3700. per annum to mission or other schools approved by the Minister which provide education for children resident in unorganized territory.

10. Grants may be paid to boards on the basis of $7.20 per student, plus $3.40 per specified handicapped students, to reimburse the board share of payments to Canada Pension Plan.

11. For private schools which have been in operation for three years, have a minimum of 25 students per certificated teacher, where the teachers are not required to teach more than three grades, and is not being operated for monetary gain, the grant is $469. per elementary student, $515. per junior high student, and $610. per senior high student, for 1977, which is increased for 1978 to 50 percent of the per pupil grants paid to school boards. The 50 percent is expected to be increased to 80 percent in 1979.

12. For the purpose of purchasing reading materials, a grant of $2.15 per student enrolled in grades one to six is paid. Private schools are also eligible for this grant.

13. For small school boards who jointly hire a superintendent of schools, a grant is paid to each board on the basis of the actual cost, which is the lesser of $13.50 per student to a maximum of $5400.

14. Where a school board contracts for the services of diagnosing and assisting students with perceptual and learning disorders, for the school year 1977/78 a grant may be paid which is the lesser of $16.50 per elementary student, the actual costs of the services, or $100,000. in total.

15. Where a board implements an approved program for the purpose of enhancing the quality of education in the elementary grades, a grant may be paid, for the period January 1, 1977 to June 30, 1979, on the basis of actual cost up to $27.50 per elementary student.

16. Up to the end of the school year, 1977, grants may be paid to boards who implement approved compensatory educational programs for disadvantaged.

17. Grants ranging from $525. for non-handicapped children to $1330. for handicapped children are paid for students enrolled in an Early Childhood Services Program. Grants are also available for limited renovations of buildings to serve early childhood programs.

18. Grants are also available to help compensate for the operation of small schools, declining enrolment areas, varying equalized requisitions, and grants to teachers teaching in certain designated "isolated" areas in Alberta.

3. Local Supplementary Requisitions. If a board determines the revenues obtained from the School Foundation Program Fund, other grants and from miscellaneous sources are not sufficient for the operation of its educational system, the board may requisition

a further amount from the ratepayers in the district. This amount would be in addition to the mill rate established for the School Foundation Program (currently 26 mills). The basis for supplemental requisitions is found in Sections 119 and 120 of *The School Act.*

119. The Minister may make regulations
   (a) limiting the amount of money a board may requisition from a municipality and may base the limit (expressed in an amount or as a percentage) on any criteria he considers proper, and
   (b) providing any method, including a vote called for by electors, by which a board may exceed the limits specified pursuant to clause (a).

120. (1) Subject to the regulations made under section 119 a board in computing its total basic requisition upon each municipality included in whole or in part within the district or division, shall deduct from its estimated total expenditures its estimated total revenues from all sources, other than requisitions, in order to obtain the estimated total sum required to be raised by requisitions.

4. Miscellaneous Revenues.
   a. From the federal government for the provision of educational services for Indians and other children who are the responsibility of the federal government.
   b. From other school authorities for specified educational services provided through agreements.
   c. From the sale of capital assets such as abandoned schools, obsolete equipment, houses for teachers.
   d. From the rental of school board owned houses for teachers and other school board employees.
   e. From textbook rentals.
   f. From rental of school facilities to community and other groups.
   g. Other miscellaneous sources.

School Board Expenditures

As with revenues, the expenditures of school boards vary from jurisdiction to jurisdiction. The following are the expenditures of one jurisdiction for one fiscal year (approximately 21,000 students).

Elementary School Instruction	$8,891,052.
Junior High School Instruction	5,432,983.
Senior High School Instruction	5,537,165.
Special Education	1,213,855.
Community Services	72,633.
Student Personnel Services	2,369,738.
Early Childhood Services	482,473.
Administration	1,390,030.
Operation and Maintenance	4,144,084.
Transportation of Students	1,194,963.
Debt Services	2,839,580.
Contribution to Capital Fund	603,279.
Total Operational Expenditure	$34,171,835.

Dividing the total operational expenditure by the number of students results in an expenditure of $1627. per student in 1976.

REFERENCES

Alban, N., "Let's Bring Financial Controls Up to Date," *Education Canada*, Spring, 1975.

Annual Reports of the Departments of Education of the Governments of the Provinces in Canada.

Atherton, P., "What's Happening in Education Finance," *Education Canada*, Winter, 1976.

Duncan, D. J. and J. W. Peach, "School-Based Budgetting: Implications for the Principal," *Education Canada*, Fall, 1977.

Gathercole, F. J., "Why Spending Controls are Necessary," *Education Canada*, March, 1971.

Giles, T. E., "Education Budget Plebiscites are Undesirable," *The Alberta School Trustee*, October, 1970.

Government of Alberta. *School Foundation Program Fund Regulations.* Edmonton, 1978.

Government of Alberta. *School Grants Regulations.* Edmonton, 1978.

Hanson, E. J. *Financing Education in Alberta.* Edmonton: The Alberta Teachers' Association, 1969.

Loken, G. Education Finance Today. A background paper for the Alberta School Trustees' Association, 1977.

Peitchinis, S. G., "Is There a Federal Role in Education Finance?" Paper presented to the Western Canada Education Finance Conference in Banff, April, 1974.

Rawlyk, S., "Some Fundamental Issues in Funding Special Education," *Education Canada*, Spring, 1977.

Rogers, D. C. and H. S. Ruchlin. *Economics and Education.* New York: The Free Press, 1971.

Seastone, D. *Economic and Demographic Futures in Education Alberta 1970–2005.* Edmonton: Human Resources Research Council, 1971.

Statistics Canada. *Education in Canada.* Ottawa: Information Canada, 1973.

Statistics Canada. *Survey of Education Finance,* Ottawa: Information Canada, 1974.

Questions for Discussion

1. Should well-to-do areas be permitted to raise additional monies so as to provide a higher quality educational program for their children?

2. Does fiscal dependency affect local autonomy?

3. Is property tax a fair method of financing education? How about income tax? sales tax? tuition fees?

4. To what extent can the quality of education be determined by calculating the revenues needed to support the educational program?

5. Many school districts are experimenting with decentralized budgets. Is this a trend to be encouraged?

6. Will the trend towards greater accountability affect present educational programs?

7. How effective has budgeting been through PPBES (Planning, Programming, Budgeting, Evaluation Systems)?

8. Should the school board fiscal year be congruent with the calendar year, the government fiscal year or the school year?

9. Should government grants be higher for costs associated with senior high students than for elementary students?

10. Compare the Alberta model of financing education with other provincial models.

11. Explain the procedure and determinants on which an assessment is made on a ratepayer's house.

12. What is the correlation between the quality of education provided and the number of dollars spent by a school board?

TEACHER RELATIONSHIPS

PART THREE

7

Legal Liability of Teachers

Introduction

The school year has barely begun before the teacher is expected to act or react to pressing statements and queries as , "I feel sick—I wanna go home," "I need an aspirin for my headache," "Jimmy poked his pencil in my ear." It may be the teacher receives a phone call from an irate parent, "My daughter was hurt while on that science field trip and I'm going to sue you," or perhaps it is the parent saying, "My son was sold marijuana during your physics class today. You will be hearing from my lawyer," or maybe it is a word of caution, "My daughter is an epileptic—you do know what to do when she has a seizure, don't you?" It is unlikely any individual teacher will be confronted with all of these situations, but a few such confrontations forces the teacher to an increased awareness of a very real problem—just what is expected of a teacher and where does the teacher stand from a legal viewpoint? The educator begins to realize there is more involved in teaching than the dispensing of knowledge.

Just as a homeowner may find, much to his chagrin, the icy patch on his sidewalk could lead to a liability action when the next door neighbor slips and breaks a leg, so too finds the teacher a wide range of opportunity for parents, and others, to attempt actions for damages. Whether the actions are justified or not is only part of the problem. When legal action is taken, and the teacher is involved, there are legal fees, loss of salary, mental stress, breakdown of parent-teacher relations, strain on student-teacher rapport and employer-employee relationships to consider, regardless of whether or not the teacher was responsible for a negligent act. If the courts find the teacher responsible, there is the possibility of payment of damages, which often are considerable. The following recent case illustrates the extent of damages which may be awarded.[1]

> Plaintiff, a 15-year old boy, was a pupil in a school administered by defendant trustees; he was a member of a gymnastic class in charge of defendant E. The boys were performing somersaults by jumping off a spring-board and landing on a pile of foam rubber chunks contained in a large net. In order to obtain a better take-off from the spring-board the boys had placed a box horse in a position from which they jump from it onto the end of the spring-board; they did this with E.'s permission. The boys were inexperienced gymnasts and they were given no warnings or instructions by E., who, while they were performing their somersaults was sitting at a desk writing report cards. One boy made a bad landing and injured his wrist, which was later found to be broken. Despite this mishap, no warning was given to the class; some additional two-inch thick foam rubber mats were placed around the perimeter of the landing area, E. returned to his desk and the somersaults continued. Shortly after, this plaintiff, attempting a somersault, landed on his head on one of the two-inch thick pads and suffered severe spinal injury which rendered him a quadriplegic. He would require total care for the rest of his life expectancy, which was found to be 49 years. In the following judgment Andrews J. reviews fully the needs of a quadriplegic requiring total care, and the cost thereof.

> Held, the use to which the gymnastic apparatus was put was inherently dangerous, a fact which E. knew or ought to have known; the first mishap ought to have put him on notice. This, and his failure to supervise closely his inexperienced pupils, or to warn or instruct them, amounted to negligence for which he was liable. Since he was acting within the scope of his employment, defendant trustees were also liable. Plantiff was not contributorily negligent. He would require total care on a 24-hour-a-day basis for the rest of his life and had lost his whole enjoyment of life and his ability to work. He was entitled to the following damages: Special damages— $42,128.87; Cost of future care, including home, furnishings and special equipment— $1,133,071.80; Loss of ability to earn income $103,858.26; Loss of amenities and enjoyment of life—$200,000 in total $1,534,058.93.

In the subsequent appeal to the British Columbia Court of Appeal, the general damages were reduced to $600,000., then raised to $810,000. by the Supreme Court of Canada. Total judgment therefore became $859,628.

Therefore, because of the very nature of the teacher's role—that of working with impulsive, capricious and adventuresome students who are the sons and daughters of worrisome, sagacious and protective parents—the teacher must be at least as cautious and responsible as the real parents. In this chapter some suggestions will be made, and inferences drawn, from the experience gained from other teachers in Canada who are now wiser, but often poorer, for their

---

[1]Thornton, Tanner et al. v Board of School Trustees of School District No. 57 (Prince George), Edamura and Harrower, (1975) 3 W.W.R. 622, 57 D.L.R. (3d) (1976) 5 W.W.R. 240, (1978) 1 W.W.R. 606.

experiences. The cases used in the discussions, even though they are actual cases, must be considered as illustrative only. The reader is cautioned that, while some generalizations are made which may be of some assistance in guiding the teachers' actions, each case is dependent upon the particular facts and value judgments involved. There are no "cut-and-dried" cases. The main purpose here is to provide some insight for novice teachers as to situations which are potentially dangerous and to give some advice which may circumvent these situations or at least strengthen the ability of the teacher to deal with the situation.

While the intent of this chapter is to consider the position of the teacher, it should be remembered that very seldom is action taken against the teacher alone. Usually, the defendants named are the teacher, the principal and the school board. There are two main reasons for this. First, the actual responsibility is usually very difficult to define and therefore the plaintiff has a better chance of winning his case if he includes all those who could in any way be implicated, namely, the teacher, principal and board of trustees. Secondly, the testimony of one party may strengthen the case against another party. That is, a teacher could be included in a damage claim whether or not he remains an actual defendant.

When an action against a teacher is imminent, the teacher is well advised to contact the professional association to which he belongs for legal advice. To attempt a defense against an action without the assistance of dependable legal counsel is foolhardy.

Teacher-Employer Relationships

The relationship between a teacher and his employer, the school board, is that of a master and servant, or for those who prefer to avoid that time-tested legal terminology, an employer-employee relationship. Under this relationship the employer can be held responsible for the tortious actions of a teacher it employs, providing these actions were perpetrated within the parameters of the responsibilities for which the teacher was hired.

Definitions of a tortious action tend to be somewhat vague. However, one of the more commonly accepted definitions is that from Prosser.[2]

"Tort" is a term applied to a miscellaneous and more or less unconnected group

---

[2]W. L. Prosser, *Handbook of the Law of Torts*, 2nd edition. St. Paul, Minnesota: West Publishing Co., 1955.

of civil wrongs, other than breach of contract, for which a court of law will afford a remedy in the form of an action for damages. The law of torts is concerned with the compensation of losses suffered by private individuals in their legally protected interests, through conduct of others which is regarded as socially unreasonable.

This relationship between the school board and the teacher passes responsibility on to the board for certain of the teacher's actions which may result in legal recourse through the courts. However, the teacher must not assume the passing on of the responsibility necessarily relieves the teacher of responsibility. There is added protection and support for the teacher because of the employer-employee relationship but this is not a blanket protection which will necessarily protect the teacher in all ways. Job security, legal costs (if not paid for by the professional association to which the teacher belongs), loss of salary while attending court are possibilities, not to mention an area of concern involving the possibility of the employer subsequently taking action against the teacher. An example of this possibility is illustrated in the following case.[3]

> The action was one for damages for injuries to a child, sustained in a collision between a school bus and farm truck loaded with wheat. The court held both drivers to have been negligent, in that they both approached a "blind" intersection, familiar to both of them, at an excessive speed, and collided in the intersection. The school bus was overturned and the child, partly thrown out of the bus, was pinned underneath and severely injured. Damages totalling $5,539. were assessed equally against the two drivers, the school board, and the farmer who owned the truck.

> The basis of the board's liability was twofold. First, it had a statutory duty to provide transportation. Secondly, the driver of the bus was not, in fact, liable for his act. However, because it was the negligence of the driver that caused the school board to be liable, the court directed that the board was entitled, on the cross-claim against the driver, to have contribution from him for any sums that the board was required to pay.

Even though boards, as employers, can be held liable for negligent actions of its employees, including teachers, the assumption should not be made that the board will, through its insurance company, pick up the tab automatically for any action arising from teacher negligence. Sometimes an assessment is made against both the board and the teacher, in which case the teacher is liable for his own share of the damages. It should be remembered, however, that the master-servant relationship exists and may provide some protection for the teacher only if the teacher was acting as a teacher, that is, within his professional competencies. This means that if the board is able to show the actions of the teacher which led to the legal action were, in fact, not within his normal circumambient authority

---

[3]Sleeman v Foothills School Division (1946) 1 W.W.R. 145.

as a teacher, or if the teacher did not act in ways approved or con-
doned by the board, the master-servant relationship does not exist
and therefore the teacher could be left on his own.

The following case illustrates the importance to the teacher of this
master and servant relationship but still holding the teacher in an
almost untenable position.[4]

> Infant plaintiff was seriously injured when he fell while practising on parallel bars
> at the school where he was a pupil. He and other students were practising under the
> general supervision of a teacher. The action against the teacher was withdrawn after
> considerable legal dialogue pertaining mainly to the teacher-board relationship. An
> award of $183,900. was determined for the boy against the board for the very serious
> injuries sustained from the accident.

Even though in this case the action against the teacher was dropped
this did not prevent prohibitive expenses being incurred. This is
forceably stated in a communication from the solicitors to the
Saskatchewan Teachers' Federation.[5]

> Since damages as well as costs in the McKay and Molesky case were over $200,000.
> the legal costs are accordingly tremendously high. In effect we suggest that if the
> Teachers' Federation was not looking after the interests of the teacher, the costs in
> itself may well be prohibitive to any teacher to fight such a law suit because even if
> the teacher is released pursuant to the above mentioned authorities from legal
> liability, the efforts that his solicitors will have to put into this case are well beyond
> what the teacher will ever recover in legal costs from his opposing sides, even if
> he wins.

The McKay case also illustrates the importance of a section of the
School Act of Saskatchewan which is unique in Canada and which
provides more protection to teachers than in other provinces. This
section states, in part, "Where the board, the principal or the teacher
approves or sponsors activities during the school hours or at other
times the teacher responsible for the conduct of the pupils shall not
be liable...for personal injury suffered by pupils during such activities." The extent of this blanket-type protection will no doubt be
tested through the courts in the years to come.

While the discussion in this section focusses on negligence within
the framework of a master-servant (employer-employee) relationship,
the teacher should be aware this relationship affects a number of
other areas of concern besides negligence, for example, ownership
of copyrights and patents.

---

[4]McKay et al. v Board of Govan School Unit No. 29 et al Saskatchewan, (1967) 60 W.
W.R. 513; (1968) 64 W.W.R. 301; (1967) 62 D.L.R. (2d) 503.
[5]Letter from Francis, Gauley, Dierker and Dahlem, Barristers and Solicitors to the
Saskatchewan Teachers' Federation, February 22, 1965.

Accident and Liability Insurance

Although negligence suits have not been as numerous in Canada as in the United States, the number that have been referred to the courts, and the magnitude of some of the judgments makes the educator quite concerned about protection for himself. The employer-employee relationship helps but further protection is needed. One of the areas of further protection is through insurance, keeping in mind that insurance is not a complete coverage either and sometimes results in a false sense of security.

The first clear distinction a teacher must make is between accident insurance and liability insurance. Most school boards in Canada either provide accident insurance for their students or permit this to be done on a group basis through an insurance company, with the premiums paid by the individuals. When there is this accident coverage and a student is injured, payment of most, or all, of the incurred expenses could be expected from the insurance company. This could be regardless of whether or not the accident arose as a result of a negligent act of the board, principal or teachers. Because the immediate expenses are paid for by the insurance company, usually promptly, the parents are less likely to bring court action against the teacher. After all, if the accident did not actually cost the parents anything there would be little point in trying to convince a judge they should receive extra remuneration. However, the limitations of the accident insurance policy may be such that all the costs are not recovered from the insurance company, or there may be aspects which are not covered by the policy. For example, even though the policy may pay a certain sum for the loss of an arm, the parents may feel this sum would not compensate for the loss in earning power throughout the lifetime of the child. Consider also the price of disfigurement of the face of a pretty girl, the loss of mental capacity of a child, facing the future having to wear artificial limbs and braces, and other such possibilities. There are many cases where the insurances does not really cover the costs and parents may feel inclined to seek additional compensation for their children.

Some school boards insist students, engaging in school activities which are potentially more hazardous than others, be covered by accident insurance. These activities are usually competitive sports, such as football and hockey, but sometimes are vocational subjects, such as automotives and welding. Such insistence will result in duplication of insurance for some students but the cost of accident insurance for the individual student, on the basis of a group plan, is usually minimal.

Even if the parents are satisfied they have been suitably compensated through the insurance coverage, this does not mean the insurance company is necessarily satisfied. They have paid out a sum of money which may have been for the result of a negligent act of a teacher. If so, there is the possibility of the insurance company instigating action against the negligent teacher to recover costs incurred. Therefore, as desirable and as useful as accident insurance for students may be, it still cannot in any way be considered as liability insurance.

For some school boards in Canada it is compulsory to carry liability insurance to protect the interests of both the board and its employees. For example, section 65(3) of the Alberta School Act states, in part, a board shall, "keep in force a policy of insurance for the purpose of indemnifying the board and its employees in respect of claims for damages for death or personal injury..." Teachers would be well advised to check the policy the board carries to determine the actual coverage the teachers have (provided they are prepared to unscramble the complexity of terms of the policy). This would enable the teacher to decide whether he is adequately covered, if in fact he is covered at all. The limitations of the policy should be carefully considered. If covered at all, the coverage probably would be limited to actions of the teacher acting within the responsibility and authority as teacher. As with any protection the master-servant relationship may provide, so too the protection afforded by a school board by way of liability insurance, is often limited.

The Teacher in Loco Parentis

Defendant J. M. was employed by defendant board as co-ordinator of the outdoor educational programme of one of the board's high schools and at the relevant time was one of the supervisors of a "field trip" organized by the school and sponsored by the board...Two girls, M and G, both 14 years old, were drowned in a swimming accident during the trip. On the evening in question a small group of the children persuaded defendant to take them swimming, for which purpose they went to a swimming area created by a conservation authority. A natural creek had been dammed and the surrounding area flooded, and an artificial sand beach had been made. There was an area of shallow water but along the line of the old creek bed there was a sharp drop-off and the water became suddenly deep. The safe area had not yet been marked with buoys but there was one marker in the water and defendant, who knew the area well, had explained the limits of the shallow water carefully to the children and instructed them to stay within it, which they did. Defendant himself was unable to swim as was also the infant G. The infant M was an average swimmer. A fresh breeze suddenly developed which created a surface current on the water. As a result G and another child were carried over the drop-off area into the deep water. The infant M immediately swam to their assistance and though successful in rescuing the other child she drowned in her attempt to rescue G, who also drowned despite the efforts of others, including J. M. who ran into the water as far as he could, to save them.

Held, J. M. was liable in negligence for the death of G. The duty owed by a teacher or supervisor towards children in his charge is to take such care of them as a prudent father would of his children. It was therefore the duty of J.M., within the scope of that duty, to guard against the foreseeable risks to which G was exposed...Since he was acting within the scope of his employment the defendant board was also liable.

Held, further, he was also liable for the death of M. When a person by his negligence exposes another to danger it is a foreseeable consequence that a third person will attempt to rescue the one in danger...[6]

When the student is at home, he is under the effective control and responsibility of his parents. When the student is in the classroom at school, he is under the effective control and responsibility of the teacher (as well as the administrators and school board). That is, at school the teacher stands *in loco parentis;* the teacher is the substitute for the real parents. Where the responsibility of one set of parents ends and the responsibility of the other set of parents begins is not very clear. It seems there is much over-lap; the real parents must assume some responsibility for the actions of their children while in the classroom but, on the other hand, the teachers must assume responsibility for providing adequate care of the children somewhat beyond the bounds of the classroom door. In general, the courts indicate the teacher stands *in loco parentis* with respect to the student during the time he is under the jurisdiction of the school. Being under the jurisdiction of the school is not the same as being at school. Resources beyond the school grounds are often used to supplement the educational program, for example, field trips to the legislative buildings and to the local airport, or, as in the case cited in this section, swimming during an outdoor educational field trip. During these times the students are under the jurisdiction of the school. Conversely, the student may be in the school or on the playground during times beyond which the school could normally be considered in session. In the first instance, the teacher normally continues to assume certain responsibilities but in the second instance the teacher normally is exempt from responsibilities.

Supervision

The claim resulting from accidents beyond the school grounds (excluding those happening on school sponsored excursions of var-

---

[6]Moddejonge et al. v Huron County Board of Education et al. (1972) 25 D.L.R. (3d) 661.

ious types) as well as on the school grounds or within the school building but after normal school hours invariably are against the school board but sometimes can include the principal and teacher. An important distinction is made by the courts in these cases as to the status of the individual concerned—whether he be a "compulsee", "invitee", "licensee", or a "trespasser". As a trespasser he would have no right to be on the premises, or certain parts of the premises, and therefore courts are very reluctant to provide any compensation for injuries sustained. This is illustrated in the case where a school boy was using the grounds of his school during a holiday with tacit permission of the school authority and playing on a descending fire escape on which he knew he was not supposed to play.[7] The judge ruled that, as he was a trespasser he was unable to receive compensation for his injuries sustained on the fire escape. In the case the judge ruled also that the boy was a bare licensee as to the school grounds. The following case illustrates the attitude of the courts to those seeking compensation for accidents sustained when they were considered as a licensee.[8]

> A previous award of $7,200. was quashed on appeal. An eight-year-old boy, who was blind in one eye, was watching his nine-year-old brother high jumping after school hours. The broken end of the crossbar struck the boy, causing him to lose his good eye. The jury in the original trial held that the equipment was dangerous. However, the appeal court held that the boy could claim against the school board only as a licensee, not as an invitee, because he was on the school property after school hours.

One might speculate on the outcome of the case if the court had considered the injured boy an invitee instead of a licensee. Within reasonable limits, therefore, a trespasser and, to a slightly lesser degree, a licensee must accept the conditions of the property as he finds them—if he is hurt in some manner, he must assume the responsibility himself. But where the student becomes an invitee or, more especially, a compulsee, the onus on the school board and its employees becomes much greater. For example,[9]

> Damages of $519.36 and $350. were awarded for fracture of the fibula and tibia of the right leg. A fourteen-year-old boy fell on the school ground during a recreation period and when he was "lawfully and properly playing in the school ground." It was shown that the ground had been littered with stones and brickbats for some time.

---

[7]Storms v Winnipeg School District No. 1 [Man.] (1963), 44 W.W.R. 44 (1963–64) 41 D.L.R (2d) 216.

[8]Edmondson v Moose Jaw School Trustees (Sask.), (1920) 3 W.W.R. 979; 13 Sask. L.R. 516; 55 D.L.R. 563 (C.A.).

[9]Pook, et al. v Ernesttown School Trustees [Ontario] (1944) 4 D.L.R. 268; O.R. 465; O.W.N. 543.

It appears obvious the school board has a responsibility to provide reasonable and safe facilities for the students—in the school as well as on the school grounds. But it must be remembered that the board must have some way of obtaining information about potentially hazardous conditions—that broken step, that hole in the school grounds, that light fixture in a state of collapse. This information is usually obtained through the employees of the board, including the teachers. Who is in a better position to be acquainted with potentially hazardous conditions than the teacher who uses them with his students? The responsibility of the teacher is not necessarily to correct these conditions but to ensure the message is given to the appropriate authorities so they can act on the matter. A teacher who knows there is a hazardous condition but does nothing about it should expect to be involved in legal actions resulting from injuries obtained therefrom. The usual channel of communication of the teacher would be to the principal of his school. If the situation persists, then the teacher has an obligation to report the matter in writing to his employer, the school board.

The successful actions against teachers resulting from accidents within the school or on the school grounds during school hours or within the school out of school hours invariably emphasize the lack of sufficient supervision and that this lack had a causal effect. This is usually used to show negligence. From the standpoint the word "negligence" is used here care must be taken not to equate this with "incompetency". Although incompetency would point towards negligence, it would not be right to use these in reverse order. That is, a competent, conscientious person can be shown to be legally negligent in some cases. Prosser states four elements which must be present in order for a cause of action to show negligence, but the four points, in and of themselves, do not define negligence. The four points are:[10]

> 1. There must exist a legal duty for a person to maintain a standard of conduct for the protection of others against hazardous risks.
> 2. There must exist a failure on the part of the same person to conform to the standard required.
> 3. There must exist an injury to another person or persons as a result of the failure of the first person to maintain the proper standard of conduct.
> 4. There must exist a causal connection between the failure of the first person to maintain an acceptable standard of conduct and the resulting injury sustained by the other party.

It has been stated earlier that teachers are expected to act in lieu

---

[10]W. L. Prosser, op. cit., p. 426.

of the real parents, that is, to become *in loco parentis*. Added to this is the question as to whether the teacher acted in those circumstances as would a reasonable man under similar circumstances. Bargen quotes the characteristics of this artificial and unreal character as follows (note the potential conflict between points 3 and 5):[11]

1. The reasonable man will vary his conduct in keeping with the circumstances.
2. The reasonable man will be made to be identical.with the actor in the matter of physical characteristics. The man who is blind, lame or deaf is not required to do the impossible by conforming to physical standards.
3. The reasonable man is accorded no allowance for lack of intelligence short of insanity. For a defendant to do the best he knows is not enough.
4. The reasonable man is considered to be an adult. Children, therefore, are not required to meet the same standard of conduct as that of the reasonable man.
5. The reasonable man will be accorded special abilities and skills and will be held responsible for them when the circumstances so warrant. In other words, the law will take knowledge of the fact that some people are of superior knowledge, skill, and intelligence.
6. The reasonable man is required to maintain a higher degree of standard of conduct when he has had time to reflect on his course of action than when he must act in an emergency.
7. The reasonable man, under many circumstances, will be charged with the duty of anticipating and guarding against the conduct of others. For instance, where children are in the vicinity, greater caution and anticipation are required than if they were adults.

If the novice teacher now knows the basic elements to proving negligence and how a reasonable man would act, he then is in a better position to adjust his actions so as to act as a reasonable, careful parent would. As the degree of supervision seems to be basic to much of the difficulties in which teachers find themselves, consider further what good supervision is.[12]

Ramsden had left his bench to get a chisel. Instead of returning directly to his bench, as he had been warned to do on previous occasions, he flicked the chisel at the sanding wheel. The chisel caught in the wheel, driving it into Ramsden's thigh, resulting in a leg amputation below the knee. It was held that the sanding machine was not inherently dangerous and did not require a guard even if it were possible to devise one. Supervision was held to have been sufficient and the action defeated on the grounds that the negligence was completely that of the sixteen-year-old plaintiff.

Courts recognize that in spite of the best of supervision, accidents will happen. Perhaps the above case would have been different, however, if the teacher had been absent from the room at the time.

---

[11]P. F. Bargen, *The Legal Status of the Canadian Public School Pupil.* Toronto: The Macmillan Company of Canada, 1961, p. 137.
[12]Ramsden v Hamilton Board of Education Ontario, (1942) 1 D.L.R. 770.

In the following case the teacher was absent.[13]

> Damages of $8,000. and $1,208.75 were awarded. The case was appealed to the Supreme Court of Canada but with no change, the liability of both board and teacher being upheld. A boy attempting to light a gasoline stove to serve a hot lunch was burned after the teacher left him. Hot lunches were not part of the statutory or public duties of the board. However, the board knew of and encouraged the serving of hot lunches in the school and was therefore liable for negligence through the teacher.

It is sometimes possible for the teacher to be absent but still provide adequate supervision, as was shown in the following case.[14]

> A fourteen-year-old boy was injured in the gymnasium work at Lisgar Collegiate. The instructor was absent, but two senior boys were present. The boy's elbow was damaged to the extent that it caused fixation of the joint at a right angle. The action was dismissed because:
> 1. The senior boys were capable.
> 2. The cause of the accident was not known.
> 3. The plaintiff was *sciens et volens* (knowing and willing).
> 4. Fourteen-year-olds must exercise reasonable and intelligent care of their own safety.

Sometimes negligence, through lack of supervision, can be shown even when the teacher is present. The first case in this chapter illustrates this situation.

Supervision of the playground during recesses and noon hour should be on a planned, organized basis, as is illustrated in the following case.[15]

> On appeal from a previous judgment which had dismissed the action, the board and principal were found negligent. Damages of $1,000. and $160.25 were awarded. A six-year-old girl fell from a swing in the school grounds at morning recess. In this case no evidence was given of the provision of supervision. The local handbook seemed concerned with discipline supervision rather than supervision for safety.

Where there is a lack of organization for supervision, much of the burden of responsibility must rest on the shoulders of the principal. However, when supervision is organized, it is up to the individual teachers to fulfill the responsibilities set out for them.

The extent of supervision sometimes necessary is illustrated in the following case.[16]

---

[13]Gray et al. v McGonegal and Trustees of Leeds and Lansdowne Front Township School Area Ontario, (1949) 4 D.L.R. 344; O.R. 749; O.W.N. 127; app. (1950) 4 D.L.R. 395; O.R. 512; O.W.N. 475; app. (1952) 2 D.L.R. 161; 2 S.C.R. 274.

[14]Butterworth et al. v Collegiate Institute Board of Ottawa Ontario (1940) 3 D.L.R. 446; 1940 O.W.N. 332.

[15]Brost v Tilley School District Alberta (1955) 15 W.W.R. 241 (C.A.).

[16]Dziwenka et al. v The Queen and Mapplebeck (1972) W.W.R. (Vol. 1) 350.

An eighteen-year-old deaf-mute, a student in the Alberta School for the Deaf was seriously injured when his hand came into contact with the blade of a power saw in an Industrial Arts class. It was shown that the teacher was competent with power tools and that the student was shown how to use the saw. The teacher was 15 to 25 feet away, helping other boys and occasionally glancing over to the student using the power saw.

Damages were assessed at $10,716.60, with 40 percent responsibility of the student and 60 percent for the teacher and the Crown (the school was operated by the Government of Alberta) by the trial judge. The Appellate Division of Alberta reversed the decision. The Supreme Court of Canada subsequently re-instated the original judgment.

Field Trips

The supervision of students during an excursion or field trip is often much more difficult than within the school premises. There are different dangers in unfamiliar surroundings, making it necessary to provide greater supervision than in the school. Even though it is commonly recognized that field trips are an important adjunct to the school program, they must be organized and conducted in such a manner that the chance of accidents is minimal. This entails a more detailed planning, including procedures for emergencies.

A common practice adopted by most schools is the consent slip, sometimes erroneously called a waiver slip. This is a form which is signed by the parents indicating their approval of the proposed field trip. To call this slip a waiver is erroneous in that a parent is not able to sign away the rights of his child in this manner. Even if the parent has indicated in some manner that he waives the right to take legal action in the event of some accident to his child, the parent is not bound by this. The consent slip does provide other useful purposes, however. The communication between the school and the parents usually is quite inadequate—the parents usually do not know what is going on in school. The consent slip is an opportunity to describe a particular activity so that the parent not only knows what the activity is all about but also has an opportunity to indicate his approval. By indicating knowledge of the excursion to be undertaken, the parent thus gives written acceptance of the corresponding inherent dangers involved, thus strengthening the stand of the teacher should litigation occur. A teacher is well advised to check the written policies of the school board regarding field trips and to plan field trips only with the knowledge and consent of the principal and school board.

An unfortunate aspect of this manner in gaining approval is the gentle, and sometimes not so gentle, inclusion of coercion. What parent dares to indicate disapproval when the message, through the child, is that every other parent involved has said yes. Teachers should do as much as possible to avoid this type of situation as, from a public relations standpoint, more harm may be done than benefits achieved. Also, consent obtained under coercion is not consent.

As there must be a greater freedom of action in surroundings which are not very familiar, there is often a greater chance of injuries being sustained on a field trip than in the classroom. To compensate for this, it is suggested additional adult personnel be included so that the ratio of students to responsible adults is considerably lower than in the classroom. Also the students must be fully appraised of what is expected of them, what the purpose is of the trip, and some of the potential dangers involved. There is a fine, wavering line between over-supervision and inadequate supervision. There is no real way of knowing just where this line is, but the teacher apparently is expected to know. The courts are aware of this, as is illustrated in the following court decision.[17]

> The courts' realization of the necessity of developing a sense of responsibility has led to a changing attitude and a more practical approach to the question of supervision by school authorities. While there is a duty to supervise certain activities, such duty bears some relation to the age of pupils, the special circumstances of each case and particularly the type of activity.

A 1924 court decision continues to remind us of the importance of a board being informed as to anything different or special the school is doing. This is particularly true of any field trips—if the board is not aware of a field trip, and there is an accident, there is the opportunity for the board (or the insurance company which carries the insurance for the board) to claim the teacher was acting beyond his expected scope as a teacher. This would leave the teacher (and possibly the principal) to face the action on his own. This 1924 case is summarized as follows.[18]

> Damages of $2,000. against the board were awarded, but the action against Thomas, the principal of the school, was dismissed. The appeal dismissed. The board had decided that all schools should have a sports program for the 23rd of May holiday. Specific arrangements were, however, left in the hands of the individual principals. Thomas decided to have a shooting contest and asked the boys to bring rifles. One of the rifles was defective. There was some trouble and after a second try with the same cartridge, the gun backfired and a particle went into

---

[17]Schade v Winnipeg School District No. 1 and Ducharme (1959) 28 W.W.R. 577, affirming (1959) 27 W.W.R. 546, 66 Man. R. 335, at 360, (1959) 19 D.L.R.(2d) 299.

[18]Walton v Vancouver Board of School Trustees and Thomas British Columbia, (1924) 2 D.L.R. 387; 34 B.C.R. 38.

Walton's eye, which became inflamed and later had to be removed. The board claimed that the shooting contest was outside the powers of the school board and that Thomas was acting beyond the scope of his authority. It was held that the board knew that such contests had been held for several years, and that it was, therefore, their duty either to prevent the contests, or to insure that they were properly supervised.

Had the board been able to show they were, in fact, not aware of the shooting contests, principal Thomas probably would have found himself on his own in the action.

First Aid

Whether teachers should, or should not, give first aid to injured students is a question often discussed with some concern. The answer invariably is, naturally a teacher will always do whatever is in his power to assist a student who is injured or ill. Sometimes this means giving first aid and sometimes this means obtaining help for the student through more competent personnel (medically competent, at least).

When a student is injured and the teacher does not give first aid, with resulting aggravation of the injury, the teacher may have acted negligently. However, when the teacher gives first aid, and as a result of the first aid the injury is aggravated, the teacher may also have acted in a negligent manner. Knowledge of first aid is not usually a legal requirement for teachers but, viewed from the parent's viewpoint, there is the expectation of the teacher possessing at least minimal first aid expertise.

The professional competence of a teacher is an educational competence, not a medical competence. The teacher should never attempt to play the role of a professional physician. When a student is ill or injured, the competence required is that of a doctor or nurse rather than an educator. However, the educator, the teacher, must remain in control of the situation until relieved by another person, whether this be the parent, the school nurse or physician. Further, teachers must never prescribe drugs for students (aspirin, 222's, etc.).

The teacher must familiarize himself with emergency procedures established by the school. Where is the emergency list of phone numbers for parents at home and at work? Who is the family doctor? Are there special medical situations the teacher should be aware of and prepared for (possibility of epileptic seizures, etc.)? Where are the first aid kits and what are their contents? How is transportation provided in emergency situations? How is the reporting of accidents to be conducted? What is the procedure to be followed when students become ill during school hours? These and other questions should be considered before an emergency arises, not after.

The following Saskatchewan case emphasize the need for alertness and establishment of reasonable procedures to be followed.[19]

> The plaintiff, aged 17, came to live in residence and attend grade 11 at the defendant school. The defendant S was a teacher in the school. S was in charge of the residence in which plaintiff lived, and was coach of the hockey team on which plaintiff played. At the beginning of the hockey season the plaintiff got a cut on his big toe from ill-fitting hockey skates, which he had bought. The plaintiff did not regard this as a serious injury. He received an antiseptic for it from S. A few days later the plaintiff was hit on the hip by a hockey puck. Over the next several days the hip injury became progressively worse as a result of an infection in the region of the hip, apparently caused by the cut on the toe. On a number of occasions the plaintiff asked S to let him go to see a physician but S refused him permission. S forced the plaintiff to dress for hockey games when he was in no condition to play. Eventually the plaintiff became so seriously ill that he was taken to hospital by some of his fellow students. At one stage the plantiff was near death but he eventually made a good recovery...

> In a negligence action by the plaintiff against the defendants to recover damages for personal injuries and for loss of clothing, held, the plaintiff was entitled to succeed. The standard to be applied in judging S's conduct was that of a careful father. Applying this standard, S was negligent. A careful father, when faced with requests from his son for medical attention, would have arranged for such medical attention or, at the very least in the case of a 17-year-old, would have urged him to seek or consented to his seeking medical attention. The defendants were not at fault with respect to the cut on the plaintiff's toe or the injury to his hip. Nor did the plaintiff establish that the infection was caused by any fault on the part of the defendants. However, it is probable that earlier treatment with antibiotics and an earlier presentation of this infection for medical attention would have had a beneficial effect. Under the circumstances, damages should be more, but only slightly more, than nominal.

REFERENCES

Bargen, P. F. *The Legal Status of the Canadian Public School Pupil.* Toronto: Macmillan, 1961.

Dahlen, H. H., "The Doctrine of In Loco Parentis," *Education and the Law: Emergence of Legal Issues.* Saskatoon: University of Saskatchewan, 1977.

Enns, F. E. *The Legal Status of the Canadian School Board.* Toronto: Macmillan, 1963.

Lamb, R. L. *Legal Liability of School Boards and Teachers for School Accidents.* Ottawa: Canadian Teachers' Federation, 1959.

McCurdy, S. G. *The Legal Status of the Canadian Teacher.* Toronto: Macmillan, 1968.

Ontario Institute for Studies in Education. *The Interaction of Law and Education.* Working Notes Towards a Selected Bibliography. May, 1974.

Prosser, W. L. *Handbook of the Law of Torts.* Second Edition. St. Paul: West Publishing, 1955.

Revised Statutes of each of the provinces.

Robbins, M., "Noon-Hour Supervision—Voluntary or Compulsory?" *Education Canada,* Fall, 1976.

Singleton, J. R., "Gross Negligence and the Guest Passenger," *Alberta Law Review,* No. 1, 1973.

Thomas, A. M. *Accidents Will Happen.* An Inquiry Into the Legal Liability of Teachers and School Boards. Toronto: Ontario Institute for Studies in Education, 1976.

LAW REPORTS

A.C.	Appeal Cases, Canadian Reports
Alta. L.R.	Alberta Law Reports
B.C.R.	British Columbia Reports
D.L.R.	Dominion Law Reports
Man. R.	Manitoba Reports
M.P.R.	Maritime Provinces Reports
N.B.R.	New Brunswick Reports
N.L.R.	Newfoundland Law Reports
N.S.R.	Nova Scotia Reports
O.L.R.	Ontario Law Reports
O.R.	Ontario Reports
O.W.N.	Ontario Weekly Notes
O.W.R.	Ontario Weekly Reports
Q.K.B.	Quebec King's Bench Reports
Que. Q.B.	Quebec Queen's Bench Reports
Sask. L.R.	Saskatchewan Law Reports
S.C.R.	Canada Supreme Court Reports
T.L.R.	Territories Law Reports
W.L.R.	Western Law Reports
W.W.R.	Western Weekly Reports

Questions for Discussion

What are the possibilities of a teacher becoming involved in legal action in each of the following situations?

1. A grade one student was pushed from a swing and was hurt. The supervising teacher was at the far side of the playground when the incident happened.

2. An eleven-year old boy falls from the climbing rope in a gymnasium during a physical education period and fractures a hip.

3. A teacher is called to the office by the principal. While the teacher is out of the room, a boy throws a piece of chalk, injuring an eye of a classmate.

4. A grade two student tells his teacher he is feeling ill and wants to go home. The teacher agrees. The student goes home to find the house locked. The child is subsequently hospitalized for frost-bite.

5. A beaker breaks during a high school chemistry experiment. The spilled chemicals injured a student.

6. A student volunteers to help the teacher arrange a display after school. The ladder slips and the student is injured.

7. At a year-end picnic held by a lake, a sixteen-year old girl drowns.

8. A teacher offers a ride to two students to an evening school party. There is an accident and the students are injured.

Each of the following cases is relevant to the discussion in this chapter. Determine this relevancy.

1. Storms v School District of Winnipeg no. 1 (1963) 41 D.L.R.(2d) 216.

2. James et al. v River East School Division no. 9 and Peniuk (1976) 2 W.W.R. 577; 64 D.L.R.(3d) 338; (1975) 58 D.L.R. (3d) 311.

3. Dyer (otherwise Venables) et al. v Board of School Commissioners of Halifax (1956) 2 D.L.R. (2d) 394.

4. Moffatt et al. v Dufferin County Board of Education et al. (1972) 31 D.L.R.(3d) 143.

5. Board of Education for City of Toronto and Hunt v Higgs et al. (1959) 22 D.L.R.(2d) 49.

6. Durham et al. v Public School Board of Township School Area of North Oxford (1960) 23 D.L.R.(2d) 711.

7. Thiessen v Winnipeg School Division no. 1 (1967) 62 D.L.R.(2d) 1.

8. Sombach et al. v Board of Trustees of Regina Roman Catholic Separate School District of Saskatchewan (1969) 9 D.L.R.(3d) 707; (1970) 18 D.L.R.(3d) 207.

9. Mattison et al. v Wonnacott et al. (1975) 59 D.L.R.(3d) 18.

8

Community Involvement in Education

Introduction

Community Involvement in Education — a catchy phrase, a call for
teacher awareness of the public and the need for better public relations, a slogan for riders of bandwagons, a determined effort to involve parents in the educative process, another phrase in the dictionary of educational jargon. Like many educational terms, this term
conjures up a great variety of ideas as to its meaning, these varying
from individual to individual. To some the term is a call to arms —
it is time to revolutionize education and awaken the somnolent
public, to others it is a new way of expressing the opinion that the
public continues to be interested in education as they always have.
Either extreme does not do justice to the term — some place in between there is an optimum acceptance of meaning.

Does education direct the path that should be followed by society?
There are many who believe so, but there also are many who maintain the educational system is strictly a tool of society, the method
by which society is mirrored to the younger people so that the youth
will perpetuate the developed culture for generations to come. Probably education embraces both views — a leader of society as well as
a reflection of society. Either way there is societal involvement,
people involvement, community involvement. In this context, the
community is not limited to the people who live adjacent to the
school, but also those who live in the surrounding area, the surrounding province and the surrounding country. In this particular
chapter the more conventional meaning will be used, which refers
to the immediate community, the people directly associated with a
particular school or schools. However, the view is taken that educa-

tion is too important to be left entirely to the whims of the local populace.

Community Interest in Education

From the standpoint of self-interest, which is often subsumed under the aura of community interest, educational matters of most concern to the majority of people are those which are particularly local. This is quite understandable, as parents are more concerned about their children than those of the neighbors, community members are more concerned about the children in the immediate environs than those further away. Perhaps it would also be fair to state the populace in any province is more concerned with education in that province than in any other province. Maybe this is over-stating the situation somewhat, but it must be remembered that self-interest, or a little more broadly stated—community nationalism, is one of the pervading forces in education. Of course, people are concerned about, and interested in, the education of their children. True, many people give the appearance of non-interest but educators must work on the basic assumption that, no matter how dormant, the interest and concern is there.

The majority of students will not remain in the immediate locality after completion of their educational program. This means the local populace concerned with the educational program must be cognizant of the fact that education is far more than a local matter. Each community has workers and home-builders who have received their education elsewhere, and therefore the local community has a vested interest in the educational programs in nearly all other parts of Canada. That is, the interest in education must be broad enough to prepare local youth for living elsewhere and for the satisfactory assimilation into the local community of those from further afield.

Direct involvement of residents in Victoria in the planning of educational programs in Halifax is an impossibility; even direct interest and involvement from Calgary to Red Deer is extremely difficult. Therefore, mechanisms are necessary to balance the local and more distant interests. There needs to be provision for local involvement for local purposes, local involvement for provincial and national purposes (and even international), and for provincial and national involvement in the local scene. This is an extremely difficult framework within which the schools are expected to operate. The thesis being stated here is, basically, education is too important and too precious to be left to the whims of the local populace, but on the other hand, too important and precious to be removed from the hands of the local populace. Somehow an optimum mixture must be maintained of the interests of the local, regional and provincial, national, and even international, communities. That is, the local residents have an important role to play, as has the school board, the Department of Education, and other groups—no one group must be permitted free reign.

While aware of the appropriate roles of the various levels of community, the discussion will now focus on the more immediate community.

The Community and Curriculum Development

The major aspects of curriculum planning and curriculum approval takes place at the provincial level. This is understandable, granting the Canadian design of education discussed in chapter four. The method used by the departments of education is usually the formation of committees and sub-committees with representation from the Department of Education professional staff, teachers seconded from the classroom, and lay people representing various aspects of the public (home and school associations, farm groups, for example). Usually these committees are temporary in nature in that they meet as a committee only until a particular task is accomplished. Some provinces have more less permanent main committees (elementary, junior high and senior high) which consider for approval the work of the various sub-committees. The point being made here is that at the provincial level there is lay representation, both through committees and the fact that the Minister of Education is an elected official whose retention in office is subject to the goodwill of the lay public.

What is taught in the schools and when it is taught is basically not the prerogative of the classroom teacher. Teachers do participate in such decision-making but their particular area of expertise is how the subject matter is taught. Whether sex education is taught in the schools, for example, is a political decision rather than professional.

Additional to provincial concern regarding curriculum, is local concern. There is need for some curriculum planning at the local level to meet local needs not satisfied by the provincial curriculum. Here again lay representation is required to assist in the determination of the pertinent goals, and even to some extent in the operationalizing of these goals. However, their role should not include smaller details of content, within grade sequencing of content, or in the methodology to be utilized in the instruction of the content.

Further, the local community is also always involved in the evaluation of the schools—usually informal and somewhat ethereal, but important nevertheless. The novice teacher must remember the student members of his classroom belong to parents who normally are very concerned for the welfare of their children.

Community Use of School Facilities

In the earlier history of this country, and even up until a generation ago in many parts, the schoolhouse was the focal point of the community. Church services were held in the school on Sundays, community dances and socials on Saturdays, community picnics during the summer, campaign meetings during elections, annual meetings for the municipal and school boards, and in numerous other ways the neighborhood school was in considerable demand in addition to functioning as a school. There was no question—the school belonged to the people of the community and they used it as they saw fit. Gradually, as the communities grew, other public buildings appeared—the churches, the community hall, the church hall, then to more specialized buildings such as the theatre. With the improvement of roads, travelling time to larger centres was shortened, thus reducing the requirements of the school building in the local community.

Beginning in the 1950's and before, and gaining momentum in the 60's and 70's, was the extension of academic and interest courses for adults. The best equipped and most comfortable facilities for these courses were found in the schools, particularly the senior high schools. As schools included home economics, industrial arts and other specialized programs, the public expressed interest in the particular facilities and instructional expertise for themselves. From the early 1960's, with the advent of the industrial vocational program additions to many of the senior high schools, and thus industrial-style equipment and space, public interest in welding, electricity, carpentry, and other do-it-yourself skills increased. Government money became more readily available for recreational and cultural pursuits; Canada Manpower developed job-retraining programs. In general, public interest in utilizing the staff, equipment and buildings increased.

The use of the small, older type school building by the public was no particular problem. Whichever group used the school moved the desks to the side or carried them outside, lit the fire, provided the gasoline lamp, swept the floor and returned the desks in preparation for the next day's classes. Supervision needed was minimal. As the school buildings gained in size and complexity, the previous rough treatment of the facilities was no longer acceptable. The teachers and administrators began to discourage, and even prohibit the use of the schools for many of the previous activities. Therefore, at the same time there was an increased need for the school facilities, there was increasing resistance to their use for outside groups. The public prevailed however—these were their schools, built with their tax money and they were going to use them.

Now nearly every school board has definite policy as to the use of school facilities by outside groups. In some cases the arrangements are made through the principal of the school, in others the school board considers each request, in others committees are formed (principal, caretaker, trustee, for example) to approve requests. Where the requests are extensive, and the recreational branch of the municipal board is well organized, agreements are sometimes made whereby the recreation branch assumes complete control of the school facilities for out of the usual school hours.

The Community Library

The sharing of the school gymnasium, some of the classrooms, the swimming pool, the playground, and other school areas with the public outside of regular school hours has become an acceptable arrangement in most of the schools—or at least, where not acceptable, then tolerable. But one area of the school which generally has not succumbed to this kind of partnership is the school library. Gradually this pocket of resistance will no doubt also be eroded away, but at the present time the amount of sharing or cooperation is more token than real.

Libraries exist to serve users—whoever those users are. The library in the school then, is to serve the students and staff in that school. The library staffing is selected with this in mind, as is the selection of books, periodicals, records, filmstrips, films and other materials found in libraries. To be more specific relative to the purpose of the school library, the following is a statement of aims developed by the Canadian School Library Association.[1]

The specific aims of the school library are to:

Acquire books and other materials of instruction in line with the demands of the curriculum and the interests of pupils, and to organize these materials for effective use.

[1]Canadian School Library Association. *Standards of Library Service for Canadian Schools.* 1967.

Guide pupils in their choice of books both for personal and curricular purposes. Develop in pupils skill and resourcefulness in their use of libraries, and to encourage the habit of personal investigation.

Help pupils establish a wide range of significant interests.

Provide aesthetic experiences and to develop an appreciation of the arts.

Encourage good social attitudes.

Work cooperatively with the instructional and administrative staffs of the school.

Promote and participate in the acquisition and development of a collection of professional materials for use by the staff.

Interpret its resources and services to the teaching staff, students and administration, and also interpret the services of other cultural agencies of the community to pupils and staff.

Another common type of library is the public library, a facility which is for the public. This simple statement becomes important as will be seen later. The objectives of the public library, as stated by the Canadian Library Association are as follows:[2]

1. To provide opportunity and encouragement for continuous education for every individual in the community—children, young people, men and women.

2. Through guidance, stimulation, and communication of ideas, to promote an enlightened and enriched citizenry.

3. To assemble, preserve and administer in organized collections the library's print and non-print materials to support the educational, cultural and recreational program of the community.

4. They provide an accurate, reliable information service.

5. To support and cooperate with groups and organizations in the community in presenting educational and cultural programs.

As expected, there is some common ground to both of these statements. Further, in defining the public and the students, some difficulty is encountered. When a student enters a public library to borrow a book which gives information on a school assigned topic, is the student a "student," or is he a "public?" That is, the definition of public includes a sizeable group of people who are also students. Libraries are for users—if the student wishes to borrow a book from the public library to assist him in his classroom work, then of course this must be permitted, but in so doing the public library serves a school purpose. On the other hand, a housewife enrolled in a chemistry course by correspondence may find the particular reference

---

[2]Canadian Library Association. *Canadian Public Library Standards,* 1969.

book she requires in the school library, so why shouldn't she use the school library?

More and more, as teachers use the project method of teaching (and sometimes as an excuse for not teaching) the demand on public libraries for references will be increased. Also, school libraries invariably are not available to students in the evening and weekends (and sometimes not during noon hour, before, or after school). This forces the students to use the public library instead of the school library.

To summarize, students need public library materials, the public need school library materials, the mechanical skills of the public and school library staffs are almost identical as is much of their expertise in assisting the clientele, the non-school public generally patronize libraries during other than school hours, and therefore why not join forces and provide a community library. To the cost-conscious public, better value can be obtained for each dollar spent because less money needs to be diverted for capital and operating costs. The placing of public library books in a school library does not constitute a community library—neither does the sharing of facilities. The literature is full of descriptions of library-sharing arrangements which did not work. In the same way that there is not a public police force and a school police force but just a police force, there is a place for a library service which is neither public, nor school but both. The public and school components of a community library must be indistinguishable for a successful community library.

Through a community library the staff and students will have access to a far greater collection of library resources and a greatly extended service—at the same time the general public will also profit. There are difficulties but any school staff that really wants to can make this arrangement work for the benefit of all. This is a relatively new trend that is still in its infancy but should become much more acceptable in the future.

The Community School

As with the community library, the community school is not merely a sharing of school facilities with the public but rather a facility (called a Community School) which serves both the students and the public. The facilities, staff and buildings of the school and public services are integrated to the extent there is no real school, non-school separation.

The school that permits the ladies of the community to use the gymnasium one evening a week for keep-fit classes does not, on that basis, qualify as a community school. There is however, an element in this example which moves towards the community concept and that is the school has matched an expressed need (the ladies wishing keep-fit instruction) with the facilities (the school gymnasium) and with the program and staff to conduct the program. This is assuming the school undertook the responsibility for all that matching.

The true community school embraces the philosophy of community education. The school assumes responsibility for all, or nearly all, aspects of education as it relates to that community. The clientele then becomes the pre-school, the usual school age, the post-school and adult ranges. The programs include everything this clientele needs and wants as being educational. The school assumes major responsibility in determining these needs, encouraging community members to the satisfying of these needs and then being the facilitator to ensure the program development and the facilities in which to house the program. This gives the school an activist role, or perhaps better expressed, a catalytic role.

The community school, by the definition just given, is somewhat idealistic but is a direction that some communities are encouraging. A school does not become a community school just by placing the word "community" before its name, but at least this step would serve all as a reminder of the direction in which the educative process in that school and community should move. The designation is a commitment and any teacher who is not willing to accept that commitment for himself should move to more traditional territory (and certainly no derogatory evaluation of more traditional schools is intended).

The very definition of teacher becomes fuzzy. Does the instructor who teaches a group of adults ceramics in the evening require teacher training and certification? How about if the class is conducted during the traditional school day in a classroom in the school? What happens if a fifteen-year-old student joins the class? How about when most of the class are students who will receive recognition for the course on their high school transcripts? The problems along this line of reasoning are numerous, but so are problems of financing, decision making and control.

The development of the community school concept has been somewhat piecemeal. The four main types which are emerging are:[3]

1. The school with community centered curriculum. In such a program the school

sees the community as a resource for the enrichment of the program. Such a plan determines greatly the learning experience of a child.

2. The school with the vocation centered curriculum. The school here uses the opportunities provided by the community for work experiences.

3. The community centered function. In this type of school the emphasis is put upon developing the fullest use of the physical facilities of the school by various community groups.

4. The community service program. Here the aim is to improve the conditions of life in the community. Efforts are made to co-ordinate the activities of many agencies with the school.

Truly, the concept of the community school is a challenging one. Many schools in the future will accept this challenge and gradually work towards the community school idea. Most schools however will remain in the realm of community involvement and community awareness, only getting their feet wet in the somewhat hazardous journey to the community school.

Public Relations

Whether the school is very traditional, has an attached community program, includes a community library, or is a real community school, the importance of good public relations remains paramount. The classroom teacher is the key to good public relations—others in the school plant can assist—the administrators, the caretakers, the office staff—but good teaching by professional teachers is crucial to maintaining good public relations in every school.

Public relations is more than window dressing or the big smile and a hearty handshake. Basically it is the sum total of activities designed to improve the relations between the school and the community. This means public relations is a two-way street—it is not only helping the public become aware of the functioning of the school but also assisting the school in being more aware of the public, their thoughts and their wishes. Interpreting the school program to the lay public means the teaching staff themselves must know the intricacies of the school programs and why the school is proceeding as it does. Explaining the school program forces the professional staff to develop greater insight and depth of understanding of their own programs. At the same time, a knowledgeable public is usually a supporting public.

---

[3]Campbell, "Accountability Through the Community School," in *Educational Accountability.* T. E. Giles (ed.) (Calgary: Council on School Administration, 1972.)

There is little doubt that the very best program of public relations is good teaching—this really is the fundamental basis and the key. Good teaching naturally includes suitable management procedures and satisfactory teacher-student relationships. The teacher who achieves this will have the support of nearly every parent of his students, a very solid basis for public relations—a good beginning, but not a complete public relations program.

The novice teacher soon determines that many, and even the majority, of his students' parents never make themselves known to the school, never make substantial contact with the teacher. Often this is discouraging and leads the teacher to believe the parents don't care. This usually is a very wrong interpretation—almost every parent does care, but most parents have no desire to fall all over themselves trying to show their concern to the school. To many parents, if the student is doing well in school (as reflected in the report card marks and grades on tests and assignments), is supportive of the teachers (as evidenced by comments at the dinner table), and appears to be working hard (appropriate amount of homework, notebooks with meaningful notes and in some organized format), the parents will be satisfied. If the parent is satisfied, then why should he take up the teacher's valuable time and his own, discussing the student's satisfactory progress? This is overstressing the point somewhat, but the beginning teacher should not interpret no contact as no concern.

There are other reasons why parents are reluctant to contact the teacher or school. To some parents the school is a formidable place, sometimes bringing back memories of their own very unhappy experiences in schools. The school is not a very inviting place to most people, larger schools can even be places in which the stranger gets lost. The very presence of so many students can be intimidating to many people; some parents are reluctant to show their ignorance of the educational program; others may have a speech or some other physical defect about which they are sensitive; students, particularly in the higher grades, are inclined to discourage their parents from contacting specific teachers. These reasons are illustrative of a host of reasons why many parents do not make contact with the school, either on their own initiative or even on requests and invitations from the school.

Whether the grade is one or twelve, the students will bring their parents to the school to watch, and enjoy, a program. Certainly the modern-day school could learn much from the one-room country school of a few years ago. One of the most pronounced expectations the public had for the teacher and his class of students in these schools was the annual Christmas concert—complete with its make-shift stage, plank seating for the over-flow audience, the bedsheets for stage curtains, the Christmas tree, Santa Claus, and the gifts for every child, followed by a lunch for everyone. This probably was the greatest public relations project of any school—it was an absolute must. Every parent came, and brought their neighbors. Every student participated. There was no need to coax parents to attend, and for various excellent reasons. First, their child was participating, second, the concert was a social occasion, third, the program was enjoyable, fourth, there was no pressure on any parent—they were made welcome as individuals and as members of the community, and fifth, this was their school, and let there be no doubt about this latter statement.

Perhaps Christmas is not necessarily the only time for a school program, but it certainly is an opportune time. Programs there must be—they are tremendous learning events, motivators, and have excellent public relations opportunities. Teachers must never let a year go by without at least one program involving the whole school, plus one or two more specialized programs such as the band performance and the dramatics class presentation. After these programs, and other school events, the lunch and coffee period will give parents and teachers an opportunity to mingle and become better acquainted. Parents like to meet, in a non-threatening atmosphere, that teacher his child talks about at home—and this includes the poor teacher as well as the good.

The cocktail party can sometimes be a contributor to teacher-parent relations, but to the ill-informed teacher can be a disaster area. The public expect teachers to be knowledgeable about education and its problem areas, and rightly so. The teacher must be able to carry on a meaningful conversation about federal aid to provincial education, the effect of vocational education, the legal school leaving age, salary negotiations, removal of the mill rate for school purposes, the effect of empty classrooms in the older parts of the city, and a host of other topics. Whether the stand is right or not, the teacher who cannot discuss school affairs in a professional manner leaves some doubt as to his ability in the classroom. Not that the teacher should take these opportunities to deliberately lead the conversation into the educational field, but certainly not to display ignorance in the field in which he is supposedly professionally trained.

The design, decor and certain arrangements within the school can create an inviting atmosphere which will encourage the parents and public to visit. Items such as the distance and direction from the front door to the general office can be important. Parents prefer not to walk down long hallways, sometimes jammed with students at period change, in order to locate the general office—there is a sense of intimidation. Location of the various offices and facilities must be readily discernable by even the most reluctant parent. The school which houses a community library must have that library located so as to serve both the students and public, and must not be located in some hard-to-reach area of the building. A school should be a pleasant place, a reaction which can be assisted by appropriate choice of paint, some houseplants strategically located, comfortable reception areas, offices tastefully furnished, intercoms used only at scheduled times and, as part of the important furnishings of the school, a pleasant receptionist provided with sufficient time to permit unhurried communications with a caller. Extravagant architectural taste is not required, nor even desired—but neither is the obviously cheap, inadequately planned building. The planners must remember the function of the building may change during the life expectancy of the building and therefore should be planned so as to provide for essential remodelling as time passes. For the building that is in the planning stage, why not include a few of the interested community members in the planning committee?

From time to time communications from the school to the parents or public become essential or desirable. Perhaps the grade four student can be excused spelling mistakes and even some grammatical errors and writing which is of a poor calibre, but this is inexcusable on behalf of a teacher communicating to the public. The typing must be perfect; the reproduction of a professional calibre; the spacing and attractiveness quite important. The communication is from a professional person—if the communication is worth sending home, it is of sufficient importance to present in a professional manner. Communications should be timely and be obvious in the recognition of the importance of the involvement of the parents and community. Letters must be written only in a recognized and acceptable format; receipts for moneys paid only on an official, serialed receipt (and receipts given for *every* payment a student makes). The content of communications should be understandable, reasonable, and written in a manner which accepts the parent as a partner in the important educative process. The teacher must remember these communications sent home to the parents via the student sometimes don't arrive home. Students forget, the same as everyone else. It has been somewhat facetiously stated, but with some understanding of children, that if parents wish to inform themselves of the school's activities, the mother should wash her daughter's and son's jeans at least once a week.

The communication from the school that is paramount in importance in the minds of the parents, is the report card. The school board may change the format of the annual report of the board so that it eventually becomes a presentation of meaningless utterings, but the school report must never succumb to the same ignominy. The report card is a report of the progress of a student in school over a specified period of time—it must be intelligible and meaningful to the parent and student alike. The school may mean well in the designing of a format of a report card which matches a philosophy they feel appropriate, but unless the report card is meaningful to the parents and student, the whole exercise is an exercise in futility. Perhaps stanines present what the teachers wish presented, but if the parents do not understand stanines, then the opportunity to inform the parents is lost. Every teacher must be able to substantiate everything that is placed in a report card and must be able to explain in an intelligible manner the derivation of every mark. Remarks such as, "Johnny could do with additional help from his parents," are clearly out of order. The professional teacher's competency is on the line—the report card must be regarded a very professional communication between the teacher and the parent about the progress of a child in school.

The report card itself is not sufficient—it must be supplemented by at least one interview per year with the parent. As with any other type of communication, the parent-teacher interview must be well structured, thoroughly planned and conducted in a professional manner. The basic premise must be that the parent and teacher pool their thoughts and efforts so the student will receive maximum benefit from the educational program in which he is enrolled. Neither the parent nor the teacher should be placed on the defensive, but certainly the teacher must be able to explain, in an intelligible manner, the pertinent parts of the program and the progress the student is making. The teacher must be able to demonstrate clearly that he really knows the student.

No matter how difficult a student has been in the classroom, surely there is something good which can be reported to the parent. Some preliminary positive reinforcement will assist in gaining parental acceptance of some of the negative things which also may need to be said. The conference should be in private and confidences must be honored. There is no need to view forthcoming interviews with trepidation but rather the opportunity to meet the parents should be welcomed.

One or two short, but meaningful interviews per year should suffice for most parents but provision must be made for either the parent or the teacher to initiate other interviews as needed. It is not realistic to expect a parent to lose wages from a job because of an interview, which means that teachers may have to adjust their schedule on occasions to accommodate these special timing problems. To force a parent to lose wages will probably mean an irate parent before the interview even starts—certainly not a satisfactory basis for an interview. Remember, in all interviews and other contacts with the parents the welfare of the student is the important issue.

A very useful organization which is designed to improve public relations is the home and school association or parent-teacher organization. Unfortunately most schools do not have an active organization, sometimes the result of teachers not expending sufficient effort to ensure meaningful contact with the public through these organizations. True, these organizations invariably represent a minority of the parents and general public, but they are the people who demonstrate greater interest and can be the most supportive of the school. This is an excellent opportunity to explain programs to parents and provide for that two-way communication that is so essential to good public relations.

REFERENCES

Beach, R. *An Analysis of Current "Joint-Use of Facilities" Agreements in Alberta.* Community Education Project D Report. Edmonton: Government of Alberta, 1976.
Conway, J. A., R. E. Jennings and M. M. Milstein. *Understanding Communities.* Englewood Cliffs: Prentice-Hall, 1974.
Dotten, V., "The Case for Home and School," *Education Canada,* June, 1972.
Driscoll, R. H. *A Survey of Informed Thought in Alberta Concerning Community Education.* Community Education Project E Report. Edmonton: Government of Alberta, 1976.
Fusco, G. C. *Improving Your School-Community Relations Program.* Englewood Cliffs: Prentice-Hall, 1967.
Gayfer, M., "Candid Comments from a Community School Notebook," *Education Canada,* Summer, 1977.
Giles, T. E. *Educational Accountability.* Calgary: Council on School Administration, 1972.
Giles, T. E. and J. A. Siqueira. *The Community Library: A Study of the Sir Winston Churchill Community Library.* Calgary: Calgary Board of Education, 1973.
Giles, T. E., "The Library is For Users," *Ontario Education,* March/April, 1977.

Hiemstra, R. *The Educative Community: Linking the Community School and Family.* Lincoln, Nebraska: Professional Educators Publications, 1972.

Hoen, R. R., "Community Advisory Committees: A Warning," *Alberta School Trustee,* March, 1976.

Hoke, F. A., D. D. Basile and C. R. Whiting, "How to Improve Community Attitudes," *Phi Delta Kappan,* September, 1971.

Murray, A. R. *An Analysis of Community Education Related Provincial Government Policy in Alberta.* Community Education Project C Report. Edmonton: Government of Alberta, 1976.

Ontario Institute for Studies in Education. *Volunteer Helpers in Elementary Schools.* Toronto, 1971.

Pellegrino, J., "Parent Participation," *Education Canada,* March, 1973.

Phi Delta Kappan. Community Education: A Special Issue, November, 1972.

Prout, P. F. *A Study of Current and Emerging Community Education Developments at the Provincial and Territorial Level in Canada.* Community Education Project A Report. Edmonton: Government of Alberta, 1976.

Roberts, W. G. *Synthesis and Suggestions: Project Summary.* Community Education Project F Report. Edmonton: Government of Alberta, 1976.

Schindler-Rainman, E. and R. Lippitt. *The Volunteer Community: Creative Use of Human Resources.* Washington: NTL Institute for Applied Behavioral Science, 1971.

Seaton, E. D. A Survey of the Utilization of Selected School Facilities by Community Groups in the Province of Alberta. Unpublished Master's Thesis, The University of Calgary, 1971.

Shuttleworth, D., "Whatever Happened to Community Involvement?" *Education Canada,* Summer, 1977.

Sullivan, K. C. *An Analysis of Community Schools in the Province of Alberta.* Community Education Project B Report. Edmonton: Government of Alberta, 1976.

Wells, T. L., "Parents and Public," *Education Canada,* Spring, 1975.

Questions for Discussion

1. Should the school initiate the formation of a home and school association?

2. Obtain a selection of report cards from the nearby schools. Critically analyze them and then design a report card which you feel is most appropriate.

3. What is the desirable extent of community involvement in education?

4. How can an advisory committee be structured from the local community to assist the local school?

5. Explain the role played by paraprofessionals (teacher aides) in the development of a good public relations program.

6. Develop an agreement form suitable for use by a school for requests for use of school facilities by "outside" organizations. Develop a suitable school board policy for use of school facilities by "outside" organizations.

7. Explain suitable staffing and purchasing practices for a community library.

8. Explain suitable financing procedures for a community library.

9. What preparations are needed for an anticipated successful interview with a parent?

10. Should the student be invited to attend, and participate in, a parent-teacher conference?

11. What is the attitude of the provincial teachers' association relative to teacher aides, community libraries, and community schools?

12. What reasonable restrictions can be placed on teachers' communications to parents and public by the school board, the professional association and by the principal?

9

Classroom Management

Introduction

One of the major problems facing the beginning teacher (and some experienced teachers) is how to maintain discipline and control. Effective learning and teaching cannot take place when pandemonium reigns. That is, there are appropriate classroom 'climates' which are more conducive to a learning situation than others. The professional teacher is able to determine, and maintain, the appropriate learning environment considering the activity undertaken, the interests and abilities of the students, and the factors external to the classroom but which nevertheless impinge upon the classroom situation. This ability is both an art and a science. It can be learned, but, as with learning to play the piano, some natural talent helps.

The beginning teacher who expects to have suitable classroom management simply by following a set of rules-of-thumb is bound for disappointment. Rules-of-thumb may help the individual teacher to determine what he is doing and perhaps form a framework from which the teacher can form his own management techniques. Rules-of-thumb can be compared to the use of medicines for various maladies. There appears to be certain medicines or drugs which have more universal application in that they are effective for almost everyone for a certain specified malady. Penicillin could perhaps be placed in this category for certain treatments. On the other hand certain medicines and drugs have been found useful for a very limited number of individuals.

The comparison of the medical use of medicines and drugs by the medical profession with the techniques for classroom management by the professional teacher could be considered a spurious analogy.

However, it may be helpful in reminding the beginning teacher that for each classroom management problem there is not necessarily a treatment that can be prescribed with guarantees of one hundred percent success. The techniques that one teacher uses in a particular situation may be quite inappropriate for another teacher. The medical doctor builds up a repertory of possible medications. He uses his professional judgment (and some professional experimentation) in the selection of the appropriate medication. The teacher does the same—he becomes aware of techniques which hold promise and uses his best judgment in selecting the right, or appropriate, technique for the situation. The point being made here is there are no pat answers to classroom management. What works for one teacher may be disastrous for another teacher.

Further, as with medicines, where each medicine used by a patient may have proven benefits, but put together in certain combinations with other equally proven medicines, the results can be devastating, the same applies to control and discipline techniques. Nevertheless, even with these cautions, the teacher can be given some very sound advice. The best advice will not be to prescribe a remedy for each malady but rather to give some basis from which the teacher can determine a course of action which he determines best in his professional judgment. Some teachers will consider the remainder of this chapter a set of rules—others will give serious consideration to the suggestions and then work out his own courses of action. It is hoped that the latter will be the more prevalent procedure.

How common a problem is discipline? The answer to this is readily obtained by listening to teachers in the staff room and listening to family discussions around the supper table. Discipline is a recognized problem by staff, students and parents. The two illustrations following are typical of research evidence showing the concern for discipline.

In 1972-73 the Canadian Education Association surveyed Canada through the distribution of 1680 questionnaires to determine "The Purposes of Education". One of the questions asked was, "What do you think is the biggest problem with which your schools have to deal?" The responses were:[1]

---

[1]Joseph Lauwerys, "The Purposes of Education: Results of a C.E.A. Survey," Toronto: Canadian Education Association, 1973. (as quoted in S.C.T. Clarke, *Alberta School Discipline Study*. Edmonton: Department of Education, 1977.)

1. Lack of discipline 21 percent
2. Difficulty in getting "good" teachers 22 percent
3. Lack of parents' interest 33 percent
4. Other (mostly lack of students' interest) 22 percent
   No response 2 percent.

While not the greatest concern, Canada wide, lack of discipline was designated as the biggest problem by 21 percent of the respondents. The percentages changed from province to province, as might be expected. Alberta, for example, placed lack of discipline as the main problem.

The second illustration is taken from the Ninth Annual Gallup Poll of Public Attitudes, by George H. Gallup. The respondents, randomly selected adults from across the United States, in reply to the question, "What do you think are the biggest problems with which the public schools in this community must deal?", indicated the top problems were as follows:[2]

1. Lack of discipline
2. Integration/segregation/busing
3. Lack of proper financial support
4. Difficulty of getting "good" teachers
5. Poor curriculum
6. Use of drugs
7. Parents' lack of interest
8. Size of school/classes
9. Teachers' lack of interest
10. Mismanagement of funds/programs

The percentage of respondents choosing lack of discipline as the biggest problem was 26, slightly more than the comparative figure for Canada, which was 21 percent. Because of differences in the overall questionnaires, population sampled and purposes of the surveys, comparison of the results of only one point in the overall questionnaires is not entirely valid. However, the point being emphasized is there is considerable concern as to discipline within the schools.

The Student in Today's Society

A generation ago the position of expectancy for control and discipline was from an authority base. That is, students were told what was expected of them and discipline was meted out from a base of unquestioned authority. The teacher knew best; the student was ex-

---

[2]George H. Gallup, "Ninth Annual Gallup Poll of the Public's Attitudes Toward the Public Schools," *Phi Delta Kappan,* September, 1977.

pected to acquiesce. Since then, both the student and society have changed somewhat in their expectations (hopefully, so has the teacher). No longer does the student accept unquestioningly the dictums of his teacher (or his parents). No longer has the teacher full freedom to discipline and control as he sees fit. We are in a new era. Whether we, as teachers, approve of the trends of today is not the point here. The point is, within reasonable limits, teachers must face the situation as it is and work from there.

At first glance this appears to be a do-nothing attitude, but such is not the case. It is expected education will reflect society at the same time as it helps to lead society, and a proper balance between these must be maintained. As an illustration, there are many youth today experimenting with drugs. Certainly the school cannot condone drug use by students and must set the stage to help combat this problem. However, students are taking drugs and this fact must be recognized. Just because the school does not approve does not mean the students involved should be sent off to Baffin Island (or wherever a Canadian Siberia exists). We must accept the student with the problems and work from there.

At a more generalized level is the believed extent of freedom young people have today. They question their parents; they question their government; they seek answers to some of the most sociologically baffling problems. At home they are more inclined to not obey the dictums of the parents than were the children a generation ago. This is more than just a generation gap—generation gaps have always been with us and will continue in the future. Society itself has moved more into a permissive society. Like it or not, that is the case.

So what does this have to do with classroom management? Basically, it points out the necessity to understand the youth with whom teachers work. The child who goes to bed when he feels like it has some initial expectations that he can come and go as he pleases in school. He will need to have explained some of the differences between what he perceives as home control as opposed to control at school.

Just because some students give the impression they believe in being granted full freedom to do whatever they please, this is not necessarily what they really want. Structure and organizations are still important to the students in the schools. They want direction; they want control; they want guidance. Perhaps the situation is similar to the case of the fifteen-year-old girl requesting permission from her father for her to attend an all-night party to which she has been invited. She is asking in a manner which indicates that she wishes to gain this permission. But what she really wants is for her father to not let her go. As with this girl, our students in school wish direction and control. They really do not want the teachers to 'cop out', in spite of what many students are inclined to say.

This, however, is not an argument for the return to the autocratic type of control which was prevalent in our schools not many years ago, but it is a call to a reasoned approach to classroom management. The students want and need the help of the teacher in this somewhat baffling society of today. The role of the teacher is not of less involvement than formerly. However, the teacher must be prepared to examine his role more critically so that he can be of the most help to the students with whom he works.

Student Rights

Students as citizens and/or residents of Canada have certain rights which are protected by law. This appears to be a needless statement to make because this is true of all people residing in Canada. However, it bears remembering as, too often, teachers and administrators get into difficult situations when they deal too lightly with student rights. It appears more and more that students today in high schools (and even below high school) like to find an issue and then stretch it as far as possible. The issue itself may not be very important but it can provide a 'focal point and a base from which to draw support. Parents also sometimes are quite displeased with something relating to the school or with certain teachers. Not being able to obtain satisfaction with their main 'bone of contention', they sometimes turn to issues which will provide a legally or socially accepted base for retaliation. The whole field of students' rights lends itself admirably to the students and parents who wish to find issues to pursue. Considering this problem from a more positive approach, there is no doubt that Canadian residents need certain personal rights; they were legislated for real purpose. Therefore individuals should ensure their personal freedoms are not being eroded away. Schools, in particular should set a good example by the proper observation of civil rights of individuals.

Students' rights problems are usually solved within the school itself but sometimes present themselves as problems for central office and school boards to cope with. Court cases, although not frequent in the past, probably will become more frequent in the future. For the classroom teacher, the legal hassle in the courts probably is not the worst side of an issue. As inconvenient, costly, time-consuming and embarrassing as a legal action may be, it is the side effects which usually are more harmful as far as the classroom situation is concerned. The emotional strain on both the students and the teachers mitigate against a classroom environment which is suitable for effective learning.

Most of the students' rights cases involve length of hair and dress regulations. The following, a case involving length of hair, is an example of the type of litigation which Canadian educators can expect to become more commonplace in the years ahead.[3]

Ward et al. v. Board of Blaine Lake School Unit No. 57

One S., an 11-year-old Grade VI pupil at a school administered by the respondent Board, was temporarily suspended until he obeyed a resolution of the Board defining the maximum length of haircuts for male students. S. and his mother were informed of the resolution and of the principal's decision to suspend S., and the reasons therefor, and were also told that they could, if they wished, attend a special meeting and make representations regarding the resolution. They chose not to do so but sought relief to quash the resolution by way of certiorari, and for orders of prohibition and mandamus.

On a full review of the relevant legislation and of the authorities, it was *held* that the applications must be dismissed; it was clear that there was statutory authority both for the Board which passed the resolution to suspend; the principal's action was purely ministerial and not judicial or quasi-judicial and was well within his statutory powers to act in the interest of the well-being and discipline of his school. Nor could it be said that there was any bad faith or failure of natural justice in what was done. Neither the resolution of the Board nor the action of the principal was reviewable on certiorari. Applicant had failed to show a "clear legal right" to attend the school and it followed that the applications for mandamus and prohibition must also fail.

As interesting as litigation procedures may be, they really aren't the main focus for classroom management problems. They are to serve as reminders to teachers there are legal restraints and there are those people who are willing to pursue possibilities of legal redress.

Teachers and administrators can reduce the possibilities of legal involvement by being more aware they are working with other human beings who have rights and privileges which must be protected. School rules and regulations must be fair, consistent, understandable and acceptable. They should receive the sanction of the school board and, as much as possible, the approval of parents and students.

---

[3] Ward, et al. v. Board of Blaine Lake School Unit (Saskatchewan) *Western Weekly Reports.* Vol. 4, 1971, p. 161.

Knowing the Students

Basic to good classroom management is knowing the students. A decade ago much was said about the whole child coming to the school, a saying which is just as true today as it was then. The child doesn't completely shut out all his out-of-school background just because he walks through the door of the school. If his father and mother are in the midst of divorce proceedings, the child may react in different ways than ordinarily in the classroom. Perhaps the child wishes to vent his antagonism on something, anything, because of a poor home situation, and the school, the teacher and other students are handy vehicles.

It is with very good reason that teachers, in their training programs, undertake studies in the discipline of psychology. This discipline provides many insights into why children act as they do. The message is brought home forcefully that the students are very individual but at the same time are group members, which modifies their individualistic nature.

Knowing the students as individuals and in groups helps explain, sometimes even excuse, their actions—or more appropriately, aids the teacher in deciding courses of action, or inaction, which would be most appropriate to the situation. This is not a violation of the principle of being consistent but more the development of the ability to say the right thing at the right time, to know when to be very firm or merely suggestive, to know when the student needs help or is acting as a spoiled child, to know when to encourage or when to help. As indicated previously, the most appropriate blending of all capabilities is the art which the teacher must accomplish.

The nursing profession's dictum of T.L.C.—tender, loving care—is apropos to the teaching profession. Teachers are in a loco parentis situation, and as interim parents of the students the teachers are teaching, surely there must be available a goodly supply of T.L.C.

Psychological studies helps teachers to understand students' vagaries but this needs to be coupled with sociological foundations. Perhaps an illustration may assist here. In some communities there are a considerable number of people who express a disbelief in Christmas as a celebration of Christ's birth. How fruitless would it be for the teacher to attempt to have a Christmas pageant in which all students are compelled to participate and all parents are invited to attend. Issues of saluting the flag and reciting the Lord's Prayer can trigger protests from certain groups of people. Discussing Canada's Food Rules, involving the eating of meat, can be an area of protest for others. Many other examples can be given—at least enough to frighten the teacher into believing that no matter what he does, or what he says, he will be violating someone's basic tenets.

There obviously is some support for this concern but this does not mean the teacher cannot do anything. Rather, the message is that the teacher in knowing his students may better be able to work with items which are potentially troublesome because of religious or ethnic beliefs. It is not a matter of avoiding entirely these issues but rather of developing a more effective and sensitive manner of dealing with them. There really isn't any sense in insisting on a student attending a dance on a Friday evening if the student belongs to a religious group which prohibits dancing and has its sabbath beginning at sunset Friday. History gives us too many examples of religious wars, large and small, for us to be unaware of the possibility of a "mini-war" within the school.

Teacher Preparation

A real asset to the establishing and managing of satisfactory classroom control is to be prepared—academically, organizationally, physically and mentally. Each of these preparations is important in its own right plus its contribution to the overall image that is produced.

Whether a teacher teaches grade one or grade twelve, academic or vocational, fast learners or slow learners, the teacher must have a substantial academic background. The teacher must be quite knowledgeable in the field in which he teaches—it is not enough to be one chapter ahead of the students. The students sense the teacher's level of understanding of the material and will react accordingly. Naturally, there will be questions which the teacher cannot answer but this is different from having a shallow understanding of the material. Fields of knowledge alter and extend very rapidly and therefore the teacher will need to up-date the very considerable background which he has acquired mainly through university studies. The updating may be further university studies, in-service studies, reading or through personal contact. Students respect the educated teacher.

Academic knowledge must not be limited to the subject being taught but must also include a sufficient knowledge of pedagogy of teaching, an understanding of students as individuals and as group members, and a broad general education. Knowing the subject matter under discussion is important, but so is the knowledge of how to teach it.

Organizational preparation is essential on both a long-range and short-range basis. The teacher must organize on a yearly basis, on a unit basis, and on a daily basis. When the teacher steps into the classroom he must know exactly what he wants, the purposes or goals towards which he is working, and how he intends to get there. Thorough planning is essential for suitable classroom control. The unprepared teacher is asking students to misbehave—the students are well enough aware when the teacher is not prepared and is trying to bluff his way through.

The physical preparation must be accompanied by an appropriate mental preparation or mental set. Even a well-prepared lesson can fall flat if the teacher isn't "really there". The teacher who carries in his mind that fight he had with his wife at the breakfast table will not have an adequate mental set. The teacher who knows his material, is well prepared and can present in an enthusiastic manner will enthuse the class. This motivation alleviates most of the bases from which discipline problems stem.

The image the teacher presents is important. The mental set must be there, supplemented by a physical-mental image which can be enhanced considerably by being suitably groomed—wearing clothes which are clean, pressed and well chosen. Students appreciate a bit of color and something different on occasion. They notice poorly chosen combinations of clothes, styles which are inappropriate for the year, the season, the person, or the occasion. Students are very quick to stereotype. They have not developed an adult level of maturity and frequently judge the inner person by the exterior.

Rules, Regulations and Expectations

Permitting hundreds of students in a school to do anything they wish, when they want to, is enhancing a situation far from a satisfactory learning situation. Permitting two or three dozen students in a classroom to act under no regulation achieves the same probabilities. Some semblance of order and control are obviously necessary. The questions are: how much control? how many regulations? who establishes the rules and regulations? what sanctions are brought to bear for regulation infractions? Again, there are not firm and fast benchmarks for the novice teacher, but at least there are some useful guidelines.

The fewer written rules, the better. In fact, the fewer rules the better. It must be assumed that any rules established by the school, or by the classroom teacher are fair, impartial, just, necessary, and acceptable. Rules must reflect an understanding of the rights of other individuals. Therefore, if a basis of appreciation of the rights and wishes can be understood and accepted, most control problems are obviated. The trick, then, is to establish mutual respect and understanding, with the expectation of little necessity for formalized control.

Some rules and regulations are established at a higher level, the school board level, for example. Then it becomes the teacher's responsibility to have the higher authority's wishes followed. Should the teacher feel the regulation is too stringent, not necessary, or not fair then the teacher, in his professional conscience, should attempt to have the regulation changed. It would be unprofessional to circumvent the intent of the higher authority. Also, there are the legal obligations involved, an area where it is quite important for the teacher to set a good example.

Different teachers in the same building will have varying conduct expectations of the students. On some issues, there needs to be a school policy—on student smoking, for example. On other issues there can be different understandings. For example, the business education teacher would probably not permit gum chewing in class (as a matter of job training), while another teacher doesn't care. The industrial arts teacher may require long hair to be tightly secured (for safety reasons) but the mathematics teacher may not care. It is the responsibility of each teacher to ensure his expectations are made known to the students, that his expectations are consistent with, and compatable with, school expectations.

Students will determine the expectations of the teacher. The emphasis is on the word "will". It is a pathetic class indeed which will not test the teacher as to the limits of expectations and their sincerity. This is quite normal and must be expected by the beginning teacher. This also means it is usually a good policy to start off a new class with firmer control and then ease off somewhat as circumstances require. To start a new class with poor management, and then try to become firmer at a later stage is usually not very acceptable.

The expert car driver automatically steers into the direction of a skid. The driver develops this and many other skills which he uses almost automatically. The skilled teacher will develop automatic-type management techniques and devices—or rather, the skilled teacher will automatically set the stage appropriately so that classroom management does not become an issue or problem.

Sanctions

In spite of everything the teacher does in setting the appropriate stage, there will be students who will require some form of sanction because of behavior detrimental to the learning situation and/or his classmates. Sanctions will vary from a fairly sharp, brief comment to pay attention, to formalized suspension and expulsion procedures for sustained and extremely disruptive behavior. The rights of the individual will need to be weighed against the rights of the group. Where the individual's behavior is injurious to the group, consideration of sanctions is necessary.

Most of the considerations for the development of reasonable and acceptable rules and regulations are also pertinent to the meting out of punishment. The sanctions brought to bear must be commensurate with the offense, must be consistent, fair, understandable and as much as possible, acceptable by the offender. Often a personal talk with the offender, in private, will serve the purpose. For more sustained difficulties, assistance from the parents may be needed. The administration can also play a very effective role if not called on too frequently by the teacher. The school counselor can be quite effective in assisting, as can other student personnel staff.

The teacher must realize that providing education for students is a team effort. Even though the teacher has the main responsibility for management in his classroom, or area, there are other staff members who are involved and concerned. To discuss management problems with them is not necessarily a sign of weakness. On the other hand, the teacher should not expect other people to do his work for him.

The School Acts for the various provinces and territories indicate procedures for suspension and expulsion of students from class, school bus and school. There are differences and the teacher is well advised to become thoroughly familiar with the pertinent sections of the School Act. Generally, teachers can suspend a student from class but must report the circumstances to the principal. The principal usually has the authority to suspend a student from school and/or school bus. Reporting of the occurrence to the board (usually through the superintendent) generally is necessary, as is the reporting to the parents. Teachers must be careful not to get themselves in a situation of saying that there is no way that a particular student can be re-admitted to his class. In almost every case the higher authorities, after considering the information, will re-admit the offender at least once, often several times. The power to expel a student invariably rests with the board of trustees. Education for the student is both a right and a privilege, and these are not to be dealt with lightly.

At the classroom level, the students must know what to expect. That is, if one student must stand in the corner for five minutes for chewing gum in class, then the next person caught chewing gum (other things being equal) could hardly be "sentenced" to write a thousand lines. Consistency is important. Where punishment must be given, a range of possibilities are available through removal of privileges (the emphasis being that privileges are lost rather than the teacher takes privileges away). In this connection, school subjects are not privileges to be taken away. That is, misbehavior in a mathematics class should not result in being kept out of the physical education class. Conversely, assigning school work for punishment is ill advised.

Tempers will flare. Teachers must recognize this and be very careful not to act harshly while either the teacher or the student is emotionally charged. Excessive delay of action is not advised either, but at least tempers should be cooled, and rational thought be given before acting. Usually the student could be asked to see the teacher after class, or after school.

Teachers like to save face when caught in an embarrassing situation. So do students. Wherever possible, provide opportunities for a student to save face as this makes the situation much more bearable, and thus acceptable, for the student.

Physical force should rarely, if ever, be used. Obviously a teacher must protect himself, but the teacher is acting in loco parentis. If the parent wouldn't use force under the same circumstances, then the temporary parent (the teacher) would be hard pressed to justify force. Teachers who beat students, pull their ears and provide other physical treatment not in accord with school policy should be treated the same way as other adults would—through the courts on assault charges.

Strapping has been ignored thus far, and should probably be ignored further. Generally, strapping elementary students is not effective nor desirable. It is almost a last resort procedure, which many school authorities now prohibit. Strapping a secondary student should never be considered.

In summary, the punishment given should be commensurate with the offense. The best procedures are those which provide a learning situation where possible. However, when punishment is needed, avoid making students hate teachers, school and everything to do with schools. Remember that students grow up, marry, and have children of their own who will attend school. A parent who has had bitter experiences as a student at the hands of thoughtless educators will not be very supportive of schools.

Various Attitudes Regarding Discipline

In 1977 Dr. S. C. T. Clarke completed a comprehensive Alberta School Discipline Study for the Department of Education. The following is a summary of the findings of the study, based on a stratified sample of 100 schools resulting in returned questionnaires from 1489 teachers, 973 students, 274 trustees, 1715 parents, and 112 central office and regional office personnel.[4]

Forty-one percent of the participants felt school discipline as it was in 1975–76 was just about right. Parents especially endorsed this position.

Thirty-two percent felt school discipline was a bit too lenient. Trustees and teachers especially held this view.

Thirty-four percent felt school discipline should be stricter.

The suggestion that after elementary school, in order to improve school discipline, pupils be allowed to quit school, was strongly opposed by parents, students and trustees in that order.

Respondents rated good to very good the suggestion that students and teachers having discipline problems be offered guidance services.

Students felt schoolwork should be more interesting. This idea was not strongly supported by other groups.

Students, parents and teachers did not feel that students should participate in making and enforcing school rules.

Traditional discipline (do what is necessary, including using the strap to keep discipline) divided participants, with sizeable groups holding extreme positions.

Humanistic discipline—more freedom, acceptance, encouragement—divided participants with the majority opposed.

The most frequently mentioned written suggestions for improving school discipline were participation, standards, school conditions, and understanding and acceptance of students in that order.

Reasons given by respondents for discipline problems were irresponsibility, lack of respect for authority and property, and poor attitudes. Another frequently men-

---

[4]S. C. T. Clarke, *Alberta School Discipline Study.* Edmonton: Department of Education, 1977.

tioned cause was lack of discipline in the home. Others were inappropriate action by teachers, poor parent-teacher rapport and poor student-teacher relations.

A total of 9110 causes of poor school discipline were noted. Seventy percent felt they were located in the school, 21% out of school and the remainder in the relationship between the school and the home. Most participants felt the school should act to improve discipline.

Female teachers were more opposed to letting students quit school, more in favor of parents backing up the school and teachers who were having discipline problems than were male teachers. Teachers over 30 and mathematics and science teachers held more traditional views on discipline than did younger teachers and those teaching English and social studies.

Parents over 30 and "two-parent" families were more conservative in views on school discipline than younger or "one-parent" families.

Students in matriculation programs were more traditional in their views on school discipline than non-college-bound students. However, the first group were also more in favor of humanistic measures of student control. These findings agree with the common view that non-academic students misbehave.

The findings of the Alberta School Discipline study are less alarmist and show more satisfaction with school discipline than Gallup poll results. This may be because the Gallup poll did not provide opportunity for respondents to rate the state of school discipline in America nor to make an open-end statement about what they thought of school discipline.

The views of the trustees and teachers were close together on what discipline is like and what is should be like. At the opposite end were students and superintendents. Parents and students were most opposed to letting students quit after elementary school.

Although groups differ in their views on school discipline, group differences were overshadowed by the diversity of views within any one group.

There was little difference in views on school discipline between participants associated with different grade levels and some differences between urban versus rural schools. In the view of participants with respect to school discipline, big was bad and small was good. The implications of the findings about the relationship between school size and participants' views of school discipline are most important.

REFERENCES

The ATA Magazine. Edmonton: The Alberta Teachers' Association. (The March-April, 1975 issue contains 14 articles on discipline.)

Buxton, T. H. and K. W. Prichard, "Student Perceptions of Teacher Violations of Human Rights," *Phi Delta Kappan,* September, 1973.

Chalmers, Ronald. *1,000,000 Opinions: A Report of the Social Values Survey.* Montreal: The Protestant School Board of Greater Montreal, 1972.

Clarke, S. C. T. *Classroom Discipline.* Edmonton: The Alberta Teachers' Association, 1968.

Clarke, S. C. T. *Alberta School Discipline Study.* Edmonton: Department of Education, 1977.

Dreikurs, R. D., B. B. Grunwald and F. C. Pepper. *Maintaining Sanity in the Classroom: Illustrated Teaching Techniques.* New York: Harper and Row, 1971.

Gallup, G. H., "Ninth Annual Gallup Poll of the Publics' Attitudes Toward the Public Schools," *Phi Delta Kappan,* September, 1977.

Gnagey, William J. *Maintaining Discipline in Classroom Instruction.* New York: Macmillan, 1975.

Good, T. L. and J. E. Brophy. *Looking in Classrooms.* New York: Harper and Row, 1973.

Hudgins, B. B. *The Instructional Process.* Chicago: Rand McNally, 1971.

Jessup, M. H. and M. A. Kiley. *Discipline: Positive Attitudes for Learning.* Englewood Cliffs: Prentice-Hall, 1971.

Keene, M. *Beginning Secondary School Teacher's Guide.* New York: Harper and Row, 1969.

McFarland, H. S. N. Intelligent Teaching. London: Routledge and Kegan Paul, 1973.

Phi Delta Kappan. (The January, 1978 issue contains 15 articles on discipline.)

Sheviakov, G. V. and F. Redl. *Discipline for Today's Children and Youth.* Washington: Association for Supervision and Curriculum Development, 1956.

Skinner, B. F., "The Free and Happy Student," *Phi Delta Kappan,* September, 1973.

Silberman, M. L. *The Experience of Schooling.* New York: Holt, Rinehart and Winston, 1971.

Ward, et al. v. Board of Blaine Lake School Unit. *Western Weekly Reports.* IV, 1971.

Questions for Discussion

1. What do you think are the biggest problems with which the public schools in this community must deal? Compare your answer with those from the Gallup Poll.

2. To what extent should
   (a) elementary students
   (b) junior high students
   (c) senior high students
   participate in the decision-making processes in relation to their educational programs?

3. Will the extent of permissiveness in our society increase?

4. To what extent should the school assume responsibilities for the upbringing of the youth of today?

5. Develop a set of regulations for student grooming and dress which you feel would be acceptable to high school students, the teaching staff, administration, and the parents.

6. What is an appropriate procedure to follow when a teacher is confronted with a student who apparently is under the influence of drugs?

7. Should a smoking room be permitted in a junior high school? in a senior high school?

8. What are the provisions in the School Act relative to suspensions and expulsions?

9. How effective are parent-teacher interviews in establishing good classroom climate and control?

10. How effective is a "student court" for working with student discipline problems?

11. When should the teacher call upon the principal for assistance with discipline problems?

12. To what extent should each teacher be responsible for maintaining discipline and control of students from other classrooms?

10

Student Personnel Services

What are Student Personnel Services?

The phrase "Student Personnel Services" is used extensively in educational literature and by educators in the field, usually with the impression that, of course, everyone knows what is meant by student personnel services. However, this really is not the case. This is one of the vaguest and most ill-defined terms in educational jargon today. Meanings in the literature appear to range from a very all-encompassing definition which appears to include everything to do with educational services for students, to a very limited definition which describes the counseling function of the guidance personnel in the school. In this book the term will include some of the services supporting the teaching function, such as the counselor, activities director and the attendance officer, to specifically name three of many. Even though there obviously are administrative tasks involved in student personnel work, the emphasis does not include the general administrative tasks associated with the general operation of the school (hiring teachers, supervising caretakers, purchasing books, for example) which would normally be within the jurisdiction of the principal, the assistant and vice principals, or the school office manager. As is the case with teachers, administrators are constantly associated with student personnel services work, sometimes in an administrative capacity and sometimes in a supportive role.

The most important relationship in the school is the relationship between the teacher and the students. The teachers work towards the achievement of goals set for them by society (including educators). Student personnel services, and other support services involving the school and the students, are supportive of the means by which the goals are achieved. That is, teaching services, student personnel services, administrative services, and other support services, form a team approach towards the achievement of goals.

These categories are not mutually exclusive—the teachers are hired for more than the dispensing of academic material—they are also hired for their involvement in student personnel services, administration and support services. For example, teachers are expected to be involved with the student newspaper (student personnel services), keep accurate record of student attendance (administration), and effect certain housekeeping standards (support services). Thus student personnel services becomes an area of emphasis rather than a discrete category. For example, the school guidance counselor does not relieve the teacher of all guidance and counseling functions. The staff of the school in general, and the professional staff in particular, must recognize that there is a job to be done and it is the entire staff's responsibility to see that it gets done. Jurisdictional disputes on a construction site are relatively common (who installs the steel beam in a building—a member of the steel-workers' union or a member of the carpenters' union?) and they can become common in the educational setting unless the professional staff learns to work together (who looks after the cumulative records—a member of the administrative staff or a member of the guidance staff?). The central position of the classroom teacher forces him to become anchor-man for the educational team. Him, of course, means him or her.

The size of the school system, the nature of the individuals concerned, the type of organization, the commitment of the board to particular services, budget restrictions, and the philosophies of the school system influence the nature and extent of student personnel services. Figures 10-1 and 10-2 will help to illustrate this point. Figure 10-1 could be representative of a relatively small school system. It will be noted there is a considerable overlap among the four major service areas. Therefore, the teacher who is employed in a small school system must expect to fill in to a very considerable extent in the three other areas (student personnel services, administrative services and other support services), in addition to the teaching function.

Figure 10-1 could also be representative of a system where the expectations for the other three service areas are very minimal. Figure 10-2 would be more representative of a larger system, or one where there is a greater commitment to other service functions, for example, pupil personnel services.

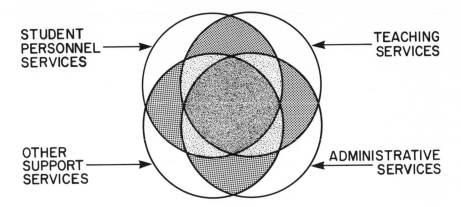

Figure 10-1
Relationship of Services in a Small System

Much of the overlap between the services noted earlier is really indistinguishable and the expectations held for the teacher in these areas will vary with the wishes and capabilities of the administrators and fellow colleagues. No teacher should ever assume his job is solely that of dispensing an academic curriculum to the students.

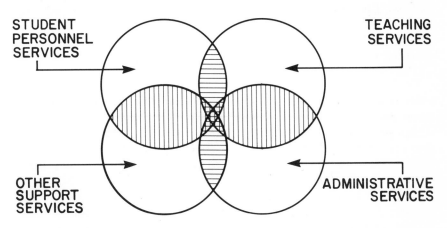

Figure 10-2
Relationship of Services in a Large System

Perhaps this aspect is basic to the role of the teacher, however, teachers do have responsibilities for organizational maintenance, setting of the stage for the best learning situations possible, and the provision of a full school curriculum for each student. Many of the curriculum associated activities (track meet, newspaper, yearbook, for example) are not mere additions designed to keep students busy and thus out of mischief. They are part and parcel of the curriculum for the students and must be considered as such. Involvement by the teachers is essential. This type of involvement is different from that of classroom instruction in a specified subject in the sense that additional opportunities are afforded the students to learn how to organize, manage and provide activities with limited assistance and guidance of the professional teaching staff. The situation is somewhat similar for the activities which are not as closely related to particular curricula but which are important to the providing of a relatively full educational program. Examples of this category of experiences would be the school dance, the cheerleaders and the photography club. The teacher has an important role to play in these activities—the teacher's concern and assistance is necessary. Mention should also be made at this time of other activities, or chores, which the teacher has as part of his teaching responsibilities. These are the usually non-structured, often spontaneous items—for example, assisting the grade one student with his boots. Such an item sounds trivial, and could perhaps be performed as well by a non-professional. However, it is opportunities such as these, and even the more structured co-curricular and extra-curricular activities, which provide the opportunities for the fuller development of teacher-student relationships. The teacher becomes a human being, someone approachable, someone understanding, all of which assists in the learning environment and better enables the teacher to fulfill his intended role.

In larger schools and school systems the teacher is able to call upon these other service areas to assist in the provision of an encompassing learning environment. In the smaller systems the teacher may not have the same degree of back-up services, however, too extensive a back-up service may well rob the teacher of much of his opportunity for involvement in fuller teacher-student relationships. Insufficient back-up service will place such a burden on the teacher that he would not be able to fulfill the expectations held for him. Somewhere in between, there exists an optimum provision of support services.

Organization of Student Personnel Services

The first professional position obtained by the novice teacher will invariably be one of teaching—not administration, not counseling, not managing, but teaching. This is comforting in the sense that most beginning teachers have had little preparation or experience in these other areas. However, it will soon become obvious that a certain amount of administration work is necessary and expected. The teacher must administer his classes—organize, prepare, and structure. A certain amount of record keeping is required—books, supplies, attendance, grades. Leadership skills are soon put to good use—in the professional organization, in the classroom, at staff meetings, and in student affairs. In the early months, perhaps even in the early days of his employment, the teacher will be asked questions, such as, "Will you be the staff advisor to the Glee Club?", or, "Will you organize and supervise the track meet?" The development of administrative skills is necessary in the growth towards becoming a very effective teacher. The following discussion is not aimed at telling teachers how to become good administrators in three easy lessons, but rather to summarize a few principles which experienced administrators believe to be basic to good organization. It should be realized that working with student personnel services assumes a certain degree of administrative knowledge and ability. The following points should assist in focussing attention on areas of particular concern. Consider, then, the following basic assumptions:*

1. Leadership is not confined to those holding status positions in the power echelon.

2. Good human relations are essential to group production and to meet the needs of individual members of the group.

3. Responsibility as well as power and authority can be shared.

4. Those affected by a program or policy should share in decision-making with respect to that program or policy.

5. The individual finds security in a dynamic climate in which he shares responsibility for decision-making.

6. Unity of purpose is secured through consensus and group loyalty.

7. Maximum production is attained in a threat-free climate.

8. The line and staff organization should be used exclusively for the purpose of dividing labor and implementing policies and programs developed by the total group affected.

9. The situation and not the position determines the right and privilege to exercise authority.

10. The individual in the organization is not expendable.

11. Evaluation is a group responsibility.

Whether the teacher is responsible for the organization of an activity

---

*Adapted from E. L. Morphet, R. L. Johns and T. L. Reller, *Educational Organization and Administration* (Englewood Cliffs: Prentice-Hall, 1974).

which involves other professional personnel, or an activity which involves only students, whether the activity is extensive and more or less permanent or minimal and transient, whether the activity is within the school environment completely or extends beyond into the surrounding neighborhood, the basic principles apply.

An effective leader will permit and encourage leadership to develop from within the members of the group, thus extending rather than restricting the leadership capabilities available. The greater the leadership capabilities forthcoming from the group, the greater will be the need for the status leader (in many instances this is the teacher) to serve more in a coordinating rather than in a leadership or directing role. Leadership capabilities may develop from within the group because of a certain type of personality, knowledge of the matter under discussion, a felt need of an individual, or the need to buffer differing viewpoints. The status leader should capitalize on these strengths. The teacher should encourage the development of student leadership as a necessary, and desirable, part of their educational program. This is often easier to do in activities supplemental to the classroom situation, and thus what is ostensibly viewed as an extra-curricular activity becomes co-curricular and more properly curricular if one holds a holistic view of education.

Individuals within a group, whether they are teachers or students, each have personal needs. This should be recognized in order that there may develop a closer correlation between the individual needs and those of the group, thus resulting in greater group productivity. Good human relation skills will help to develop this. Much more can be accomplished, and in a more meaningful manner when there is good group morale.

In the same manner that leadership can be developed and shared, so can responsibility. Neither all the credit nor all the blame should accrue to the status leader. Responsibility should go hand-in-hand with authority and power—responsibility should not be assigned unless it is accompanied by adequate authority. Individuals within an organization should not be required to take orders directly from more than one person. Acceptance of this principle of administration requires that each member in the organization should know to whom, and for what, he is responsible. This applies equally to students and relates directly to both classroom management and the less formally structured student activity program.

Too liberal an interpretation of the premise that everyone affected by a program or policy should share in decision-making with respect to that program or policy could result in a very chaotic state. However, within reasonable limits, greater acceptance, and thus greater success, with a program should be anticipated if those who are particularly affected have been asked to contribute towards that program or policy. It must be noted this premise does not indicate the decision-making activities with respect to such programs and policies are necessarily made by a majority vote of the individuals affected—rather, it indicates the provision for the opportunity to contribute towards the decision. This principle is reflected in many statements of codes of ethics or standards of professional conduct. The individual who shares in the responsibility for decision-making is more likely to feel that the decision arrived at was part of him, and thus is more inclined to work towards the successful fulfillment of that decision. He feels more secure when working on a basis of understanding.

When goals, policies and programs are developed by the group, there will be greater acceptance of them. This works towards a greater unity of purpose and greater group loyalty. This is important to each individual and also to the group as a whole.

Threats and pressure tactics will not increase long-term production. Short-term production may increase but these procedures in all likelihood will be more damaging to the long-term picture. If the individual participates in the determination of the aims and objectives, these are more likely to become part of him, and thus he will strive harder towards the achievement of them, thus achieving greater production. The exerting of pressure develops increasing resentment, particularly if the pressure involves the forced acceptance of aims and objectives which the individual feels are not part of him.

Some type of line and staff organization, showing channels of authority and assistance relationships, is necessary in any organization to assist in carrying out policies and decisions that have been made. The determination of the policies and programs can best be achieved by utilizing the involvement of others within the organization, regardless of where these people fit within the line and staff organization. However, when the policies and programs are determined, there needs to be a structure to carry them forward. A line and staff organization is best suited for this purpose. Within any effective organization there needs to be a coordination of activities, a function which can best be done by a single executive head.

Although a certain degree of authority rests with status positions within an organization, such as the legally sanctioned position of principal, it should be recognized that, generally speaking, authority arises from the situation rather than from the status position. This means the authority to act should be placed as close as possible to the point where decisions must be made. This statement is made on the assumption that when responsibility is delegated, sufficient authority must also be delegated in order to permit the group or individual to cope adequately with the responsibility delegated to that group or individual. Each person within an organization must know for what he is responsible, and to whom he is responsible. No individual should be placed in the position of having to take direct orders from more than one person.

The structural aspects of an organization such as a school or school system are frequently stated or appear to be independent of the persons within the organization. No person should be indispensable to the organization, however, the functional organization realizes the individuals within it are not expendable items. The worth of each individual within an organization must be considered and recognized. Each individual should have a feeling of security within the organization.

Working on the assumption there is broad participation within the organization on the development of goals, policies and programs, then there should be broad participation in the evaluation of these items. The organization becomes stronger and more productive when the individuals have the opportunity to become involved in the evaluations. The meanings of the evaluations become more personalized and therefore more understandable to those concerned.

The framework through which these basic assumptions can operate will vary from organization to organization. There is no one structure which is best, but the structure must make possible the purposes for which the organization exists. Figure 10-3 is an example of the organization of Student Personnel Services within a school system. The figure shows the organization within the division of Student Personnel Services as well as the relationships of this division to the other divisions within the school system. Internal organization of the other divisions are not elaborated upon in this figure. The policy handbook for this school system, as well as in other school systems, would serve the purpose of clarifying relationships, intent and purpose for structuring in this particular manner. There are some services which could work equally as effectively within a different branch of the organization but could be allocated a particular place because of the background and interests of the people concerned. Other reasons may be balancing work loads, efficiency and geographic locations.

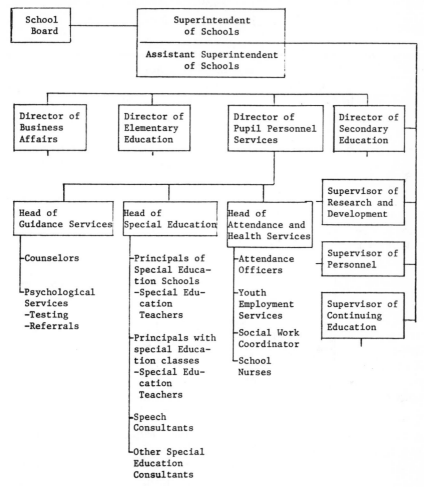

Figure 10-3
Organization of Student Personnel Services

In most provinces the Department of Education has consultative or administrative personnel who are particularly involved in areas within Student Personnel Services. The school system needs to clarify the role of these people and to provide arrangements for the best possible coordination with the appropriate personnel within the school system.

The Counseling Continuum

The classroom teacher has an important role to play in the counseling continuum. The extent of this involvement, in relationships which could be considered counseling, depends upon each individual teacher, but all teachers will be involved to some extent. A teacher is not a trained medical officer but nevertheless does assist the young student with the cleansing and bandaging of a cut or bruise. The teacher is not a trained psychologist or counselor but does have an important part to play in certain areas of psychology and counseling. The extent of involvement in the various components of counseling services by the teaching, guidance and referral staffs is illustrated in figure 10–4.

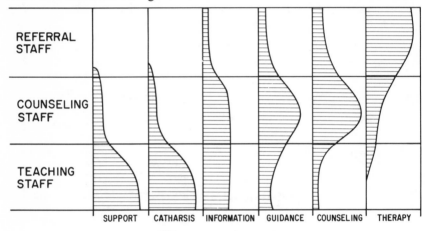

Figure 10–4
The Counseling Continuum

Each of the six areas is important. They range from the easier, or less intense, aspects to the most complicated. At the least complicated of these levels, support is given to the student which increases his confidence and makes what he is doing more important and realistic. The teacher may say, "That was a good basketball game you played yesterday", or give a friendly pat on the back for a suitable performance in the school play. Support comes from a variety of sources, including the classroom teacher. At a slightly higher level, that of catharsis, the student needs non-threatening opportunities to ventilate his thoughts and feelings. Having dispensed with the "over-burden", the student is then more capable of viewing his problems more objectively and with less emotion. The classroom teacher can provide many of these "ventilating" opportunities—they need not all be done by the counselor. As with the other levels of support and information, the teacher must be alert to the possibilities of the student using a low-key approach in order to open the door to the real problems with which he needs help.

The classroom teacher is quite capable of providing considerable information needed by students. Routine information is readily available from the teacher, but more specialized information requires preparation and organization which may be beyond the time and expertise capacities of the teacher. Career information is an example—complete, accurate and current information is best obtained from the school counselor. Guidance goes beyond the dispensing of information—guidance, or advising, is the assisting of the student in the utilization of information so as to best solve his problem. This is not to be confused with directing, but there is the element of giving advice, often in the form of suggesting viable alternatives. For example, a student indicates a desire to go to university upon completion of high school. In the selection of a mathematics course, the student may be advised to take the "academic" mathematics course instead of business mathematics.

The counseling aspect is in large measure beyond the capabilities of the classroom teacher and should be left substantially to the trained and experienced counselor. Counseling is a somewhat sensitive relationship in which, traditionally, the student is assisted in the solving of his own problems. The involvement of the counselor in the less intense aspects of the counseling continuum (support, catharsis, information and guidance) will assist in establishing relationships which will make the counseling aspect more effective. In the area of therapy, the role of the teacher is to carry out instructions from the professionals in this field.

The boundaries discussed here are not clear-cut. Much will depend upon the availability and competence of the teaching and counseling staffs, the attitude of administration, the wishes of the students, the personality of staff members, and many other related factors. The teacher's role in the counseling continuum is very important. The beginning teacher is well advised to determine the counseling services available and to develop himself as a teacher who is a real human being who cares.

Curricular, Co-Curricular and Extra-Curricular Activities

The curricular program is the structural basis for providing educational opportunities for students. The curricular program, including curricular activities, needs to be fleshed out with co-curricular and extra-curricular activities in order to provide a suitable or full educational program. Educators must provide not a minimal program but rather as complete a program as possible, realizing, of course, there are limitations and restrictions which are beyond the control of the educator.

There exists today some confusion as to what is meant by the terms curricular, co-curricular and extra-curricular. This is understandable because the terms are relative and the boundaries fuzzy. An examination of these terms according to various criteria soon forces the individual into deciding what really is part of the curriculum and what is extra. One stand can be that the educational program consists of the various subject components and that student council, sports program, yearbook and other similar activities, are actually extra to the program, something some teachers become involved in but is not really part of their job. At the other end of this continuum is the stand that these other activities, even though not associated directly with a specified subject, are important to the overall educational program and are indeed a definite responsibility of the teaching staff. The author tends towards this latter view.

Each of the provinces has stated aims and objectives which point the directions in which education should proceed. While stated in different ways, the desired directions are consistent. There appears little doubt that, if we are to be serious about achieving these aims and objectives, the subject matter must be supplemented by an interesting and full program in sports, social, and the many other activities designed to permit self-exploration and self-satisfying needs of students. Becoming a better citizen of this country doesn't happen by chance. It is a learning situation in an experimental setting. The school must make this setting the best possible.

Assuming all the activities within, or connected with, a school setting are part of the educational program, then the differences between curricular, co-curricular and extra-curricular become differences in emphases. Let us compare these emphases according to the criteria of compulsion, teacher-pupil direction, time, financing, non-teaching personnel and location.

Generally, curricular activities are compulsory or nearly compulsory, as compared to extra-curricular activities, which are generally non-compulsory. Co-curricular activities are usually of a nature where the students are expected to participate but can often opt out. Curricular activities are more teacher-dominated and teacher-directed, whereas extra-curricular activities are more student-dominated and student-directed, with the teachers playing an advisory role. Curricular activities are primarily within time-tabled time allotments whereas extra-curricular activities tend to be not included in the time-table, and usually out of the regular school hours or during the noon recess. Co-curricular activities tend to be within regular school hours, either with period readjustments, or during the noon recess or directly "after school."

Curricular activities are generally financed through taxation and grants, whereas extra-curricular activities are usually financed directly by the student (and his parents). Co-curricular activities usually involve a heavy financial subsidy arrangement by the school, with the students contributing part. All three types of activities often involve the use of adult "non-professional" personnel, but the emphasis in curricular activities is on professional involvement (supplemented by non-professional) as compared to extra-curricular where involvement is more frequently by non-professional personnel. Curricular activities usually are located in the school building whereas co-curricular and extra-curricular are not necessarily within the building. Here the difference in emphasis is not as great as with some of the other criteria.

Exceptions can be noted to each of the directions indicated, but there is an emphasis that signifies the differences. Obviously, however, there are many learning activities which are important to the student but which are not associated with the school in any direct way. For example, church, scouting, guides and other youth groups, have no direct connection with the school in a formal curricular sense. They also contribute to the complete education of the child and they may also call for the teacher's commitment and contributions. However, the teacher would be contributing as a teacher-citizen, rather than teacher-teacher.

Integration of Handicapped Children

Since early times in Canada there has been integration of boys and girls for most educational purposes in most schools. There never has been any question of integration of tall and short children, blue-eyed and brown-eyed, left and right handed. There always has been an acceptance of the fact that in any classroom there is the integration of children with a mosaic of characteristics. Somehow however, over a period of years educators, usually with the consent and blessing of parents and trustees, decided certain individuals and groups would receive a higher quality education by being removed from the regular classroom and placed in segregated classrooms or segregated schools or in another institution, or just left at home. A way of restating the previous sentence would be to state certain classrooms would operate "better" if certain individual students were removed, not as sound from an educational stand, but a fact of educational life.

Through the 1950's, 1960's and into the 1970's, segregation of certain students into either special classrooms or special schools became an accepted practice. This trend was supported by educationists and encouraged by provincial departments of education. In general, school systems attempted to provide an educational program for those who were "educable" but were not ready to provide for the "trainable but not educable". Until recently the trainable were more the responsibility of charitable organizations or larger institutions under the auspices of departments other than education. The more severely handicapped, mentally at least, generally were provided with no programs or inadequate programs. By 1960 there were 1200 classes for mentally retarded children operated by local parental associations for the mentally retarded in an effort to remedy the situation.

Gradually more and more physically handicapped children were being educated in regular school systems, but this move for the mentally retarded was slower. For the mentally retarded the movement of normalization became accepted in the late 1960's and in the 1970's. This idea of even the severely mentally retarded being provided a life style as congruent as possible with the life styles of other people began to change living and training patterns for the mentally retarded, associating more and more of these individuals with the normal community. Schooling and training programs were thus being developed on a community, rather than an institutional, base. By the late 1960's some school boards were beginning to recognize their responsibility for education and training of those who were mentally retarded (the right to an education, regardless of handicap, is not yet fully accepted in Canada but the principle is gradually gaining acceptance). By 1970 some of the more than 5000 classes for the mentally retarded were under the auspices of school boards. By 1975 integration into public schools and school systems was underway on a large scale.

Parents, in the middle 1970's, were often not satisfied with the progress being made in integrating the handicapped, mentally handicapped in particular, and therefore associations developed with the expressed purpose of forcing school boards to extend their integration practices. Many misunderstandings have developed and, unfortunately, pro integration and con integration have tended to become two very rigid views regarding integration. The real question is not whether there should or should not be integration but rather to what extent. The following discussion is based on the premise that, of course, there will be, or should be, integration of handicapped children into the publicly supported school systems. Certainly this poses certain challenges to the classroom teachers and to administrators but realistically, teaching is far more than teaching only those students who are most capable of doing without teacher services. The students who really need teacher assistance is what teaching is all about.

There are four levels of integration, with variations within these levels. First, there is integration at the administrative level. An example would be a parent organization which operates a training or education facility for handicapped children. The school board, acting on the request of the parent group, "integrates" the facility into the school system. In this type of situation the measurable effect upon the students concerned would be negligible. The teachers would receive their cheques from a different source and probably would have some different personnel from head office to assist them. Even though the facility is integrated with the school system, the facility operates in much the same way that it always did. The first level of integration then is the incorporation of a facility or facilities into a larger system.

The second level of integration is the provision of segregated classrooms within schools. Instead of the handicapped children being segregated into special schools, they are still segregated but placed within an overall normal school environment. They would attend the neighborhood schools, use the same washrooms and the same playground as the other students. The integration would be mainly casual contact at recesses and noon hour, before and after school. As in the first level of integration, staffing patterns probably would not change.

The third level of integration would have two emphases. The handicapped have a segregated classroom as home base but are integrated into specified programs within the school, such as in the music class or the physical education class. The reverse of this also provides varying degrees of integration. In this situation the handicapped are in the normal classroom as a home base but are taken into segregated classrooms or resource areas for certain specified activities and instruction.

The fourth level of integration could be called complete integration wherein the handicapped are placed in the regular classrooms and programs. In this situation the additional assistance they require would be given primarily within the regular classroom environment. As is the case with all students in regular classrooms, there is provision for individual assistance for students.

These four stages are an oversimplification but are important to remember in discussions relative to integration. Too often the response of a classroom teacher to integration is horror at the thought of increasing his already crowded classroom by two or three additional students who are severely handicapped and may or may not be toilet trained, all this with no additional help. The beginning teacher should be assured this is not what is intended. Whether the handicapped are in a segregated or integrated classroom, additional assistance is needed, commensurate with the extent of handicap. If the type of handicap requires a maximum teacher-student ratio of one to ten in a segregated classroom, then a teacher who has one "regular" student replaced by a handicapped student, then at the very least the teacher should expect additional assistance of at least one tenth professional and non-professional staff as was provided to the segregated classroom.

When a teacher teaches a new unit of work, preparation is required. When a teacher acquires a student with a handicap, the teacher prepares accordingly. The teacher will become acquainted, through consultation with experts and reading, with the handicap. A teacher would not expect to have the depth of background a special education teacher would have, but any intelligent teacher can acquire necessary background information. Remember, there always will be additional help available, from professionals and from the parents, as examples.

School systems often plan integration on some adaptation of models such as the Cascade Model. This is a very realistic approach to the integration situation which was developed over a period of years, particularly since 1962. Figure 10-5, one version of the cascade system, was developed by Evelyn Deno and appeared in *Exceptional Children* in November, 1970.

The student whose handicap is being left-handed is not going to be placed in a segregated classroom, or institution for left-handed people. Rather, the teacher will accommodate this handicap by acquiring a left-handed desk and placing the desk to avoid troublesome shadows on the student's work. At the other extreme, there

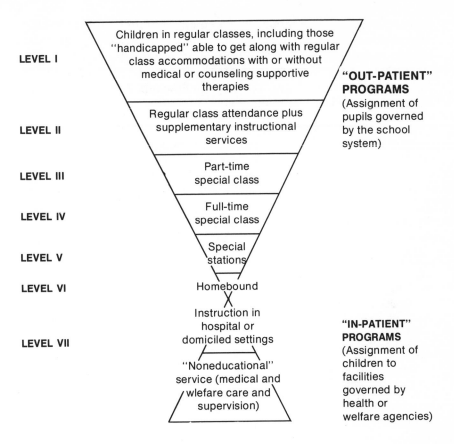

LEVEL I — Children in regular classes, including those "handicapped" able to get along with regular class accommodations with or without medical or counseling supportive therapies

LEVEL II — Regular class attendance plus supplementary instructional services

LEVEL III — Part-time special class

LEVEL IV — Full-time special class

LEVEL V — Special stations

LEVEL VI — Homebound

LEVEL VII — Instruction in hospital or domiciled settings

"Noneducational" service (medical and wlefare care and supervision)

"OUT-PATIENT" PROGRAMS (Assignment of pupils governed by the school system)

"IN-PATIENT" PROGRAMS (Assignment of children to facilities governed by health or welfare agencies)

Figure 10–5
Cascade System of Special Education Services

never has been any suggestion that integration, or mainstreaming, means the placement of a severely mentally retarded child in an academic grade twelve mathematics class. Integration means to place each handicapped person in as normal an educational setting as possible, commensurate with the extent of handicap. Constant reassessment of each handicapped student in conjunction with discussions with the parents, the student and others concerned, ensures a realistic degree of integration.

The everyday classroom receives most of the children, with diminishing numbers for the regular classroom with consultants, and so on until only a very small number are located in the hospital school and residential hospital. Once placed does not mean permanently placed. If the placement was inopportune, the next step lower could prove to be the best temporary placement. Throughout there is the constant effort to have more and more children progress to the next step, or steps, higher. For some, integration into the regular classroom would be a distant goal which will not be realized, but with the development of programs for the handicapped, more and more are moving further along the integration route than was thought possible even a few years ago.

REFERENCES

Alexander, W. E. and J. P. Farrell. *Student Participation in Decision-Making.* Toronto: Ontario Institute for Studies in Education, 1975.

Arbuckle, D. S. *Pupil Personnel Services in the Modern School.* Boston: Allyn and Bacon, 1966.

Berry, K. *Models for Mainstreaming.* Sioux Falls, South Dakota: Dimensions Publishing, 1972.

Crawford, Leonard. *One Million Children—The Celdic Report.* Toronto: Canadian Association for the Mentally Retarded, 1970.

Deno, E., "Special Education as Developmental Capital," *Exceptional Children* November, 1970.

Hummel, D. L. and S. J. Bonham. *Pupil Personnel Services in Schools.* Chicago: Rand McNally, 1968.

Interchange. Vol. 8, Nos. 1-2, 1977, 1978. This volume has 16 articles on "Children's Rights: Educational and Legal Issues".

Jones, R. L. *New Directions in Special Education.* Boston: Allyn and Bacon, 1970.

Keogh, B. K. and M. L. Levitt, "Special Education in the Mainstream; A Confrontation of Limitations," *Focus on Exceptional Children,* March, 1976.

Kirk, S. A. *Educating Exceptional Children.* Boston: Houghton Mifflin, 1972.

Kolstoe, O. P. *Teaching Educable Mentally Retarded Children.* New York: Holt, Rinehart and Winston, 1970.

Kowitz, G. T. and N. G. Kowitz. *Operating Guidance Services for the Modern School.* New York: Holt, Rinehart and Winston, 1968.

Levin, B., "The Silent Partner—the Role of the Student in School Governance," *The Politics of Canadian Education.* Canadian Society for the Study of Education, 1977.

Living and Learning. The Report of the Provincial Committee on Aims and Objectives of Education in the Schools of Ontario. Toronto: Ontario Department of Education, 1968.

Morphet, E. L., R. L. Jones and T. L. Reller, *Educational Organization and Administration.* Englewood Cliffs: Prentice-Hall, 1974.

National Institute on Mental Retardation. *Orientation Manual on Mental Retardation:* Toronto: Canadian Association for the Mentally Retarded, 1977.

Paterson, J. G., "Emerging Trends in Administering Pupil Personnel Services," in F. D. Oliva, and E. L. Koch. *Designs for the Seventies.* Calgary: Department of Educational Administration, The University of Calgary, 1970.

Purnell, R. F. *Adolescents and the American High School.* New York: Holt, Rinehart and Winston, 1970.

Rhodes, H. C. *The Alberta Special Education Study.* Edmonton: Department of Education, 1977.

Rogow, S., "The Right to an Equal Education: Is it Happening for Blind Children in Canada," *Education Canada*, Fall, 1976.

Sangster, C. H. and G. Adamson, "Nurturing Gifted Children," *Education Canada*, Winter, 1977.

Silberman, M. L. *The Experience of Schooling*. New York: Holt, Rinehart, and Winston, 1971.

Stevenson, H. A., R. M. Stamp and J. D. Wilson. *The Best of Times/The Worst of Times*. Toronto: Holt, Rinehart and Winston, 1972.

Strom, R. D. *Teachers and the Learning Process*. Englewood Cliffs: Prentice-Hall, 1971.

Treslan, D. L. Student Participation in Senior High School Governance: A Control Assembly Model. Unpublished doctoral dissertation, University of Calgary, 1977.

Wolfensberger, W. and H. Zauha. *Citizen Advocacy and Protective Services for the Impaired and Handicapped*. Toronto: National Institute on Mental Retardation, 1973.

Questions For Discussion

1. To what extent should the school be responsible for "extra" and "co" curricular activities?

2. Should credits (that is, recognition in the same manner as for subjects) be given for student participation in "extra" and "co" curricular activities?

3. Should participation from all teachers be required for the planning, advising and conducting of student activities?

4. What are the essential differences between a counseling program for elementary and secondary students?

5. Draw an organization chart for student personnel services in
   (a) a 1000 student senior high school.
   (b) a 1000 student junior high school.
   (c) a 1000 student elementary school.

6. How accurately does The Counseling Continuum (figure 10-4) describe your expectations of the role of a classroom teacher?

7. What is the relationship between the extent of subject specialization of teachers and the extent of specialized counseling services required in the school?

8. To what extent should special education (the physically handicapped, the mentally handicapped, the neurologically impaired) be integrated with and segregated from, the regular classes?

9. Describe the student personnel services which were available in the school in which you were last a student.

10. Is there any significant difference between the expectations of the teaching staff and the general public as to student personnel services in the schools?

TEACHING AS A PROFESSION

PART FOUR

11

Teaching As a Profession

Introduction

Is teaching a profession? The answer to this question is not a simple yes or no but rather an impression, or a feeling. The answer does not lie strictly with the collection of facts or opinions. Rather, it is something more personal, somewhat emotional. The purpose of this chapter is not to arrive at a definite answer to this somewhat evasive question but rather to discuss a few of the measuring sticks which may assist the individual in his deliberations. In making our decision, we can be assisted by a knowledge of the generally acceptable criteria used by others. The question is an important one though, because how teaching is considered influences how teaching is done. That is, there is an emotional involvement which affects the teacher's expectations of others, and referent groups' expectations held for the teacher.

How do we know whether teaching is a profession or not? One measuring stick frequently used is to compare teaching to other occupations which have received common acceptance as professions. There may be some question in many peoples' minds as to whether occupations such as mechanical engineering, optometry, accounting and paleontology are in fact professions, but there seems to be acceptance for recognizing medicine, law and the ministry as professions. Therefore, much of the literature regarding professions focuses mainly upon these three and not many more. The writers generally attempt to analyze the accepted professions in order to determine what these people have in common and what they have that other groups of people do not have, the assumption being the difference between these groups, i.e., doctors, lawyers, ministers and other work groups can somehow be interpreted as being the characteristics of professionalism.

This type of reasoning is similar to that used in much of the leadership research. Particularly in the earlier leadership studies, the basis of study was the determining of who was accepted as being an effective leader. Subsequently, the main traits of these leaders were ascertained. The assumption appeared to be that if other people could somehow develop these same traits, then they too would become effective leaders. While there is little doubt that these trait studies did further the knowledge about leadership, it must be accepted this reasoning really was not adequate to the situation. This type of converse thinking also may assist in this problem of profession-determining, but we must not accept at face value the results of such research as having universal application, or providing us with the full answer.

Characteristics of Occupations Recognized as Professions

The following discussion emphasizes some of the features of occupational groups which, by general consensus, are considered professions. It does not necessarily follow that if an occupational group acquired a similar listing of characteristics they would automatically be considered as a profession. No doubt this would help somewhat in the professionalization process but is not a method which would guarantee results. There is more to being a profession as further discussion will show.

The earlier recognitions of professionalism involved a degree of mysticism. The professional (the medicine-man) was the intermediary between man and unfathomable mysteries of nature. This early type of professional activity gradually divided into two categories or occupational groups—one the mystical healer of physical ills and the other, the intervener of the spirits for the good of man. Later, other groups of people, such as those interpreting the vagaries of institutionalized regulations, laws, to the usually uneducated individual, began to be accepted as professions.

Dr. Abraham Flexner, in 1915, stated that a profession was based mainly on six criteria. The first of these was that a profession was intellectual. Second, it was learned. That is, a profession was based on a substantial body of knowledge which developed over a long period of time and which was transmissable to students through a lengthy training program. Third, a profession was practical in that its knowledge could be used to solve problems in important recurring situations, such as birth, death and marriage. Fourth, a profession had skills or techniques that could be taught. Fifth, a profession was organized into associations which regulated entrance into the association and guided further education for its members. Sixth, a profession was guided by altruism, that is, a desire to serve mankind.

Many other descriptions of characteristics of occupational groups considered as professions have been developed since 1915. There are variations, mainly according to differences of opinion as to which occupational groups are professions. Generally, however, the characteristics can be summarized as follows:

1. A profession serves a unique, essential service to mankind.
2. A profession is based on a body of knowledge which has taken a long period of time to develop, and active, planned efforts are made to understand this knowledge and further it for the betterment of mankind.
3. Members of a profession undertake a long training period plus an internship period before being recognized by their particular association, and the public, as being competent to practice.
4. The public accepts and respects the opinions and practices of the members of the profession.
5. The life-style of the members of the profession reflect an above-average standard educationally and culturally. Usually, this is accompanied by an above-average monetary entitlement.
6. Members of professions organize into closed-shop associations which protect the public from "unprofessional" practices and protects the profession from unscrupulous members of the public.

There still exists a certain mysticism about the professions. The ordinary, lay public are awed by the amount of knowledge and skill possessed by professionals. Invariably, this is accompanied by a technical language indigenous to the profession and not readily understood by other groups of people—adding to the impression of the possession of a great wealth of knowledge. What the professional does is usually not completely understood by the lay public. They must place their faith in the judgment of the professional—even life and death decisions. For this kind of confidence, the public readily pays comparatively high fees, usually without questioning the validity of the fee. The public accepts a closed shop arrangement whereby the members admit new members to the profession, police their own members, and provide an area of insulation between the lay public and the individual professional members—all with the acceptance of the public. All members of the professions are not necessarily rich, but there is usually the acceptance that professional people should be able to enjoy a higher standard of living than most people, and to be able to enjoy the finer things of life. Often the opinions of professional people are respected above those of other people in matters which are not necessarily related to the particular profession. That is, the trust placed in the hands of the professional people extends beyond the necessary professional competencies of these control individuals.

In order to police their own members and to provide a degree of protection from the public, a profession, through its professional association develops a code of ethics which reflects expected ethical behavior of its members and sets the framework for standards of professional work. An example of a code of ethics from a recognized profession, medicine, is as follows.

The Canadian Medical Association Code of Ethics

Principles of Ethical Behavior for all physicians, including those who may not be engaged directly in clinical practice.

1. Consider first the well-being of the patient.
2. Honour your profession and its traditions.
3. Recognize your limitations and the special skills of others in the prevention and treatment of disease.
4. Protect the patient's secrets.
5. Teach and be taught.
6. Remember that integrity and professional ability should be your only advertisement.
7. Be responsible in setting a value on your services.

The medical profession also developed a guide to the ethical behavior of physicians. This guide operationalizes the code of ethics in that the responsibilities are indicated in a more specific manner (for example, "An ethical physician...will recognize that he has a responsibility to render medical service to any person regardless of colour, religion or political belief."). The guide specifies the ethical physician's responsibilities to the patient, to the profession and to society.

Teaching—A Profession

However important the various characteristics commonly accepted as being professional-based aspects are, it appears acceptance is the important criterion. That is, do the individuals within the occupational group really accept themselves as professionals, and does the general public also accord them with the same acceptance? If teachers wish to be professionals they will need to do more than attempt to meet the standards of measurement which reflect already established professions. Teachers will need to feel professional and to gain public acceptance of professional status, both of which are difficult tasks.

In order for teachers to arrive at professional status, one of the first requirements is to analyze where they stand in the characteristics of accepted professions. As fallacious as this method may be, the self-image of the teacher needs to be measured. He must have confidence in himself as a professional or he never will be one. The measuring sticks are vague and ethereal, but at least something to start with.

Teaching provides a service which is somewhat unique. However, every member of the public has had the experience of going to school. This makes it more difficult to incorporate an aura of mystique surrounding teaching comparable to other accepted professions. The general public feels there is nothing special about teaching spelling—anyone can do that. The teaching of arithmetic facts can also be done without training—at least in the eyes of most of the public. Many other phases of teaching fall into the same realm. The present movement to individualized instruction, often misunderstood, coupled with greater teacher visibility, has not helped the situation much. Non-professional people—the teacher aide, the parent, the school secretary—see teachers at work, more so now because of the open-area school concept. Too often they see a teacher sitting at a desk giving instructions to the students—"do pages seven and eight, if you have any difficulty, see me." When a student seeks help he is often told to find out for himself. Real individualized instruction is a different matter. However, the impression given by the misuse of an important concept, individualized instruction, or any other important concept, emphasizes to other teachers, and to the public, that there is very little that is unique about teaching. Our present teaching methods are more open to public scrutiny than ever before—the uniqueness is more and more difficult to attain.

Education is an essential service to mankind. However, its essential nature is frequently determined in the long-term sense. The public would agree with this essential aspect but they are also quick to point out there is much that is non-essential.

The training period for teachers has increased considerably since the early settlement days of Canada. Appendix B, Teacher Certification in Canada, illustrates that most provinces now require teachers to have three and four years of formal training (university) before they may receive permanent certification. Compared with medicine, law and other professions, however, the one and two years of training possessed by many teachers presently teaching in Canada seems quite inadequate for the task to be performed and for development of a scholastic-academic image of the practitioner.

Practice teaching is invariably a part of the training program but to date internship has not become a general requirement for certification. Teacher training programs are gradually including more school-related experiences in their programs. Internship is being discussed in a number of provinces and perhaps will become an integral part of the preparation period for teachers.

The base of knowledge for teachers has taken a considerable time to develop. Efforts are being made continuously to analyze, understand and further this knowledge. The lag between research and practice in education is notably long but research is becoming more acceptable as a basis on which knowledge is furthered. It is only recently that increased periods of training for certification have been required and therefore most of the teaching force in past years has had insufficient background on which to utilize to the fullest advantage the knowledge as it developed.

There appears to be some difference of opinion, as reflected in the literature, as to the acceptance and respect of opinions and practices of teachers. This may be, in part, because the general level of education of the general public has increased faster, comparatively, than that of the teaching force. With this in mind, it appears teachers are at least holding their own as to acceptance and respect.

The life-style of teachers has not been above-average educationally and culturally. Their life-style reflects a middle class perspective —one which is shared by many non-professionals. In the past, the professional person has been one who has been considerably ahead of the majority of the people. Now other groups of people who in the past have not been considered as professionals, and are not now so considered, are developing life-styles analogous to the professional. Thus the increase in the life-style of the teachers is not as obvious as it once might have been. That is, the teachers must struggle to keep comparative pace, let alone increase noticeably.

Lastly, teachers are organized into associations, some of which are closed shops. There have developed codes of ethics and standards of professional conduct. The code of ethics and standards of professional conduct of The Alberta Teachers' Association exemplify the ethical basis which provincial associations hold for their teaching force.

Code of Ethics*

The Code of Ethics shall apply to all members, and the term "teacher" as used in this code includes all members of The Alberta Teachers' Association. A complaint of violation of this code made to the Association by any person or group shall be regarded by the Provincial Executive Council of the Association as a charge of unprofessional conduct under the Discipline Bylaws of the Association. Excessive or flagrant violation of the Standards of Professional Conduct by any member of the Association may also lead to discipline charges being laid against that member.

1. The teacher does not criticize the professional competence or professional reputation of a colleague except to proper officials and then only in confidence and after the colleague has been informed of the criticism.

2. The teacher recognizes the Association as the official spokesman of the teachers in Alberta. Individuals or groups purporting to speak on behalf of teachers to the officials of colleges, institutions or universities, or to the government, its members or officials, on matters affecting the interests of teachers generally, do so only with the prior consent of the Provincial Executive Council.

3. The teacher provides documents relevant to engagement or advancement requested by the employer.

4. The teacher adheres to collective agreements negotiated by the Association.

5. The teacher fulfills contractual obligations with an employer until released by mutual consent or according to law.

6. The teacher does not apply for nor accept a colleague's position before it has been declared vacant.

7. The teacher does not divulge information received in confidence or in the course of professional duties, except as required by law, or where, in the judgment of the teacher, it is in the best interests of the child.

*The Code of Ethics and Standards of Professional Conduct are reproduced here with the permission of The Alberta Teachers' Association.

8. The teacher does not accept pay for tutoring his own pupils in the subjects in which he gives classroom instruction.

9. The teacher does not use his professional position for personal profit by offering goods or services to his own pupils or their parents.

Standards of Professional Conduct

The Standards of Professional Conduct shall apply to all members, and the term "teacher" as used in this statement of standards includes all members of the Alberta Teachers' Association. This statement does not attempt to define all items of acceptable conduct. These items are minimum standards of professional behavior which members are expected to observe. Excessive or flagrant violation of the Standards of Professional Conduct by any member of the Association may lead to a charge of unprofessional conduct under the Discipline Bylaws of the Association.

In Relation to Pupils

1. The teacher shall diagnose needs, prescribe and implement instructional programs and evaluate the progress of students and may not delegate these responsibilities to any person who is not a teacher.

2. The teacher may delegate specific aspects of instructional activity to noncertificated personnel on a short-term basis only.

3. The teacher treats pupils with dignity and respect and is considerate of their circumstances.

In Relation to the General Public

4. The teacher does not engage in activities which adversely affect the quality of his professional service and acts in such manner as to maintain the honor and prestige of the profession.

5. The teacher endeavors to improve the quality of education.

In Relation to Employers

6. The teacher does not accept a position with an employer whose relations with The Alberta Teachers' Association are unsatisfactory without first consulting the Association.

7. The teacher intending to terminate employment with a school authority gives notice of intention as early as possible.

8. After accepting a position, the teacher notifies other boards to which applications were submitted.

9. The teacher protests both the assignment of duties for which he is not qualified and conditions which make it difficult to render professional service.

In Relation to Colleagues

10. The teacher does not undermine the confidence of pupils in other teachers.

11. The teacher submits to the Association disputes arising from professional relationships with colleagues which cannot be resolved by personal discussion.

12. The teacher observes a reasonable respect for the authority of school administrators and recognizes the duty to protest through proper channels, administrative policies and practices which he cannot in conscience accept; and further recognizes that if administration by consent fails, the administrator must adopt a position of authority.

13. The teacher as an administrator respects staff members as individuals and provides continuous opportunities for staff members to express their opinions and bring forth suggestions regarding the administration of the school.

14. The teacher, before making any report on the professional competence of a colleague, provides him with a copy of the report and forwards with it any written comment that the colleague chooses to make.

In Relation to the Association

15. The teacher adheres to Association policy and seeks to change such policy only through the proper channels of the Association.

16. The teacher accepts service to the Association as a professional obligation.

17. The teacher who has requested representation by the Association honors commitments made on his behalf.

In Relation to Professional Growth

18. The teacher strives to improve his educational practices.

The compatability of union and profession is being more accepted than even a few years ago. It is now recognized that some forces behind professions such as medicine are the same as for unions. The medical doctors' strike in Saskatchewan demonstrated clearly professionals will use union tactics when it is necessary to protect the profession. There are many examples of professionals working on negotiated salary schedules rather than on a fee for service. The closed shop of the professional organizations resemble that of unions; the control and discipline which unions have over their members is often as strict as professional organizations have for their members. Thus it is not easy to separate professionalism on the basis of their organization. Teachers often are associated with other labor unions through their association in the Labor Acts. Teacher associations maintain union tactics are necessary to upgrade teaching through obtaining a better standard of living and working conditions commensurate with professionalism, that is, provide the climate within which professionalism can operate.

For teaching to be considered a profession, the individual teachers must personally feel they are professionals and must be able to gain the respect and acceptance of the public as have other professions.

REFERENCES

Carver, F. D. and T. J. Sergiovanni. *Organizations and Human Behavior.* New York: McGraw-Hill, 1969.

Chalmers, J. W. *Teachers of the Foothills Province.* Toronto: University of Toronto Press, 1968.

Chapman, S. L. G., "Teacher Militancy: Trend for the 70's? For Administrators," *Quill and Quire*, October, 1974.

Flexner, A., "Is Social Work a Profession?" *Proceedings of the National Conference of Charities and Correction.* Chicago: The Hildmann Printing Co., 1915.

Guy, A. J. Y., "Teaching as a Profession," *The Saskatchewan Administrator*, May, 1970.

Hennessy, P. H. *Teacher Militancy: A Comparative Study of Ontario, Quebec and New York Teachers.* Ottawa: Canadian Teachers' Federation, 1975.

Jesse, K. A. Dimensions of Professionalization Among Junior High Teachers. Unpublished master's thesis, University of Calgary, 1970.

Keeler, B. T. and H. A. Doherty. *The Rights and Duties of Teachers.* Edmonton: The Alberta Teachers' Association, 1972.

Lieberman, M. *The Future of Public Education.* Chicago: The University of Chicago Press, 1960.

Lynas, E., "Reluctant Militants," *Educational Courier*, February, 1973.

McCurdy, S. G. *The Legal Status of the Canadian Teacher.* Toronto: The Macmillan Company, 1968.

McGlothin, W. J. *The Professional Schools.* New York: The Center for Applied Research in Education, 1964.

McLeish, J. A. B. *The Advancement of Professional Education in Canada.* Toronto: Ontario Institute for Studies in Education, 1973.

Members' Handbook, 1977 Edition. Edmonton: The Alberta Teachers' Association, 1977.

Myers, D., "Teacher Militancy: Trend for the 70's? For the Teachers," *Quill and Quire*, October, 1974.

Ohles, J. F. *Introduction to Teaching.* Toronto: Random House, 1970.

Paton, J. M., "Crisis of Confidence in the Teaching Profession," *Teacher Education,* Spring, 1975.

Reeves, A. W., H. C. Melsness and J. E. Cheal. *Educational Administration: The Role of the Teacher.* Toronto: Macmillan Company, 1962.

Richey, R. W. *Planning for Teaching.* New York: McGraw-Hill, 1973.

Segall, W. E., A Study of Collective Professionalism in Western Canada. Unpublished doctoral dissertation, The University of Arkansas, 1967.

Questions for Discussion

1. The result of some of the government statutes and regulations has been firmer structures which encouraged, and forced, the development of professionalism for teachers. What are some of these statutes and regulations?

2. Is there any other recognized profession which has as great a proportion of female members as has teaching? Is there any valid connection between sex and professionalism?

3. Should there be a formalized and compulsory internship program as part of the training program for teachers?

4. Should the permanency of teachers' certificates be subject to evidence of continual professional upgrading?

5. Should education develop a greater "mystique" (such as law and medicine) in the pursuit of greater professional recognition?

6. Are there factors, other than those mentioned in this chapter, which are pertinent to the concept of professionalism?

7. Each year there are a number of teachers' strikes in Canada. To what extent does this affect the public acceptance of teaching as a profession?

8. If it was your responsibility to revise the Code of Ethics and Standards of Professional Conduct of your professional association, what changes would you recommend?

9. Do you consider teaching as a profession?

10. How will the over-supply of teachers and decreasing school enrolments affect teaching as a profession?

11. Should a teacher's membership in his professional association be terminated because of misbehavior outside the direct teacher-student relationship (for example, shoplifting, drunken driving, fraud, moral incidents)?

12

Teachers' Associations in Canada

The Beginning of Teachers' Associations

It is not possible to pin-point a particular date in Canadian history as being the date of organization of the first Canadian teachers' association. Groups of workers tend to form, and dissolve, organizations—both formal and informal. When the formation of a group becomes the formation of an association is mainly an exercise in semantics, an exercise of which there is no intention of pursuing here. From the earliest times in Canadian history, teachers naturally formed interest groups comparable to those formed by other groups of workers. For example, the mathematics teachers in a certain geographical area, or perhaps, the teachers who taught in a certain parish school, may have formed a group, or association. The purpose of this chapter is to consider teachers' associations which bear resemblance to the provincial organizations now common in Canada, and in particular, those which contribute substantially to the development and protection of teaching as a profession.

One of the first of the more formal educational organizations which had some of the attributes of a professional association was the Teachers' Association of Canada West formed in 1861 (from 1867, called the Ontario Teachers' Association). However, this organization probably should be described as a group of people, some lay, who were interested in education, rather than being an organization of teachers interested in themselves for welfare purposes as well as professional interest in education generally. The Provincial Association of Protestant Teachers of Quebec, founded in 1864, and continuing under the same name today, came closest to being what today we would call a professional teachers' organization, or association. They obtained a provincial charter in 1889, the first in Canada.

Other teacher organizations subsequent to this time were formed and dissolved, for example, the Ontario Teachers' Alliance of 1908, and the Educational Society of Ontario in 1886. This latter organization aimed "to combine the advantages of a labor union and of a fraternal benevolent society." More substantive beginnings of the organized teacher movement included The Nova Scotia Teachers' Union in 1895, The Newfoundland Teachers' Association in 1890, The New Brunswick Teachers' Association in 1902, the Territorial Teachers' Association before 1907, the Alberta Teachers' Alliance in 1917, and The Manitoba Teachers' Federation in 1919.

Even though the movement toward the formation of professional organizations began early in Canadian history, it was not until after the First World War that substantial results were obtained in developing organizations which could be more professional in nature. Prior to the war, the teachers were not strongly organized, nor did they generally have clear aims regarding professional recognition. Most of the organizations were educational in nature but usually not professional, that is, they did not concentrate on education as a profession. Undoubtedly, the comparatively low salaries and poor working conditions experienced by teachers in the early 1900's spurred the development of teachers' associations.

Today, there are provincial teachers' associations or organizations in each of the provinces, as well as in the Yukon and North West Territories. For most provinces, there is one association representing the teachers of that province, however, Ontario, Quebec and New Brunswick have multiple associations. The remainder of this chapter will discuss briefly each of the present-day teachers' associations, concluding with the national organization (CTF) and discernible future directions.

The British Columbia Teachers' Federation

Prior to 1914 institutes along the Provincial Coast and Interior, dominated by the Department of Education, provided B.C. teachers a biennial opportunity to discuss mutual problems. In 1916 delegates from the general areas of Vancouver and Victoria met to form a provincial federation of men and women actively engaged in teaching. The first annual meeting was held in 1917 with the main concerns being low salaries, insufficient training, lack of tenure and disrespect of teachers' rights by employers. Beneath these issues was the longing for professional recognition and status.

The need for unified strength, focussed by the first teachers' strike in the British Empire, at Victoria, resulted in the BCTF being incorporated under the Benevolent Societies Act in 1919. The three original objectives are still the first three objectives in the present BCTF constitution: (1) to foster and promote the cause of education, (2) to raise the status of the teaching profession, and (3) to promote the welfare of the teachers in British Columbia.

The first permanent office was established in Victoria in 1920 and moved to Vancouver in 1926. Progress was slow during the recession and World War II. Subsequent to this time, salaries increased and other benefits were achieved—pension plan, sick leave, group insurance, medical coverage, educational leave and tenure protection. Mandatory automatic membership was achieved in 1947 and was in effect until 1971, when it was removed by the government. Very few of the teachers, however, opted out of membership since it became legally possible for them to do so.

The prime concern for basic teacher welfare has gradually been supplemented by other professional activities such as curriculum development, educational research projects and involvement in the responsibility for education decision making in the province.

The head office of the BCTF is at 105–2235 Burrard Street, Vancouver. The Executive Committee consists of the president, two vice-presidents, past president and seven members-at-large. The president and the first vice-president are relieved of their teaching duties with their salary paid by BCTF. The general secretary is Mr. R. M. Buzza. The legislative arm of the BCTF is the Annual General Meeting at which each of the local associations has the right of representation on the basis of one voting delegate for each 0.2 percent membership in BCTF. Between Annual General Meetings a Representative Assembly meets at least three times a year to safeguard membership interests. It is made up of 114 Geographical Representatives and the 11 members of the Executive Committee. The official magazine of the BCTF is *The B.C. Teacher*.

There are approximately 30,000 BCTF full- and part-time active members, divided into 79 Local Associations. The active members pay annual fees of 0.91 percent of the mean salary of all members. No rebate is paid to the local associations, which set their own fees in addition to the provincial fees. Grants are available to local associations for specific purposes.

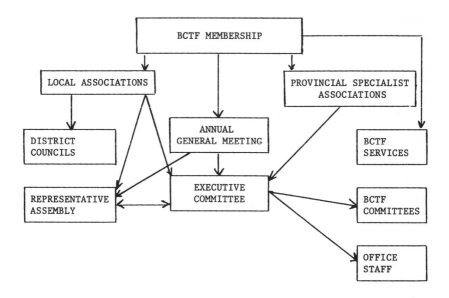

The Alberta Teachers' Association

The forerunner of the present Alberta Teachers' Association was The Alberta Teachers' Alliance, formed in 1917. The Alberta Teachers' Alliance, in turn was an offshoot of the Alberta Educational Association, which was more of a convention organization than a professional organization in that the main thrust was to organize an annual convention of the teachers and others in the field of education. The resolutions passed at the first annual meeting of The Alberta Teachers' Alliance in 1918 indicated the early concern which prompted the formation of a teachers' association. These were related to the drafting of a code of ethics, a provincial salary schedule, with a minimum annual salary of $1200., improved teachers' contracts, full citizenship rights for teachers, a pension scheme for Alberta teachers, improved government grants, publication of The ATA Magazine, and the inauguration of a federation of all teachers' organizations in Canada.

The formation of this teachers' organization was opposed strongly, and often bitterly, by school trustees and members of the government. In 1919, The Alberta Teachers' Alliance appointed a full-time organizer, followed in 1920 by the appointment of a full-time secretary-treasurer. The defeat of the government in 1921 eased the strength of opposition somewhat, but it was not until the defeat of another government in 1935 that the necessary legislative action was undertaken to ensure the permanency of this organization, now called The Alberta Teachers' Association, as a professional organization. The legislature, in 1936, provided for compulsory membership in the Association by all teachers teaching in publicly supported (provincial) schools and for discipline powers. In 1937 came provision of a Board of Reference with power to enforce its decisions and in 1939, the establishment of a teachers' pension scheme. In 1945 the training of teachers was assumed by the universities in the province, under the watchful eyes of the Board of Teacher Education and Certification, a body now consisting of twenty-seven members, four of whom represent The Alberta Teachers' Association.

The head office of The Alberta Teachers' Association is at Barnett House, 11010–142 Street, Edmonton, Alberta, with a subsidiary office in Calgary. The executive staff consists of the executive secretary, Dr. B. T. Keeler, and nineteen full-time salaried professional staff. The elected Provincial Executive Council consists of a president (full-time), two vice-presidents, past president, and fourteen district representatives, plus the executive secretary (non-voting). The legislative arm of The Alberta Teachers' Association is the Annual Representative Assembly which consists of the Provincial Executive Council and approximately 500 local representatives. The approximately 24,000 ATA members are formed into seventy-eight locals. In addition, there are four student locals. Members pay fees of $210. per year to the provincial association, twenty per cent of which is rebated to the local associations to promote the development of local professional activities and cover the operating expenses of the 78 local associations. Additional fees can be assessed by the local associations.

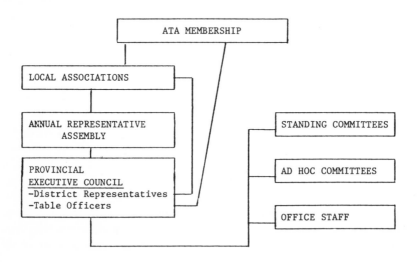

The Saskatchewan Teachers' Federation

Prior to 1905, the teachers employed in the areas now known as Alberta and Saskatchewan joined a Territorial Teachers' Association. The records of this association were subsequently lost, and thus details of the early history are sketchy. In 1907 the provincial government inaugurated the formation of The Saskatchewan Educational Association. The basis of this organization was teacher welfare and the annual conferences which were devoted mainly to addresses and discussions about schools and education. In 1914 the Saskatchewan Union of Teachers was formed. This union attempted to form within the framework of The Saskatchewan Educational Association but was refused permission to do so. Four years later this union was renamed the Saskatchewan Teachers' Alliance. After supporting the Moose Jaw Teachers' strike in 1921, the Alliance experienced a membership increase to 1600. During the depression, membership declined to approximately 600, and it was at this stage that a third organization, The Rural Teachers' Association, was formed.

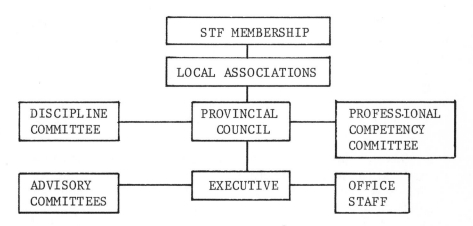

In 1934 The Saskatchewan Education Association, The Saskatchewan Teachers' Alliance and The Rural Teachers' Association banded together to form The Saskatchewan Teachers' Federation, the resultant membership of which included seventy-three percent of all the Saskatchewan teachers. In 1935 *The Teachers' Federation Act* was passed which made membership in STF mandatory for all teachers employed in publicly supported school systems. This was the first legislation of mandatory membership for teachers in the British Commonwealth.

The head office of The Saskatchewan Teachers' Federation is at 2317 Arlington Avenue (Box 1108), Saskatoon, with a subsidiary office in Regina. The administrative staff consists of the general secretary. Dr. S. McDowell, and ten full-time professional staff. The Federation publication, *The Saskatchewan Bulletin*, reports current activities of the Federation and topical events in education generally.

The elected executive consists of the president (full-time), past president, vice-president and seven executive members. The Council consists of two councillors for the first 150 members of each local association, and one councillor for each additional 75 members. The legislative arm of the Federation is the Provincial Council. The annual fee is $168., plus .50 percent for the income continuance plan. There are approximately 11,000 STF members, divided into 76 local Associations.

Manitoba Teachers' Society

In July, 1918, eighty teachers met in Winnipeg for the purposes of forming a professional organization. During Easter week of 1919, the Manitoba Teachers' Federation was formed with 62 members paying fees totalling $61. By 1924 the membership had risen to 2000 and the first issue of *The Manitoba Teacher* was printed. In 1942 the organization's name was changed to The Manitoba Teachers' Society. The provision of automatic, but not compulsory (that is, with a write-out provision), membership was also achieved in 1942.

By 1948 legislation had been passed which guaranteed the teachers the right to bargain collectively. The beginning of some tenure for teachers was made in 1956 and the salaries and working conditions began to steadily improve. A provincial pension scheme was developed in 1957. The association has also developed summer and winter courses for teachers, plus other seminars and conferences, and a one-week leadership course for division association officers.

McMaster House, in Winnipeg, was erected in 1957 as the first permanent headquarters of MTS. The present headquarters at 191 Harcourt Street, Winnipeg, Manitoba, was opened in 1967. The executive staff consists of the general secretary, Mr. W. R. Gordon and twelve full-time salaried professional staff. The elected Provincial Executive consists of a president (full-time), first vice-president (half-time), second vice-president, treasurer, past president and fourteen representatives. The legislative arm of The Manitoba Teachers Society is the Annual General Meeting which consists of about 250 division association representatives and provincial executive members. The approximately 12,000 members are formed into 47 Division Associations and thirteen Remote Locals. Within each division there may be several local associations which serve a smaller number of teachers and are advisory to the divisional associations. Members pay fees of $159. per annum to the provincial association. As well, members pay local fees which vary with the association, and may belong to one of 23 subject area groups which also have a fee.

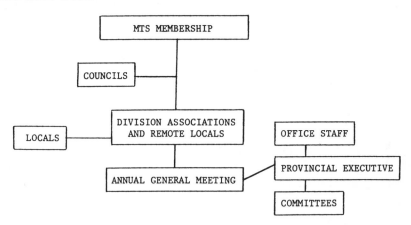

Ontario Teachers' Federation

In Ontario all teachers teaching in publicly supported schools must, by provincial statute, belong to the Ontario Teachers' Federation. This professional organization has five affiliated organizations, each of which will be described following the OTF description. The OTF members are allocated membership in one of these five affiliates according to the OTF by-laws. Thus OTF membership is mandatory, as is membership in the appropriate affiliate. The Board of Governors votes on the fee, as requested by an affiliate, which then needs to be approved by the Lieutenant Governor in Council. The fees, which include the affiliate fee, a fee for the Canadian Teachers' Federation and a fee for the OTF, are collected by the OTF and distributed accordingly.

The OTF, which was formed in 1944, is governed by a 50 member Board of Governors, with each affiliate appointing ten members. The Board meets at least three times a year dealing primarily with matters which affect all the teachers of the province. A policy developed in this manner may be reconsidered at the request of at

ONTARIO TEACHERS' FEDERATION
Approximately 105,000 members; five affiliated bodies

ONTARIO SECONDARY SCHOOL TEACHERS'
FEDERATION –Approximately 34,000 members;
55 Districts; districts divided into branches
of one school staff each

FEDERATION OF WOMEN TEACHERS' ASSOCIATIONS
OF ONTARIO –Approximately 33,000 members;
5 Regions divided into 78 Associations;
Associations by inspectorates; some associations divided into units

ONTARIO PUBLIC SCHOOL MEN TEACHERS'
FEDERATION –Approximately 15,000 members;
72 districts divided into branches

ONTARIO ENGLISH CATHOLIC TEACHERS'
ASSOCIATION –Approximately 18,000 members;
49 units

L'ASSOCIATION DES ENSEIGNANTS FRANCO-
ONTARIENS –Approximately 5200 members;
28 Regional Districts; Districts divided
into locals

least one affiliate. The Federation Executive, consisting of eleven members elected by the Board of Governors, meets once per month. Standing committees and special committees of the Board of Governors report to the Board of Governors.

The OTF is the official liaison between the teachers of the province and the Minister of Education. They meet with the Ministry frequently during the year to discuss matters of an educational and professional nature. The OTF names representatives to committees set up by the Ministry of Education. Breaches of the Code of Ethics are dealt with by the OTF, with the right of appeal to the Federation Executive or Board of Governors. The OTF concerns itself with activities which contribute to the further professional improvement of education in the province.

At least three times a year the OTF, through its official publication, *Interaction,* reports to the members on the Federation's activities and other matters of concern. The address of the OTF is 1260 Bay Street, Toronto. In addition to the secretary-treasurer, Mr. William Jones, there is a senior staff of seven persons each with a major responsibility such as teacher education, educational finance, superannuation, acts and regulations, professional education, communications.

Federation of Women Teachers' Associations of Ontario

The Federation of Women Teachers' Associations of Ontario is the only women teachers' professional organization in North America. It was established in 1918 at a time when women teachers were paid lower salaries than men. This group of women set out to obtain equal pay for similar jobs in schools, regardless of the sex of the teacher. Membership at that time was voluntary. By the time mandatory membership was established in 1944 more than half of Ontario's women teachers were already members and the goal of equal pay had been achieved. By 1978 almost 33,000 elementary public school women teachers belonged to the Federation.

For Federation purposes the province of Ontario is divided into five regions. Each region elects six teachers to serve on the Board of Directors together with the executive secretary who is employed by the organization. The positions of past president, president, first vice-president and second vice-president rotate among the five regions. These officers, along with the executive secretary, treasurer and four additional members constitute the Executive. The same ten members represent FWTAO on the OTF Board of Governors. Three past presidents form an advisory board. The 78 Women Teachers' Associations within the Federation are coterminous with the Boards of Education in the province. The associations send representatives to five Regional Assemblies in May and to an Annual Meeting in August. Approximately 700 delegates and visitors attend this four day annual meeting.

In addition to the general interests of teachers FWTAO concentrates on the needs of women and classroom teachers. Approximately ninety percent of the membership falls within this latter category.

Members of the FWTAO pay a $65. annual fee, of which there is

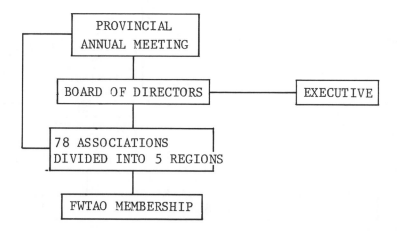

a rebate of approximately $7. per member for each Association. The FWTAO office is at 1260 Bay Street, Toronto. The executive secretary is Miss Florence Henderson.

Ontario Secondary School Teachers' Federation

In 1919 the Ontario Secondary School Teachers' Federation was formed, consisting of most of the secondary teachers in the province (that is, all except members of AEFO, FWTAO and OPSMTF). In 1928 a permanent office was set up, with a full-time staff.

The elected Provincial Executive consists of the president, 2 vice-presidents, 2 executive officers and the treasurer. The Executive Council consists of the voting members of the Provincial Executive, one executive councillor from each of the 55 Federation Districts, plus the general secretary (non-voting) and one OSSHC Liaison member (non-voting). The Provincial Assembly consists of all members of the Executive Council, the elected members of the OTF Board of Governors, three members of the Secretariat, chairmen of Commissions and Committees, and delegates from each District chosen in accordance with the by-laws. There are Provincial Standing Committees, Special Committees, and a Certification Committee and Board. The Professional Standards and Practices Council, consisting of 12 members, some of whom are elected and some appointed, is concerned with articulating acceptable principles of professional conduct and standards and competent teaching, and assisting in the maintenance of such principles and standards. The

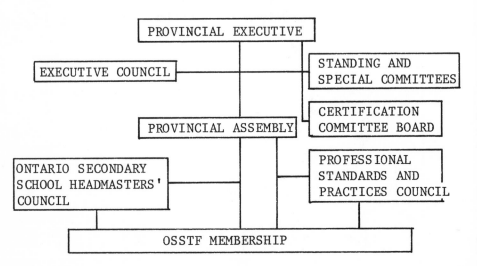

Ontario Secondary School Headmasters' Council consists of practising principals who are statutory members of OSSTF.

At the District level, OSSTF is divided into 55 districts. Each of these Districts has a District Executive, A District Council, and District Committees, paralleling those in the Provincial organization. Members pay annual fees of $9.50 per $1000. of salary plus $120. Rebates to the district organizations range up to a total of $45.30 per member. The OSSTF office is at 60 Mobile Drive, Toronto. The general secretary is Mr. L. M. Richardson.

Ontario Public School Men Teachers' Federation

The Ontario Public School Men Teachers' Federation, consisting of the public elementary men teachers in Ontario, was established in 1921, with a permanent provincial office being established in 1948. There are approximately 15,000 members in the organization at the present time.

The Provincial Executive consists of nine representatives of OPSMTF to the Board of Governors of the OTF. These nine are elected annually by the OPSMTF Provincial Assembly. They are the president, two vice-presidents, past president, and five additional members. They meet at least once a month during the school year. District Representatives are elected on the basis of one representative per 131 members for each of the 72 districts. The Provincial Executive and District Representatives plus Standing Committee Chairmen (non-voting) constitute the Provincial Assembly. The Annual Assembly in August can be attended by any member but only Provincial Assembly members may vote.

There are 16 Standing Committees plus Special Committees as

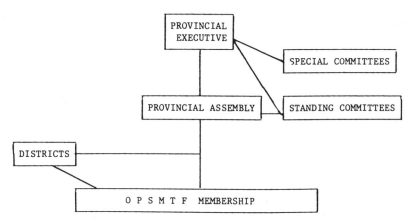

the occasion warrants. The Committees are appointed by the Provincial Executive.

The provincial office is at 1260 Bay Street, Toronto. The secretary-treasurer is Dr. R. L. Lamb. There is a deputy secretary-treasurer, two executive assistants, two administrative assistants and an assistant secretary. The association magazine, which is published jointly with the FWTAO, is *The Educational Courier.* The annual membership fee for OPSMTF is 0.85 percent of salary of which from 0.16 to 0.20 percent is rebated to the Districts.

Ontario English Catholic Teachers' Association

The Ontario English Catholic Teachers' Association was formed in 1944 as the result of an expressed need for a unifying bond between the individual Catholic teachers and the other teacher groups. There are approximately 18,000 members in the organization at the present time, which includes the teachers in the English-speaking separate schools, plus a number of voluntary members from the English Catholic private high schools. Thus the Protestants teaching in these schools become members of the OECTA.

The Provincial Executive consists of the president, past president, three vice-presidents, treasurer, two executive counsellors, executive director, and the deputy executive director. The Board of Directors consists of the Provincial Executive, the five elected members of the Ontario Teachers' Federation Board of Governors, one representative from each of the 49 Units, and chairmen of Standing Committees, plus the deputy and executive directors (non-voting). There are eleven Standing Committees. The Provincial Annual Meeting is held in Toronto each spring. All members of OECTA may attend, but voting power is invested in the Unit delegates (one per 50 members) and the Board of Directors.

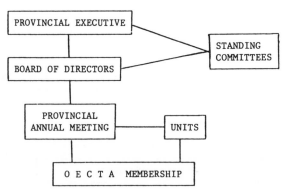

Each of the 49 Unit Executives consists of a president, past president, two vice-presidents, recording secretary, corresponding secretary, treasurer, councillors, and the representatives to the Board of Directors.

The provincial office is at 1260 Bay Street, Toronto, Ontario. The executive director is Miss M. C. Babcock. The association magazine is the *OECTA Review.* The annual membership fee is $150., of which approximately $20. is rebated to the Units.

L'Association des Enseignants Franco-Ontariens

L'Association des Enseignants Franco-Ontariens has a membership of approximately 5200 French-speaking teachers in Ontario, from the elementary and secondary schools in which French is the language of instruction.

The provincial Executive Committee consists of the president, past-president, 3 vice-presidents, secretary-treasurer, 3 counsellors and the AEFO representative to the Ontario Teachers' Federation executive. This group meets once per month. The Board of Directors consists of the Executive Committee plus one representative per 125 members in each of the 28 Regional Districts. The annual meeting of 1978 may bring about major changes in the structure of these districts. This body meets twice a year. The Annual Meeting of the Association is usually held during the winter recess. All AEFO members may attend but the voting schedule is approximately one vote per 50 members in a district.

The provincial standing committees are legislation, budget, curriculum, relations and discipline and superannuation. The provincial office is at 1427, Ogilvie Road, Suite 202, Ottawa. AEFO publishes *Entre Nous* which is the official magazine, 6 times a year and *En Bref,* a newsletter, every second week of the school year. The secretary-treasurer is Mr. Jacques Schryburt. The annual membership fee is 1.7 percent of a teacher's salary, $25.00 of which is rebated to the districts.

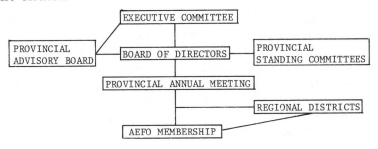

Provincial Association of Protestant Teachers (Quebec)

The Provincial Association of Protestant Teachers was formed in 1864 as a merger of the St. Francis District Teachers' Association, the District of Bedford Teachers' Association and the McGill Normal School Teachers' Association. A Provincial Charter was granted in 1889, the first in Canada.

Rapid growth in the early 1940's led to the appointment of a full-time executive secretary in 1946 and the inclusion of the provision for automatic membership in the Provincial Charter 1945. Permanent Headquarters were established at 2100 St. Mark Street in Montreal, Quebec in 1958. Better facilities gradually became more important and so newer facilities were built in the suburb of Pointe Claire in 1968–69. This was the same year of the establishment of a full-time presidency. 1969 also marked the culmination of over two years of determined collective bargaining at the provincial level, when PAPT, along with other Quebec Teachers' corporations, the school boards and the government signed the first Provincial Entente.

In 1970, with the threatened removal of the traditional confessional base to education, the Annual General Meeting recommended that the P.A.P.T. cease to be a professional corporation and transform itself into a federation of local teacher unions to be known as the Quebec Union of English Speaking Teachers (QUEST). A private bill to this effect was prepared for the National Assembly. An essential part of the motivation behind this move was a desire to create a body to represent all teachers in English language schools: the CEQ had reformed itself by abandoning its corporation charter and changing its name to Centrale de l'enseignement du Quebéc.

By 1976, it was clear that the English Catholic teachers were not prepared to unite with the Protestant teachers largely because the P.A.P.T. continued to negotiate in coalition with the CEQ, whereas they preferred to go it alone. A Special Membership Meeting in 1976 was subject to a court injunction preventing it and at the present moment the whole issue is dead.

P.A.P.T. sold its building in Pointe Claire in 1976 and moved to rented accommodation at 84J Brunswick Boulevard, Dollard des Ormeaux, Quebec, H9B 2C5. The Executive staff consists of the president, Mr. Donald Peacock, and six other full-time professional staff. The Parliament of P.A.P.T. meets in May as the Annual General Meeting which all members can attend but where only delegates may vote. There is a provision whereby the delegates may meet in January as the Provincial Delegates' Council but, of recent years, this meeting has not taken place. In attendance are the members of the Executive and the Board of Directors, the Pension Commissioner, Chairpersons of the Standing Committees and delegates from local associations. The delegates are chosen from the twelve affiliated local associations on the basis of one delegate per 50 members. The Board of Directors consists of the Executive and Directors appointed from the local associations on the basis of one director for the first 300 members and one for each additional 200 members. The Board dispatches the business of the Association, appoints standing committees, hears reports and determines the application of P.A.P.T. policy between A.G.M.s. The Executive, which traditionally was appointed on a lock step basis and consisted largely of administrators, is now elected by the teachers membership: the president, full-time, serving a two-year term, and the secretary-treasurer and four executive members at large being elected annually. A general chairman elected by the Board of Directors serves on the Executive and presides over the Directors Meeting and the Annual General Meeting.

There is a joint Curriculum Council (with P.A.C.T.), a Professional Development Council and a Teacher Education and Certification Committee. The Quebec Association of School Administrators functions as a non-geographical local representing the administrators in the Protestant system. Q.A.S.A. has no right of representation in

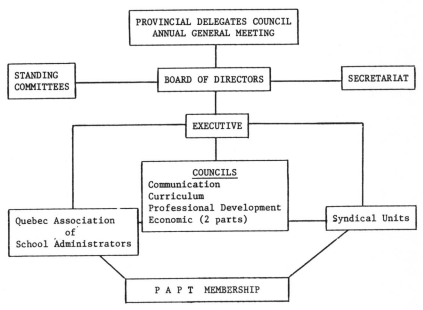

P.A.P.T. All the local teacher associations are now certified unions under the Labour Code.

The Sentinel is the official newspaper of the Association and is published at least eight times a year. The annual membership fee to the provincial association, automatically deducted under the terms of its charter, is presently $115. The local association collects union dues under the Rand Formula which vary from $70. to $115.

Provincial Association of Catholic Teachers (Quebec)

Approximately 5400 English Catholics belong to the Provincial Association of Catholic Teachers. These are divided into 34 Local Associations. Membership in PACT is automatic but there is a write-out provision. Membership fees are $40. annually. The full-time professional staff consists of the secretary-general, Mr. R. R. Dobie and three assistants. The official publication of the association is PACT.

The Provincial Council is the ultimate policy-determining body of the Association. Delegates to the Provincial Council are determined on a regional (local) basis with one delegate per fifty members. The Administrative Council members are also members of the Provincial Executive. The Executive Committee consists of the president, past-president and two vice-presidents, plus the secretary-general as a non-voting member.

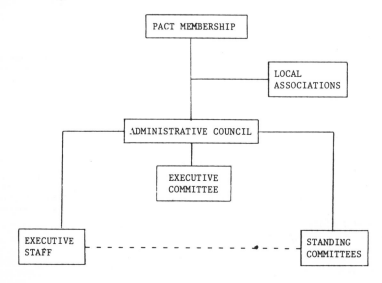

The Administrative Council consists of the Executive Council plus fourteen directors. The secretary-general is appointed by the Provincial Council.

The Provincial Association of Catholic Teachers have their headquarters at 5767 Monkland Avenue, Montreal, Quebec.

Central de l'Enseignants du Québec

La Corporation des Enseignants du Québec was incorporated as a professional organization in 1946. It was organized to assist the teachers in increasing their teaching competency, to improve working conditions and, in general, to raise the status of their profession. It is not a closed organization in that it does not control entry into the profession. However, membership is mandatory. After dropping its corporation charter, the name of the organization was changed to Centrale de l'Enseignants du Québec.

The C.E.Q. includes elementary and secondary public school teachers in Quebec, and has a membership of approximately 70,000. Membership is individual but local organizations can also become members of the C.E.Q. The C.E.Q. headquarters are at 2336 Chemin Sainte-Foy, Quebec, with a subsidiary office at 110 Cremazie ouest, chambre 709, Montreal. There are 65 local organizations. The official publication of the C.E.Q. is *Ligne Directe*. The annual membership fee ranges from $15. to $195., according to salary.

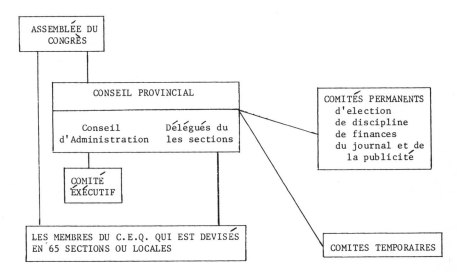

The Congrès consists of the members of the Conseil Provincial and members from the syndicates or local associations on the basis of one delegate for up to 150 members plus one delegate for each 150 members thereafter (or portion thereof). The Assemblée du Congrès meets sometime between June 15th and September 15th of each year. The Conseil d'Administration is able to call a special Assemblée du Congrès if needed.

The Conseil d'Administration consists of the president (full-time), four vice-presidents, a secretary, a treasurer, and four councillors, all elected by the Congrès (for two year terms), plus delegates from the sections or locals on the basis of one delegate per 1000 members. The Conseil d'Administration appoints an executive committee of not less than five members from itself.

The Conseil Provincial appoints members to the four permanent committees (election, discipline, finances, journal and publicity) and to temporary committees as the need arises.

New Brunswick Teachers' Federation

In New Brunswick there is one teachers' organization, the New Brunswick Teachers' Federation, with two autonomous sections— the New Brunswick Teachers' Association and L'Association des Enseignants Francophones du Nouveau-Brunswick.

The first teachers' associations in New Brunswick were formed in Albert County and Kent County in 1902. During 1902 and 1903

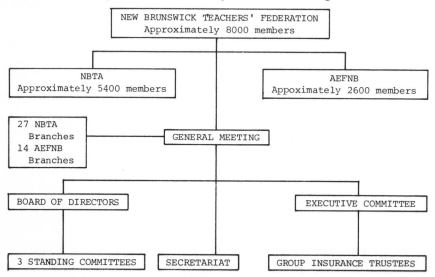

teachers' unions were formed in a number of counties. In 1903 a convention of representatives from these counties met and formed an organization called the New Brunswick Teachers' Association. The initial activity declined in a few years so that it was not long before the organization was relatively dormant. It was revived and reorganized in 1918. In 1942, it was incorporated and membership became automatic. In 1970 the NBTA was replaced by the New Brunswick Teachers' Federation (NBTF) as the organization to which all New Brunswick teachers belong. The new Federation has two sections—the English section (NBTA) and the French section (AEFNB). Both sections are autonomous but act together as a Federation in matters respecting salary, pension, group insurance and teacher certification. The chart following shows the organization of the NBTF and how the NBTA and AEFNB relate to each other and to the parent organization.

The headquarters for NBTF, NBTA and AEFNB are in Fredericton, New Brunswick. NBTF and NBTA use the same address (P.O. Box 752), and AEFNB uses the address of C.P. 712. The executive director of the NBTA, Mr. Jack MacKinnon, the executive director of AEFNB, M. R. LeBreton, and Mr. Wayne A. Nightingale are the executive directors of NBTF. The NBTF has one additional full-time professional assistant, the NBTA has five additional, and the AEFNB has three additional. The Board of Directors of each constituent part make up the Board of Directors of the NBTF. The NBTF Executive Committee consists of the president, vice-president and two other executive members from each constituent body, plus the past president and the executive director of each on a non-voting basis.

The following chart indicates the organization of the NBTA. The

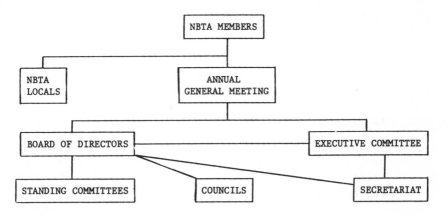

Annual General Meeting is attended by one delegate for each 100 members in each of the 27 Local Branches (with a minimum of one and a maximum of six delegates from each branch). The Board of Directors consists of the president (full-time), past president, vice-president, executive director and one director from each of the smaller Locals and two from the larger Locals. The annual membership fee is $12. per month. Three dollars per member is rebated to the Local organization, with a minimum of $400. plus additional grants for projects undertaken by the branch and approved by the Executive Committee of the Association.

The NBTA publishes a weekly bulletin entitled *Association Activities,* and a monthly newsletter entitled *NBTA News.*

The following chart indicates the organization of the AEFNB. The parliament of the organization is the Annual General Assembly. Delegates from each of the 13 Local organizations represent the teachers at the AGM. Standing Committees are appointed by the president after consultation with the Locals. The president is full-time. The annual membership fee is the same as for the NBTA, that is, twelve dollars per month. Three dollars per member is rebated to the local organization (with a minimum of $400). The official publication is *Nouvelles de L'AEFNB.*

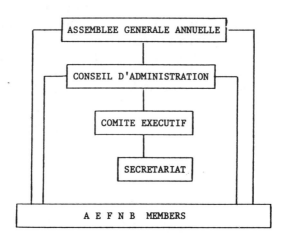

The Nova Scotia Teachers' Union

The Nova Scotia Teachers' Union was first organized in 1895–96. It was reorganized in 1921. At present the membership is approximately 11,000, with statutory membership for all teachers, but with a write-out provision.

The Provincial Executive consists of a full-time president, two vice-presidents, secretary-treasurer, past president, and fourteen members elected on a geographical basis (the second vice-president and the secretary-treasurer are selected from the already elected regional executive members). The Provincial Executive is elected by the Annual Council, which is the policy forming body. It consists of the Provincial Executive plus representatives from each of the Locals on the basis of approximately one representative per 50 members. Provincial and Local Committees report to the Provincial Executive. The Local organization offers teachers an opportunity to meet frequently to discuss common problems and participate in professional decision-making.

The Provincial headquarters are at 106 Dutch Village Road, Halifax, Nova Scotia (with a mailing address of Box 1060, Armdale). The professional staff consists of the general secretary, Mr. Norman Fergusson, five executive assistants, a business officer and a communications officer. The official publication is the *Nova Scotia Teacher.* The membership fee is $155. per annum. Twenty percent is rebated to the Locals with a minimum rebate being $750.

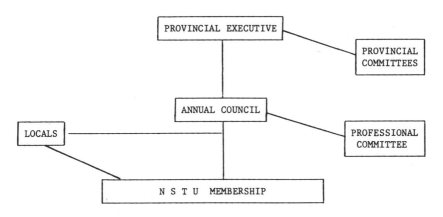

The Prince Edward Island Teachers' Federation

The first teachers' association in Prince Edward Island was formed in 1880. In 1924 the name was changed to Prince Edward Island Teachers' Federation and became affiliated with the Canadian Teachers' Federation. The PEITF was incorporated in 1945 and a Board of Governors was established to administer its affairs. At present the membership is approximately 1600. Membership is automatic, but with a write-out provision.

The Provincial Executive is elected by, and from, the Board of Governors. There is a president, past president, three vice-presidents, recording secretary and a treasurer. The members of the Board of Governors are elected at the school level in each Area Association. Basically, there is one representative from each school of at least 10 teachers and one for each thirty additional teachers. The term of office is three years, on a rotating basis. The Board of Governors usually meets twice a year. The membership is divided into 4 Area Associations, each with a coordinator and assistant coordinator. In general, the boundaries of an Area Association are determined by the geographic boundaries of a Regional School Board. There are 14 Special Associations within the PEITF which emphasize the increasing of teachers' knowledge and understanding of a special area.

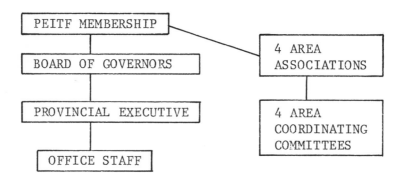

The PEITF headquarters is in Southport, with a mailing address of P.O. Box 6000 in Charlottetown. The full-time professional staff consists of the general secretary, Mr. James Blanchard and 2 executive assistants. The annual membership fee is 1.2 percent of salary. Grants are paid to the Area Associations on the basis of $1500. plus $3. per member. The official publication of the PEITF is *Prince Edward Island Teachers' Federation Newsletter.*

The Newfoundland Teachers' Association

The Newfoundland Teachers' Association was formed in 1890 but did not really perform as an association until about 1908. The Professional Bill was passed in 1951, making membership automatic, but with a write-out provision. Presently there are approximately 7950 members.

The Provincial Executive consists of the president, vice-president, and thirteen elected executive members. Seven others are elected as alternates. An Annual Meeting is held during the Easter Vacation each year. While any member may attend, only the delegates and members of the executive may vote. Delegates are selected on the basis of one to every hundred members in the Branch. Local Branches may combine to form Regional Branches but, in reality, Regional Branches ceased to exist about 10 years ago, after having been in existence in some parts of the Province for about 20 years.

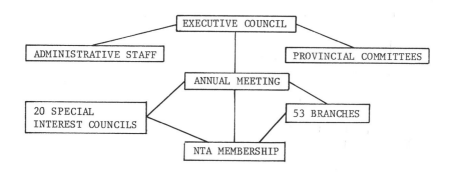

The Newfoundland Teachers' Association headquarters are at 3 Kenmount Road, St. John's. The executive secretary, Mr. William O'Driscoll, is assisted by a secretary-treasurer, director of communications, a director of professional development, a director of teacher welfare and an executive assistant, field services. The president is full-time for a maximum of two terms of one year each. The membership fee is one percent of salary, one-quarter of which is for the provision of an emergency fund. Approximately ten percent of the provincial association budget is rebated to the Branches. The official publications of the NTA are the *NTA Journal,* a professional magazine published twice a year, and *The NTA Newsletter,* published every three weeks.

The Northwest Territories Teachers' Association

The Northwest Territories Teachers' Association was established in 1953 and approved by Ordinance in 1976. Approximately 730 teachers in the Northwest Territories are members of the NWTTA. Membership is not compulsory. A limitation on membership is, "A person who in the opinion of the Commissioner is employed in the Territories in a managerial or confidential capacity is not eligible for membership in the Association." (In most of Canada "first-line" officials such as superintendents, and sometimes, "second-line" officials are permitted exclusion from the professional teachers' association.)

The Central Executive consists of the president, past president, vice-president, secretary and treasurer. Other than the past president, the executive is elected at the Annual Meeting of the Central Council. The Central Council consists of the Central Executive and regional representatives based on one per fifty active members, or major portion thereof.

The Annual Meeting is held during Easter week. It is the Central Council Annual Meeting but all teachers are permitted to attend as observers.

The eight Regions of the NWTTA are Baffin, Keewatin, Yellowknife, Fort Smith, Fort Simpson, Arctic Coast, Inuvik and South Slave. Each Region has an Executive consisting of a chairman, vice-chairman and a secretary-treasurer. Association members in one or more schools may form a Local Association.

The membership fee for the NWTTA is established at 1.15 percent of average annual salary. For 1978–79 this fee is $246. per annum ($20. for associate members and $5. for student membership). The rebate to the Regions is established on the basis of number of members, geographic location and communication problems. For 1978–79 these rebates are approximately 3.5 percent of total budget.

The official publication of the NWTTA is their newsletter *Communicate* which is published eight to ten times per year. The executive director is Mr. Winston Nettleton and the full time president/ professional development officer is Mr. Al Wolitski. The mailing address is P.O. Box 2340 Yellowknife.

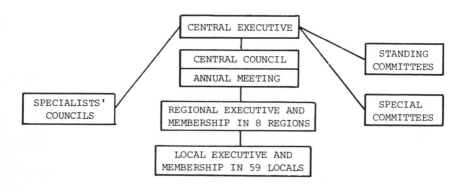

The Yukon Teachers' Association

The Yukon Teachers' Association, the youngest and smallest of the teachers' organizations in Canada, was formed in 1955. Since its inception, the YTA has served as a guardian of teachers' rights and welfare. In 1960 the right for the YTA to negotiate with the Territorial Government on matters of salary was achieved. In 1962, the right of tenure was written into the Education Ordinance. In 1964, a pension plan was made available. Other concerns have been communication, housing, code of ethics, sabbatical and educational leave. Even though membership is still not compulsory, there are approximately 290 YTA members.

The Executive consists of a president, vice-president, past president, treasurer, and chairmen of the five standing committees (one of whom is the Canadian Teachers' Federation representative). The Central Council consists of representatives for each of the twelve Areas or Schools, selected on the basis of one representative for each fifteen teachers, plus the Executive. The Annual Meeting is held once each year, with active members present having full voting rights. Standing Committee chairmen are elected by the Annual General Meeting, with the remainder of each committee appointed by the chairmen, subject to ratification by the Executive.

The membership fee is $200. per annum. The fee was increased to $200. in 1977 when the Association decided to purchase half-time release for the president who is a regular classroom teacher. The secretary of the YTA is Mrs. Phyllis Gairns. The association office is at 103–107 Main Street, Whitehorse. The official publication of the YTA is the *Yukon Teacher*.

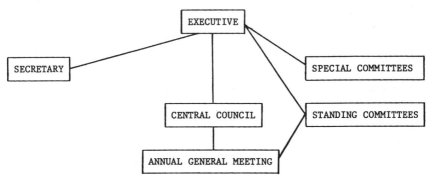

The Canadian Teachers' Federation

In 1919 the four Western Canada teachers' organizations moved establishment of an association to link the four provincial associations for certain purposes. At the inaugural meeting in 1920, the four associations were joined in their endeavours by representation from Ontario. During the next seven years, this new association, the Canadian Teachers' Federation, gained representation from every province in Canada. The development of CTF came during the same period of time as the development of most of its affiliates and thus they were able to gain strength and support from each other.

The CTF role has evolved over the years and now includes numerous activities. The CTF recognizes the need for teachers to have a strong voice at the local and provincial levels which is obtained through the provincial associations. The activities of CTF reflect emphasis on matters which are interprovincial, national and international. Some of these activities are:

—analysis and exchange of information on many subjects (working conditions, teacher aides, declining enrolments, as examples).

—development of a Canada-wide teacher consensus on the criteria of quality of education and equity and efficiency of financing education.

—continuous study on matters such as teacher education, pensions.

—information on study and service opportunities for teachers in Canada and abroad.

—national or regional seminars for study of problems affecting teachers, their work and their welfare.

—liaison with the interprovincial organizations of Ministers, departments of education and school trustees.

—study of the special problems of French speaking teachers in minority situations.

—representation to the federal government (unemployment insurance, bilingual grants, metric conversion, as examples).

—at the international level, CTF represents Canadian teachers at international conferences on educational matters, and provides opportunities for volunteers to assist developing countries.

Approximately 215,000 Canadian teachers belong to CTF by being members of the affiliate bodies and having the affiliate body pay an annual fee of $6.50 per member. Two provincial teachers' associations, the Centrale des Enseignants du Quebec and the Pro-

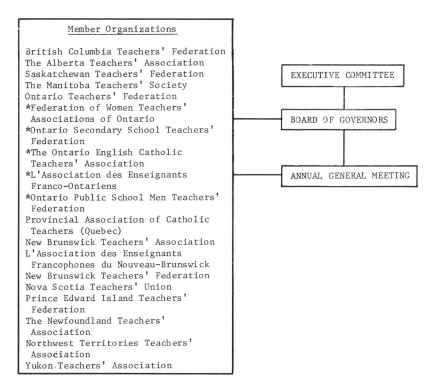

Member Organizations

British Columbia Teachers' Federation
The Alberta Teachers' Association
Saskatchewan Teachers' Federation
The Manitoba Teachers' Society
Ontario Teachers' Federation
*Federation of Women Teachers'
  Associations of Ontario
*Ontario Secondary School Teachers'
  Federation
*The Ontario English Catholic
  Teachers' Association
*L'Association des Enseignants
  Franco-Ontariens
*Ontario Public School Men Teachers'
  Federation
Provincial Association of Catholic
  Teachers (Quebec)
New Brunswick Teachers' Association
L'Association des Enseignants
  Francophones du Nouveau-Brunswick
New Brunswick Teachers' Federation
Nova Scotia Teachers' Union
Prince Edward Island Teachers'
  Federation
The Newfoundland Teachers'
  Association
Northwest Territories Teachers'
  Association
Yukon-Teachers' Association

EXECUTIVE COMMITTEE

BOARD OF GOVERNORS

ANNUAL GENERAL MEETING

*Technically, these are not member organizations in that the members hold CTF membership only through their OTF membership.

vincial Association of Protestant Teachers of Quebec are not members of the federation.

The elected officers to CTF are the president (full-time), and two vice-presidents. These three, plus the past president and the secretary general, form the Executive Committee, which reports to the Board of Directors. The Board of Directors, which is the management group of CTF, consists of from one to five directors from each member organization. The Annual General Meeting is held each July and is the final authority on policy, budget and program. The delegates represent the CTF member organizations in proportion to the membership.

The professional staff consists of the secretary-general (Mr. Norman Goble), a deputy secretary-general, five program directors and four program assistants. The CTF office is at 110 Argyle Avenue, Ottawa, Ontario.

Future Directions

Although at the present time teacher associations have a very substantial voice through membership in various provincial committees (curriculum and certification, for example), the trend appears to have the professional organizations name the individuals to the committees. At present the usual procedure for establishing membership is for a list of names to be submitted from the association from which the Department of Education selects certain individuals. Although the difference is slight in that decisions and discussions affecting education are performed by the professional educators, the basic principle becomes important to the association. The basic principle, as indicated by teacher associations, is that the professional organization speaks for the members. Therefore, on committees where the professional voice is heard, the association feels it must determine who will be the spokesmen.

At the present time, the Ministers of Education grant, or withhold, certification of teachers. This varies from action from the ministerial office only, to decisions from a certification board. The professional associations will strive, even harder than they have in the past, to be the bodies which determine entrance into the teaching profession. That is, they will strive to achieve the same extent of autonomy in this matter as is presently being enjoyed by the medical and legal professions.

A corollary of the previous point is the right of the professional association to discipline its own members. The present pattern is for the association to investigate possible violations against the association as such, and against the code of ethics or standards of professional conduct. However, teachers performing unsatisfactorily are judged by persons and committees which are not under the direct control of the associations. The future direction will be for the professional associations to not only control entry into the profession but also to police the members as professionals.

The future direction in bargaining will be more emphasis on the negotiations of working conditions—class size, hours of instruction, preparation time, determination of curriculum, representation on boards, as a few examples. That is, the future direction will be to emphasize even more than at present the establishing of a suitable framework within which teaching as a profession can emerge and be maintained.

REFERENCES

Buck, G. J. The Contributions of Teachers' Associations to the Status of the Teaching Profession in Canada. Unpublished doctoral dissertation, University of Manitoba, 1949.

Cambell, C. L. The British Columbia Teachers' Federation. Unpublished master's thesis, University of Washington, 1961.

Chafe, J. W. *Chalk, Sweat and Cheers.* A History of the Manitoba Teachers' Society Commemorating Its Fiftieth Anniversary, 1919–1969. Winnipeg: Manitoba Teachers' Society, 1969.

Chalmers, J. W. *Teachers of the Foothills Province.* The Story of the Alberta Teachers' Association. Toronto: University of Toronto Press, 1968.

Cooper, J., "Some Early Teachers' Associations in Quebec," *Teachers' Magazine,* December, 1956.

Cuff, H., "The Founding of a Teachers' Association in Newfoundland," *National Teachers' Association Journal,* May–June, 1965.

French, D. *High Button Bootstraps: Federation of Women Teachers' Associations of Ontario, 1918–1968.* Toronto: Ryerson Press, 1968.

Hardy. J. H. Teachers' Organizations in Ontario, 1840–1938. Unpublished doctoral dissertation, University of Toronto, 1939.

Hope, B. The Accomplishments of the Nova Scotia Teachers' Union in Salaries, Pensions and Professional Growth. Unpublished master's thesis, Saint Mary's University, 1961.

Hopkins, R. A. *The Long March.* History of Ontario Public School Men Teachers' Federation, Toronto: Baxter, 1969.

Kratzmann, A. The Alberta Teachers' Association—A Documentary Analysis of the Dynamics of a Professional Organization. Unpublished doctoral dissertation, University of Chicago, 1963.

McDowell, S. The Dynamics of the Saskatchewan Teachers' Federation. Unpublished doctoral dissertation, University of Alberta, 1965.

Nason, G. The Canadian Teachers' Federation: A Study of Its Historical Development, Interests and Activities from 1919 to 1960. Unpublished doctoral dissertation, University of Toronto.

Nason, G., "The Canadian Teachers' Federation: A Study of Its Historical Development, Interests, and Activities From 1919 to 1960," *Ontario Journal of Educational Research,* Spring, 1965.

Odynak, S. N. The Alberta Teachers' Association As an Interest Group. Unpublished doctoral dissertation, University of Alberta, 1963.

Ontario Teachers' Federation. OTF at 20: *Recollections of the First Two Decades of the Ontario Teachers' Federation.* Toronto.

Parker, T. *A History of the Nova Scotia Teachers' Union: Its Struggles and Achievements.* Halifax: NSTU, 1963.

Paton, J. M. *The Role of Teachers' Organizations in Canadian Education.* Quance Lectures. Toronto: W. J. Gage, 1962.

Skolrood, A. H. The British Columbia Teachers' Federation: A Study of Its Historical Development, Interests and Activities from 1916 to 1963. Unpublished doctoral dissertation, University of Oregon, 1967.

Talbot, A. D. *P.A.P.T. The First Century.* Gardenvale, Quebec: Harpell's Press, 1964.

Tyre, R. *Tales Out of School: A Story of the Saskatchewan Teachers' Federation.* Toronto: W. J. Gage, 1968.

Watson, R. E. L. The Nova Scotia Teachers' Union—A Study in the Sociology of Formal Organizations. Unpublished doctoral dissertation, University of Manitoba, 1960.

Questions for Discussion

1. Will the Canadian Teachers' Federation become the active force in the professional life of teachers as has the National Education Association of the United States?

2. Why has La Corporation des Enseignants, (now Centrale de l'Enseignants du Québec), not joined the Canadian Teachers' Federation? Why has P.A.P.T. left the CTF?

3. What is the real extent of power and responsibility of the local organizations as compared to the provincial teachers' associations in Canada?

4. There is considerable discussion regarding local autonomy in school affairs. If the provincial governments relinquish more of their central control, would this result in greater local autonomy, or would this be merely a shift from provincial central control to provincial professional association central control?

5. Compare the expenditures of the various provincial teachers' associations as to amounts spent of professional matters versus organization expenses.

6. Which provincial teachers' associations are providing the greatest leadership to their teachers?

7. What are the main similarities, and main differences, in the organizational structures of the teachers' associations in Canada?

8. Compare Canadian teachers' associations with those in the United States, England and other countries.

13

Teachers' Salary Schedules

Incentives

The viability and productivity of any organization, from the most simply structured single-purpose local volunteer group to the most complex diversified industrial conglomerate, depends to a substantial degree upon its success in getting each member or employee to direct attention and energy toward the attainment of the objectives of the organization. How is loyalty and commitment obtained, and when obtained, how is it maintained? Very simply, by the application of a system of incentives, that is, by applying rewards and punishments.

The organization, in this instance a school system and a school, operates in its essential features in very much the same way as the classroom teacher functions in the role of manager of human and physical resources. Students are rewarded for behavior which is directed toward attainment of the objectives which have been set for the lesson and are punished for other types of behavior which is extraneous or non-objective oriented. A system of incentives is being applied. Certainly, the nature of the rewards and punishments applied may vary, for example, we would not normally pay a student for attending school and devoting his energies toward obtaining an education, nor would we fire him for not learning the steps in deriving a square root. The types of rewards and punishments may vary for teacher and for student, but the consequences of their impact is no less pressing.

It is important at this time to insert a word of caution. There are factors other than motives and needs which determine the quality and efficiency of a worker's behavior. These include the ability of

195

the worker, the level of his experience, the physical conditions under which he works, and the social milieu within which he works. The worker has little direct and immediate control over these factors. Basically, there are three motives for working. Work may be done as an end in itself—work for work's sake. Work may be carried out willingly for motives directly associated with the work situation, i.e., for comradeship, status, power, or escape from other less desirable circumstances or surroundings. Work may be done for genuinely extrinsic motives—money which may then be applied to various other purposes in order to fulfill the physiological, safety, love, esteem, or self-actualization needs of the employee.

Within the confines of the school system and in a general sense, there are two rewards systems which are operative for the teacher, these being non-monetary and monetary rewards.

Non-Monetary Rewards

The non-monetary rewards system operates through a number of mechanisms. The recognition, prestige, pay-off to the teacher may come through:

(a) A lighter teaching load in the form of fewer classes to be taught, thus effectively reducing the amount of work required by the teacher or permitting him to engage in other activities, instructional or non-instructional, which are within themselves more interesting or satisfying.

(b) Having fewer students to teach or consult, either within a specific class or in total throughout the school day. This has the effect of reducing the strain upon the teacher. Incidentally, it may have desirable outcomes as well for the purposes of the institution.

(c) Having fewer different courses to teach. This type of reward does at least two things. It says to the teacher, "You are a specialist. We have confidence in your abilities in this area." Further, it may provide the teacher with a lighter work load.

(d) Being permitted the maximum allowable time for lesson preparation during the school day.

(e) Restricting a teacher's course load to those subjects in which he has special interest or special training.

(f) Assigning the teacher the most desirable classes to teach. The pay-off for the teacher usually comes through less effort being required to motivate or control students, and probably a more stimulating classroom climate in which to work.

Other types of non-monetary rewards include consulting superior teachers on curricular matters, allowing time off to attend conferences, providing desirable classroom locations, preferred parking spaces, or freeing from the extra mundane chores which are part of every school's operation. Teacher of the Year and other similar types of community or school system forms of recognition, although less frequently applied, are further illustrations of the non-monetary reward system which operates within our schools.

Monetary Rewards

Discussing teachers' salaries seems to be distasteful to some. One gets the impression that somehow teachers should live on satisfaction. Obviously non-monetary rewards contribute to our "good feeling" about our job and our performance in it, but for the young or any teacher to refuse to recognize that money is basic to our system of rewards is to deny a basic part of our social fabric.

With the exception of a few primitive societies, and these are rapidly disappearing, money is a universally accepted method of bartering our talents for those things which satisfy our needs. The teacher has talents, skills, a service which he or she supplies to the community in return for a pay cheque. This, in its turn, is applied to purchase the talents, skills, services of others. Elementary, yes, but somehow this is forgotten by some and therefore must be restated from time to time. No, the beginning teacher should not hesitate to consider the matter of salary. To do otherwise would be foolish.

The discussion of merit pay plans for teachers which follows should prove useful in that it illustrates the application of monetary incentives to the teaching profession, and further it will permit the reader to become conversant with a subject which has become almost a perennial topic of public discussion.

Merit Pay Plans

The terms merit salaries, merit pay plan, pay for meritorious service, merit rating, and incentive pay programs for teachers, when raised in educational circles by either school trustees, parents, or teachers generate much heat and very little light. The essence of the argument, and that is what it usually amounts to, centres upon the desirability of salary payments to teachers according to their level of excellence in the classroom, in conjunction, perhaps, with recognition for special research or other professional contributions. This approach is set in opposition to traditional methods which have determined payment on the basis of seniority and formal training. Excellent teachers are the most valuable asset in the educational enterprise. This is a truism. There is no dispute. Beyond this point sides are taken and communication channels become clogged by serious educational questions interspersed with emotional biases. Thus, the debate continues.

There is considerable literature on the topic of merit pay for teachers. Unfortunately, little of this literature can be classified as reported research in the sense that acceptable research procedures had been employed and thus the results could be accepted with any reasonable level of confidence. Most of the literature can be subsumed under one or the other of two major groupings. Group One, the author takes a strong unilateral, frequently emotional, stand for or against merit rating and merit pay for teachers. Group Two, the author describes how "we" did it. Unfortunately, with respect to this second group, there is little documentation or evidence supplied as to why a particular merit pay plan was initiated, and equally important, why it failed. Many plans have been initiated, particularly in the United States' school systems, and many plans have failed. It appears the only secure position which can be taken is that the reasons for introduction and failure of merit pay plans is a very complex matter.

The debate with respect to merit pay plans for teachers is still very current even though the topic is complex and the directions as pointed by the available literature is still very much clouded. The following sets forward what appears on the surface at least to be the basic affirmative and negative positions adopted 'by those who propose and those who oppose. There may be any number of hidden issues, however, since merit pay is both an educational and a political issue. Indeed, some who support merit pay state it will bring out in the open many disguised merit pay plans which are already in operation within school systems. Others say merit pay will serve to magnify the number of under-the-table deals which are already being made. Educational, yes. Political, yes.

The Arguments For and Against Merit Pay

Argument One

Affirmative: Business and industry have successfully employed merit ratings and merit pay for their employees. Business and industry, because they are competitive, place their resources where it counts, i.e., where they will receive maximum return. Excellent production or management skills increase returns and should be rewarded. In education, resources should be allocated in order to obtain maximum student growth and development. Therefore, additional resources should be applied in the form of meritorious pay increases to excellent teachers. Why should the less productive be paid similarly to the more productive? The economic system is based upon competition, why should not the educational system?

Negative: Education is not a business enterprise. The techniques for measuring production which are available to a business or industrial community are not similarly available in the classroom or school. The product of the school system is not easily measured—students are people, not things. No teacher can assume complete credit or responsibility for what the student learns or fails to learn. The results of a teacher's efforts may not become apparent for many years, and if and when they become apparent, student growth cannot be related to a specific teacher. The educational impact of one teacher cannot be separated from that of another teacher, or the influence of factors in the community or home. Further, merit rating is not as widely used in business and industry as the proponents of the scheme would have people believe. Most of the business-industrial world is unionized, and even where it is not, for example, in the office, management and executive levels, merit rating is found to have distinct limitations. Teaching is a cooperative venture, not a competitive one. Strength and progress are the result of a collegial relationship among professionals, rather than a competitive one.

Argument Two

Affirmative: By awarding substantially higher salaries to the very competent teachers, a higher calibre of personnel will be attracted to the teaching profession and to a school district. Further, these more competent individuals will remain in teaching rather than seeking more remunerative positions in business or industry.

Negative: The promise of substantially higher salaries at some unknown time in the future, particularly where such salaries are known to be dependent upon a little understood or intangible rating, is not a good recruitment device. Immediate rewards are far more effective.

Argument Three

Affirmative: Communities are sensitive to spiralling school costs. The major portion of school costs, since education is a labor intensive industry, are to be found in salary costs and particularly in teacher salary costs. To open salary discussions is to "open the season" on teachers. In spite of increasing cost, the public are still willing to pay for the education of its children provided it believes that the money is being expended wisely. Good salaries to good teachers is a wise expenditure. High salaries for poor or mediocre teachers is not a wise expenditure. Thus, in order to obtain funds for salary increases for a substantial number of teachers, school boards and their administrators must operationalize merit pay plans.

Negative: Those who support merit pay are simply disguising their true motives, which is to reduce school taxes. The salary levels of the majority of teachers will remain at a low level, and only a very few will receive higher pay. This will not raise the quality of teaching, indeed it will do the opposite.

Argument Four

Affirmative: Increasing the rewards for superior performance will raise the status of the teacher to a professional level. Identical maximum salaries for all teachers works against true professionalism.

Negative: The status of the teaching profession will not be increased by granting higher salaries to a few. The status of teaching could be increased, however, by increasing the salaries of all teachers.

Argument Five

Affirmative: Merit pay forces careful evaluation of teacher performance. Careful assessment of the work of individuals, rather than the making of snap judgments, is a sound personnel policy found to be acceptable to most employees. Recognition of excellent performance through a pay increase is very meaningful to the employee.

Negative: Since the administrator, or supervisor responsible for judgments becomes an inspector of performance, he will lose the ability to perform a leadership role in improving instruction. Hostility, frustration, resentment, and fear will characterize the relationship between teachers and their superiors. Is this a good climate within which to work? Granting or withholding merit increases is a dangerous weapon to place in the hands of the administrator. It will, whether applied justly or not, provide a divisive force in an otherwise collegial relationship. Class distinctions among teachers will emerge. The willingness of teachers to share ideas, materials and techniques will be dampened by the lure of higher salaries for a few.

Argument Six

Affirmative: Quality teaching can be measured. It can be no more difficult than measuring quality student performance. Teachers do the latter many times a day, every day. As well, teacher performance is in fact being evaluated informally at all times. Even the public and certainly the parents know who are the good teachers and they are willing to pay them more. School systems are capable of identifying excellent performance, otherwise what is the basis for promotions? School systems are able to, and regularly do, distinguish between satisfactory and superior teaching. All that merit pay plans call for, is a definition of this process and a relating of pay increases to those judged superior.

Negative: There are no accurate measures of teacher performance, even in gross terms. Evaluation to the level of at least five categories of competency would be necessary in an operative merit pay plan, these being, superior, above average, average, below average, and unsatisfactory. At present, this capability does not exist. The most we seem to be able to determine is satisfactory-unsatisfactory, or at best, satisfactory, doubtful, and unsatisfactory. Teaching techniques vary. Differences among students are numerous. How does one devise a yardstick to measure the performance of two different teachers, using different although appropriate techniques with two different classes, with the further variables of different schools, different neighborhoods, different leadership styles of school principals, different grade levels, and different purposes of instruction? The range of possibilities for variation are so staggering as to make any measurement and assessment so general as to render it useless or so specific and detailed as to make it unworkable.

Argument Seven

Affirmative: There is nothing so unjust as to reward unequal work equally. A system of pay rewards which is related solely to training and experience does just that. This does not happen in most other professions. By refusing to accept merit pay, teachers are protecting their weak members at the expense of their strong members, and the children. Those who do little and those who do much are rewarded equally provided they have equal training and experience. And further, the marginally competent are protected by tenure laws, which again thwart the public's efforts to ensure students receive excellent training.

Negative: Lawyers and doctors are prevented by their associations from practicing when they are obviously incompetent. So are teachers. However, beyond this point remuneration to doctors and lawyers as established by scaled fees, is not determined by rating teams, who travel around making judgments upon the level of performance of specific practitioners. If school systems do not dismiss unsatisfactory teachers before they obtain tenure do not blame the pay scale, put the responsibility where it properly rests, with the school system.

Types of Merit Pay Plans

A number of merit pay plans have been implemented at one time or another, in one school system or another in the United States over the past 40 to 50 years. Very few such plans have been tried in Canada, however. The merit pay plans which have operated in the Toronto area are the notable exceptions. Since merit pay salary plans have had a relatively long history, one would expect some rather explicit answers to explicit questions. Unfortunately this is not the case.

The following should be regarded as only a generalized description of the five major types of plans which seem to have emerged, with variations of course, over the past number of years and which are related in greater or lesser degree to the question of merit pay.

Type One: Straight Merit Pay

Under this plan there is no basic salary schedule which embodies payment for level of training or incremental increases for years of experience. Each teacher is evaluated, usually annually, and his or her salary, including consideration of increases or decreases, is determined on the basis of the results of this evaluation. Some teachers would receive substantial increases, others very little or no increase and in theory at least some could experience a reduction in salary. Classroom performance is the basis for determining salary. Better qualified teachers, in terms of certification and level of preparation do not necessarily receive more money. This is not a common type of plan, however, this is what the public normally thinks of when it thinks merit pay.

Type Two: Basic Salary Schedule Plus Special Allowances

A number of merit pay plans make provision for paying the teacher according to a basic salary schedule or grid with provision for the employing school board to offer special allowances for outstanding service. Sometimes these allowances relate to outstanding classroom service by a specific teacher. Frequently merit allowances are used for a number of other purposes. For example, a double salary increment is awarded when the teacher receives a permanent contract or a permanent certificate, or a special increment may be awarded when a teacher has completed three or six years of service with the board. In the example noted above, merit allowances tend to be awarded as a matter of course and do not constitute merit pay in the true sense.

Type Three: Superior Maximum Salaries

Salary schedules may make provisions for an employee to receive an additional salary increment after the regular maximum salary as determined by years of service has been reached. Although the salary contract usually states that the teacher must have given above-average service during the time of employment, or the previous year, or other similar stipulation, the superior maximum approach is more often considered to be a long-service bonus rather than an increment or allowance for superior service. Some salary schedules make allowances for more than one such increment, however, a maximum number is usually specified in the salary contract.

Type Four: Salary Schedule With Responsibility Allowances

Salary schedules frequently make provision for additional pay for additional work or responsibility. Most often this takes the form of additional pay for school principals and their administrative assistants, for example, above the salary which they would earn with their training and experience as a classroom teacher. Other examples include supervisory allowances and allowances for teaching special classes. Following the same logic, responsibility allowances make provision for classroom teachers to earn additional money for the preparation of teaching materials, television lessons, conducting in-service programs, or teaching experimental courses. These allowances are not normally considered as payment for additional hours, but are considered at least by those who draft the plan as being recognition of superior capabilities. The granting of time off for professional development is another form of the same program. Instead of receiving an additional monetary reward, the teacher is rewarded for superior service through the mechanism of a more flexible work day or week.

Type Five: Differentiated Staffing

Under this format teachers are assigned different levels of responsibility and different levels of compensation. Superior teachers are assigned the title "team leader" or "master teacher" and are given the responsibility of leading, directing and supervising a number of other teachers, interns, student teachers (perhaps), teacher aides and clericals. This type of responsibility and recognition commands a salary substantially above that of other teachers in the group and further, as those who support the concept point out, it maintains instructional contact between superior teacher and student. Other forms of advancement tend to separate the teacher from the classrooms since teachers when promoted to positions as department heads, principals, and supervisors usually have little direct classroom contact with the student.

Example of a Salary Schedule

The following example of a salary schedule, in use in Canada's fifth largest school system, has many clauses which are typical in format to clauses found in salary schedules across Canada. This schedule is called a "single salary schedule" because salary is not dependant upon whether a teacher teaches elementary, junior or senior high students. In a "positional salary schedule", a relatively common schedule one or two decades ago, a high school teacher was paid more than an elementary teacher, other factors being similar.

Most schedules provide salary differentials for the extent of teacher training or university education, as is the case in the following schedule. Determination of what constitutes a year of college or university for salary purposes is a difficult problem. In some places the hiring school board evaluates the teachers' credentials, while in other places, a provincial system is determined. In this salary schedule example, evaluation of university and college transcripts (for salary purposes) is established by one provincial agency, which is a cooperative effort of the Department of Education, the trustees' association, the teachers' association, and the faculties of education of the universities in the province.

This schedule also has a clause bringing certain working conditions within the negotiations framework, in this case the maximum number of hours of assigned teaching duties. The signing of the

1977 salary schedule was delayed because of another working condition clause which stated the date for school opening in September. Even though the date was long since past, having the clause in the schedule would have meant this item was therefore negotiable in future years. The teachers' association wish to have items relating to working conditions negotiable whereas trustees consider most such items as non-negotiable, that is, should not be within the labor legislation framework for salary negotiations.

A Collective Agreement between the Board of Trustees of the Calgary School District no. 19, herein called "the Board" and The Alberta Teachers' Association, herein called "the Association", acting on behalf of the teachers employed by the Board.

Whereas, the Association is the duly certified bargaining agent for the teachers employed by the Board, and whereas, such teachers' terms and conditions of employment and their salaries have been the subject of negotiation between the parties, and whereas, the parties desire that these matters be set forth in an Agreement to govern all the terms of employment of the teachers, The Board and Association agree as follows:

1. Application

1.1 This Agreement shall be applicable to all persons who require a teachers' certificate as a condition of their employment with the Board, with the exception of: the Chief Superintendent of Schools; the Assistant to the Chief Superintendent of Schools; the Superintendent of Instruction; the Administrative Assistant to the Superintendent of Instruction; the Deputy Superintendent, Instructional Personnel; the Director of Continuing Education; the Director of Special Educational Services; the Area Superintendents; the Assistant Area Superintendents; the Special Assistant to the Deputy Superintendent, Instructional Personnel; the Coordinator of Curriculum Services; the Assistant to the Director of Special Educational Services, and Coordinator of Media Services.

1.2 The Board may create or designate new administrative positions not covered in this Agreement. Applicable administrative allowances and salaries shall be determined after consultation with the Calgary Public School Local acting on behalf of the Association before the position is advertised or the appointment is made. No teacher shall suffer a loss of administrative allowances and salaries due only to any reorganization taking place during the currency of this Agreement.

2. Term

2.1 This Agreement shall take effect on January 1, 1977 and shall continue in full force and effect through the thirty-first day of December, 1977 and from year to year thereafter, except as hereinafter provided:

2.2 Either party wishing to amend or to terminate this Agreement shall give to the other party notice of such desire, in writing, not less than 30 days and not more than 100 days prior to December 31, 1977. A notice of amendment shall contain a list of the items which the party wishes to discuss.

2.3 If notice has been given in accordance with Article 2.2, this Agreement shall remain in full force and effect during any period of negotiations until the bargaining procedures under the Alberta Labour Act, 1973, have been completed, if applicable, even though such negotiations extend beyond December 31, 1977.

2.4 Any conclusions reached in the aforementioned negotiations shall, if so agreed, be made retroactive to the said anniversary date or the said termination date.

3. Administration of the Basic Salary Schedule

3.1 Basic Salary Schedule

Categories Representing Years of Teacher Education beyond Alberta Gr. XII

Steps	A	B	C	D	E	F
0	11810	11810	11810	13345	14170	15115
1	11810	11810	11810	14170	14995	15940
2	11810	11810	11810	14995	15820	16765
3	11810	11810	12395	15820	16645	17590
4	11810	11810	12980	16645	17470	18415
5	11810	12340	13565	17470	18295	19240
6	11810	12870	14150	18295	19120	20065
7	12280	13400	14735	19120	19945	20890
8	12750	13930	15320	19945	20770	21715
9	13220	14460	15905	20770	21595	22540
10	13695	14995	16525	21595	22420	23365
11	–	–	–	22545	23370	24315

3.2 General

3.2.1 Teachers shall be placed in salary categories, according to the statement of qualifications issued by the Alberta Teachers' Association Teacher Qualification Service in accordance with the policies and principles approved by The Teacher Salary Qualifications Board, established by Memorandum of Agreement among the Department of Education, the Alberta Teachers' Association and The Alberta School Trustees' Association, dated March 23, 1967, subject to Appendix "A" of the Collective Agreement. Pending receipt of the evaluation, a tentative salary will be established by the Board in accordance with applicable verified data in the teacher's file. The tentative salary shall be the actual salary if an evaluation is not received before June 30 of the applicable school year, unless the submission of proof is beyond the control of the teacher.

3.2.2 The adjustment dates for changes in salaries, due to category reclassification, of (a) teachers employed under a contract which continues in force from year to year, or (b) teachers employed during the previous year under a temporary contract which had a commencement date prior to November 1, and which continued through the balance of that school year, shall be the opening day of school or the first of February of each school year. The qualifications to be considered applicable to the opening day of school adjustment date shall be only those obtained prior to the opening day of school. The qualifications to be considered applicable to the February 1 adjustment date shall be only those which necessarily include some qualifications which are earned after the opening day of the school year. If the teacher does not submit proof, in the form of a T.Q.S. evaluation or an Inservice course or a music diploma, that another year of teacher education has been acquired, or prior to November 30 applicable to the adjustment date of the opening day of school or prior to April 30 applicable to the adjustment date of February 1, any adjustment in salary shall take effect from the first of the month next following the month of submission.

3.2.3 Increments shall apply only to teachers designated in Article 3.2.2 and are applicable on the opening day of school. A minimum of eleven months must elapse between increments. Teachers who teach for only part of the school year must teach at least the equivalent of 115 full days in the school year in order to become eligible for an increment. Part-time teachers who teach for all of the school year shall be eligible for an increment. In moving from one category of teacher education to a higher one, the teacher shall be placed first on the same numbered step in the higher category and then receive the increment, if applicable. The Board reserves the right, however, to withhold the increment of any teacher, for any year, if in the opinion of the Chief Superintendent of Schools, the service rendered was not considered worthy of an increment. If service is satisfactory during the year that the increment is withheld the teacher shall be placed, commencing the subsequent opening day of school, on the step applicable if the increment had not been withheld. In no case shall the Board withhold an increment for two (2) or more consecutive years.

3.2.4 Upon commencement of employment, on or after January 1, 1977, the allowance for past experience for new teachers shall be on the basis of one step for each year of previous teaching experience, to a maximum placement of Step 8, where the teacher, having such previous teaching experience, held a valid teaching certificate.

3.2.5 A teacher, not covered by Article 3.2.2, must submit (a) proof of teacher qualifications in the form of a T.Q.S. evaluation or an Inservice course or a music diploma and (b) proof of experience in writing, within two months from the date of employment in order to obtain, retroactively to the date of employment, an improvement in category placement and experience placement, respectively. Failure to do so will result in adjustments being made on the first of the month following submission of proof, unless the submission of proof is beyond the control of the teacher.

3.2.6 Any supportive data, e.g. T.Q.S. evaluation, In-Service certificates, etc., submitted for the purpose of a salary reclassification, shall be accompanied by a written request for reclassification and directed to the Personnel Services Department.

3.2.7 Teachers commencing duties on or after September 1, 1965, who require a Letter of Authority, shall be allowed one increment only, subject to review by the Interpretation Committee and recommendation to the Board. Any teacher for whom an increment is cancelled shall remain on the same salary step until the deficiency causing the cancellation is removed. When the deficiency is removed the teacher shall be placed on the step to which the teacher would have been entitled had the increments not been withheld. This placement shall be made on the opening day of school of the calendar year in which evidence of a valid teaching certificate is submitted, provided that the submission is made on, or prior to, October 31, unless the submission of proof is beyond the control of the teacher. Application will be made in the subsequent September if submission is made after October 31.

3.2.8 The Chief Superintendent of Schools shall have discretionary power to place any teacher for Vocational Schools who has been recruited from industry and who has completed successfully the teacher training courses provided by the universities in Alberta, or their equivalents in his opinion, on any step of the basic salary schedule in the category determined by the Teacher Qualifications Board.

3.2.8.1 Any teacher receiving a vocational allowance who requests and receives approval for a transfer to a completely non-vocational assignment shall be placed upon the appropriate step of the salary schedule in accordance with the number of years of teaching experience as at the effective date of transfer. The category placement shall be in accordance with the applicable T.Q.S. evaluation.

3.2.8.2 If a teacher, transferred in accordance with Article 3.2.8.1, requests and receives approval for transfer back to a vocational assignment, the former placement shall apply together with earned increments and category changes, if applicable. However, the salary plus the vocational allowance shall not exceed the maximum of the applicable category.

3.2.9 The Board reserves the right to consider any application on its merits, and to fix the initial salary above the schedule should it appear in the interest of the Board to do so, provided that the Interpretation Committee is informed as soon as possible.

3.2.10 A teacher who has been employed previously by the Calgary Board of Education, upon being rehired, may apply to the Chief Superintendent of Schools for salary reinstatement on the basic salary schedule.

4. Allowance — School Personnel

4.1 In addition to the salary earned as a teacher, a principal shall receive the applicable administrative allowance, according to the following schedule:

Class	A	B	C	D	E	F
Prof. Staff	5–16	17–28	29–40	41–50	51–60	Over 60
	$4280.	$5450	$6250	$7430	$8210	$8210 plus $180 per teacher over 60 tch. to a max. of $11000.

Comment: Principals with less than 5 professional staff shall be paid $705 less than Category A.

In addition to the salary earned as a teacher, an assistant principal shall receive the applicable administrative allowance, according to the following schedule:

Class	A	B	C	D	E	F
Prof. Staff	1–16	17–28	29–40	41–50	51–60	Over 60
Step 0	1560	2140	2540	3125	3520	4105 plus $90.
1	1850	2435	2835	3420	3810	per teacher over
2	2140	2725	3125	3715	4105	60 teachers to a
						max. of $5610.

Provided that:

4.1.1 On September 30 of each year the schools shall be classified for purposes of administrative allowances, in accordance with the above schedules and these classifications shall be the classifications of the school for the current year.

4.1.2 Part-time teachers are to be included in calculating the appropriate allowances, where they equate to full-time equivalents in a school.

4.2 Upon initial appointment to principalship, a principal shall be paid the allowance of the applicable classification of his school.

4.3 Upon initial appointment, an assistant principal shall be paid the allowance of Step 0 of the applicable classification of his school, except that in a mixed elementary-junior high school where two assistant principals are employed, each respectively shall receive the applicable allowance of Step 0 of the classification that would apply if the elementary and junior high sections were separate. The assistant principal shall be paid according to the next higher step after each year of successful service.

4.4 Transfer to another class of school shall place the assistant principal on the same step in the new category that would have applied had the assistant principal not transferred. A principal allowance for an assistant principal shall be paid on the basis of the incumbent's own period of service in the class of school involved.

4.5 Upon promotion from assistant principal to principal, or from vice-principal to assistant principal, the appointee shall be placed on the initial applicable step of the applicable class of school, provided, however, that if such placement results in a lower allowance than would be obtained in the present position, the appointee shall be placed on an appropriate step in an appropriate category with the salary amount next above that of the appointee's former position.

4.6 Schools shall have the following administrative personnel in addition to the principal:
    8 to 12 rooms—1 Assistant Principal

13 rooms or over—1 Assistant Principal, 1 Vice-Principal provided, however, that in larger schools the administrative organization may consist of a principal, and assistant principals, together with such other officials as may be necessary or desirable for the efficient functioning of the school. The principal and staff of a school, in consideration of the school's educational needs, may make application to the Chief Superintendent for the appointment of two or more Curriculum Leaders in lieu of a vice-principal where the school is entitled to such an appointment.

4.7 No decrease shall hereafter be made in the salary of a principal in consequence of a reduction in the staff of his or her school, if such principal has been employed continuously in the service of the Board for a period of not less than twenty years nor, in other cases, until such time as it appears to the satisfaction of the Board that such reduction is likely to be of considerable duration.

4.8 Any school administrative officer who is appointed to the responsibilities of a senior position for more than 10 consecutive school days shall be paid the administrative allowance of the senior position, in accordance with 4.5 for that period.

4.9 Vice-Principals; Department Heads; Coordinator, School of Language and the Dean of Girls shall receive, each, an administrative allowance of $1255. per annum.

4.10 Special Class Teachers for retarded, emotionally disturbed, learning disabled (emotional, neurological and observational), physically handicapped, socially maladjusted, visually handicapped and hearing handicapped students, shall receive an allowance of $790. per year, while so employed, in addition to their regular salaries.

4.11 Teachers who serve concurrently in two or more schools not located on the same campus shall receive an allowance of $295. per annum above their applicable regular salaries.

5. Allowances — Other Personnel

5.1 All allowances referred to shall be in addition to basic salaries.
5.2 Supervisors shall be paid an administrative allowance of $6390. per annum. The Supervisor of Physical Education and Director of Athletics shall receive an additional allowance of $860. applicable only to the present incumbent.
5.3 The Educational Coordinator shall be paid an administrative allowance equivalent to 50% of the maximum allowance of a principal plus a bonus of $540. applicable only to the present incumbent.

5.4 The Metric Coordinator shall be paid an allowance of $3735. per annum.

5.5 Subject and media specialists shall be paid $3735. per annum.

5.6 The Senior Psychologist and the Senior Speech Pathologist shall receive an administrative allowance of $3835. per annum. The Senior Visiting Teacher shall receive an administrative allowance of $4990. per annum.

5.7 Visiting Teachers shall be paid an allowance of $3735.

5.8 Speech Pathologists, Psychologists and Remedial Clinicians shall be paid an allowance of $2585. per annum.

5.9 Consultants. The current salary of each appointee at the time of appointment shall be fully protected, including the administrative increment, and the additional allowance of $1250. per annum shall be paid.

5.10 Coordinators of Corrective Reading Teachers, Curriculum Leaders and Team Leaders shall be paid an administrative allowance of $630. per annum. The Area Clinicians shall receive this allowance in addition to any other applicable allowances.

5.11 The Coordinator of Administrative Staffing and the Coordinator of Teacher Staffing shall be paid an administrative allowance equivalent to that received by a principal of a school of E category.

5.12 The Assistant Coordinator of Teacher Staffing and the Assistant Coordinator of Administrative Staffing shall be paid an administrative allowance equivalent to that received by a principal of a school of C category.

5.13 The Administrative Assistant to the Coordinator of Media Services and the Administrative Assistant to the Coordinator of Curriculum Services shall be paid an administrative allowance of $4790. (The present incumbent of the Administrative Assistant to the Coordinator of Media Services position shall be paid an allowance of $4990.)

5.14 The Special Assistant to the Superintendent of Instruction shall be paid an administrative allowance of $8685. applicable only to the present incumbent.

5.15 The Academic Coordinator shall be paid an administrative allowance of $3735. per annum.

5.16 The Coordinator of Adult Day Centre shall be paid an administrative allowance of $1255. per annum.

6. Allowances — Substitute Teachers

6.1 Substitute teachers shall be paid $39.75 per day. With 4 per cent holiday pay added, the amount will be $41.35 per day.

6.12 Substitute teachers employed for a period of 10 consecutive teaching days or more, as a replacement for a specific teacher, shall be placed on the basic salary schedule, according to teacher qualifications and experience. This period of consecutive employment during the school year shall not be considered interrupted on non-consecutive, if a holiday, teachers' convention, professional days or such other system regulated break interrupts the teacher's continuity in the classroom.

7. Allowances — Night School, Summer School, Saturday Morning Classes and Calgary Board of Education Sponsored Tutoring Classes

7.1 When a certificate of qualifications as a teacher, as issued under the Department of Education Act, is required as a condition of employment, the following allowances shall apply:

7.1.1 Teachers of In-Service classes shall be paid $16.50 per hour.

7.1.2 Part-time Continuing Education Counsellors and teachers of classes other than In-Service classes shall be paid $15.95 per hour.

8. Employment

8.1 All new appointees to the teacher staff shall submit, upon request, valid Alberta teaching authority, a birth certificate, evidence of a satisfactory chest x-ray or skin test, a medical certificate of sound health, upon a form to be provided by the Chief Superintendent of Schools, or his delegated authority, proof of previous teaching experience from previous employer(s), and any other information which may be required for official record purposes.

8.2 Teachers who wish to change their names during the school year shall provide the Instructional Personnel Department with appropriate evidence, e.g. copy of marriage certificate, at the time of request for change. Data must be submitted promptly, especially when a change in teaching certificate is applicable.

8.3 Seniority will be considered along with other factors in determining promotions but on no account will be considered the most important factor.

8.4 Seniority will have greater weight when comparing persons with relatively little service than when comparing persons with many years of service. All persons with twenty years or more service will generally be considered to have equal seniority.

8.5 Total teaching experience will be considered as a factor in determining promotions.

8.6 Promotions to administrative positions will be contingent upon the appointees being able to give at least five years' service unless there are special factors to compensate for a more limited period.

8.7 Nothing herein shall in any way restrict the Calgary Board of Education from making promotions based on ability and merit.

8.8 Teachers unable to carry on their duties, due to causes covered by the terms of the Agreement, shall give, if possible, at least one hour's notice to the central personnel officer before school assembles, so that proper substitutes may be obtained. Before returning to duty, the absentee teacher shall notify the central personnel offices of such intended return. If returning for the morning sessions, the notification must be given before 7:00 A.M., and for afternoon sessions, before 11:00 A.M. Failure to observe this regulation shall result in the loss to the teacher of one-half day's salary whether the substitute teacher is required or not, provided, however, that the Chief Superintendent of Schools may, at his discretion after investigations of the circumstances, waive the charging of a substitute teacher's salary.

8.9 Upon employment with the Calgary Board of Education, each teacher shall be given a copy of the current Collective Agreement.

8.10 Teachers will render service for not more than 200 consecutive days, commencing the opening day of school in each school year, exclusive of vacation periods, weekends, holidays and semester breaks. Notwithstanding the above, it is recognized that teachers who are in receipt of an administrative or supervisory allowance, shall accept the professional responsibility of having their units operational on the opening day of school each school term, semester or other division of the school year. In a like manner such teachers shall accept the professional responsibility of completing all activities connected with school closing.

8.10.1 Notwithstanding Article 8.10, a teacher who is not in receipt of an administrative or supervisory allowance who renders service during the summer vacation period, at the request of the Chief Superintendent of Schools, or his delegated authority, shall be paid 1/200 of his total annual salary for each day of work.

8.11 When a teacher is transferred pursuant to Section 75(1) of the School Act, or any enactment substituted therefore, the Chief Superintendent of Schools, or his delegated authority, shall, upon written request of the teacher, give, in writing, the Board's reason or reasons for the transfer.

9. General Leave of Absence

9.1 This leave may be granted at no cost to the Board for a period up to one year, as follows:

9.1.1 In case of illness when attested to by a qualified medical practitioner.

9.1.2 To attend university or take post-graduate work.

9.1.3 For any other reason which the Board may approve.

9.2 Applications shall be submitted to the Chief Superintendent of Schools, before December 1st of the school year prior to the leave, except with respect to illness.

9.3 Teachers granted leave for the purpose of further studies, or for illness which is supported by a proper medical certificate, shall be guaranteed a position upon the completion of leave as soon as possible but not later than the beginning of the subsequent school year. The applicable basic salary, upon return, shall be the salary that would have applied if the leave had not been granted. A teacher who would have been entitled to an allowance above the basic salary, if leave had not been granted, shall be designated, upon return, to an equal position, if available. Only when so designated shall the teacher receive an applicable allowance. A teacher granted leave due to illness shall submit a medical certificate verifying fitness to teach.

9.4 Teachers granted leave for reasons not stated in 9.3 shall be granted leave on the understanding that replacement on staff shall be dependent upon a position being available at the expiration of leave.

9.5 Teachers returning from leave may be required to submit a medical certificate.

9.6 Increments will not be credited to teachers for the period of leave.

9.7 Before proceeding on leave, a teacher shall submit a letter of resignation to the Chief Superintendent of Schools (a) dated March 30th, when applicable to a leave which expires on June 30th, or (b) dated November 30th of the preceeding year, when applicable to a leave which expires on January 31st. This letter of resignation shall be cancelled if the teacher notifies the Chief Superintendent of Schools (a) before March 30th, of his/her intention to return to teaching duties at the beginning of the next school year, or (b) before November 30th, of his/her intention to return to teaching duties of February 1st of the same school year. Such letter shall be written on a common form letter which has been approved by the Interpretation Committee.

9.8 The period of leave may be extended for an additional period upon written application by the teacher and approval by the Chief Superintendent of Schools.

10. Leave — President of the Calgary Public School Local #38 Alberta Teachers' Association

10.1 Upon request for leave, the President shall be seconded from the Board to the Calgary Public School Local #38, Alberta Teachers' Association.

10.2 There shall be no cost to the Board during the period of leave.

10.3 The President shall be entitled to one experience increment for each of the first two years of this leave.

10.4 The President shall be listed as a member of the Board's teaching staff.

10.5 The President shall receive an applicable salary cheque from the Board according to the Collective Agreement and shall be subject to its provisions. The Calgary Public School Local #38, Alberta Teachers' Association shall reimburse the Board for the President's salary at such periods as the Board may request.

10.6 The rights and privileges of such group plans as are specified in the Collective Agreement shall be maintained and continued as for other teachers. All normal deductions such as pension, income tax, and professional fees, shall be maintained as for any other teacher.

10.7 The President shall retain such seniority on the Board's staff as has been established prior to accepting the presidency. The President shall be considered for promotions as if still teaching and the applicable position on return to active duty shall be no less favourable than the one applicable before leaving.

10.8 In the event that approval is granted for a third year of leave due to the continuance as President all benefits and provisions shall continue, except that there shall be no entitlement to an experience increment for the third year.

10.9 The President shall advise the Chief Superintendent of Schools, as soon as possible, when an extension is applicable due to re-election.

11. Professional Improvement Leave

11.1 Teachers on permanent staff are eligible for and may apply for educational leave of one year's duration provided they have been employed by the Board as a teacher for a period of at least seven consecutive years, immediately preceding the commencement of leave.

11.2 Applications shall be submitted to the Chief Superintendent of Schools before December 1st of the school year prior to the leave and shall be accompanied by a clear statement of the purposes to be achieved. Upon return from leave, the teacher shall provide the Chief Superintendent of Schools with evidence of compliance with the application upon which the leave was granted.

11.3 The total number of teachers granted leaves of one year's duration shall not exceed one percent in any one year, unless approved by the Board upon recommendation of the Chief Superintendent of Schools. Teachers shall be chosen by the Chief Superintendent of Schools.

11.4 Leave will not be granted to teachers who are within five years or less of the obligatory retirement age.

11.5 Teachers desiring to be employed in a remunerative occupation while on leave must receive prior approval by the Chief Superintendent of Schools.

11.6 Teachers granted leave shall be paid in lieu of salary, in equal monthly installments, sixty-five (65) percent of the total annual earnings that the teacher would have been entitled to had the teacher not been on leave.

11.7 Increments will not be credited to teachers for the period of leave.

11.8 A staff member granted leave shall be on leave from the school district and not from a particular position. Placement, upon return from leave, shall be to an equal position, if available. The applicable salary shall be in accordance with verified qualifications at the time of recommencement of duties and shall include, also, the equivalent of all allowances, except the increment(s) which would have applied if leave had not been granted. This article does not necessarily apply to teachers returning to service before the expiry date of leave.

11.9 Teachers granted leave shall undertake to return to duties at the beginning of the school year following the expiration of the leave, and shall further undertake not to resign, or retire from the services of the Board for at least three years after recommencement of duties. Teachers are required to submit to the Chief Superintendent of Schools a resume of the studies accomplished during educational leave, before recommencement of duties.

11.10 The Board, at its discretion, may grant an additional leave to any teacher, such leave to be not less than five years from the conclusion of the preceding leave. Not more than one year's leave shall be granted for each seven years of service for the purpose of leave.

11.11 The Board, may at its discretion, grant a half-year leave subject to the above general conditions and to the following:
11.11.1 Teachers on permanent staff are eligible to apply for leave of one-half year's duration provided they have been employed by the Board as a teacher for at least five consecutive years immediately preceding the proposed commencement of leave. Leaves will be recommended only after full consideration has been given to the needs of the school system, to the availability of teacher replacements and to the opportunities for employment upon return from leave. Under most circumstances leaves will be granted on the basis that one-half year leave will be combined with one-half year general leave.
11.11.2 More than one leave may be obtained under this plan for half-year leaves, provided that at least five years have elapsed since the conclusion of the teacher's last preceding leave either under Article 9, or Article 11.
11.11.3 Applications for leave shall be submitted to the Chief Superintendent of Schools at least four months prior to the date of leave.
11.11.4 The total number of teachers granted half-year leaves shall not exceed one-half of one percent in any term; the number granted for the spring term shall equal that for the preceding fall term.
11.11.5 If applications for half-year leaves exceed the quota provided, precedence shall be given to applications from teachers who have not been granted leave, previously.
11.11.6 Teachers granted a half-year leave shall be paid, in equal monthly installments in lieu of salary, thirty-two and one-half (32½) percent of the total annual earnings that the teacher would have been entitled to had the teacher not been on leave.
11.11.7 Teachers granted half-year leaves shall undertake to return to duties immediately after termination of leave and shall not resign or retire, from services of the Board for at least two years after recommencement of duties.

11.12 A fund in the amount of one hundred thousand ($100,000) dollars is available to teachers or groups of teachers for the purposes of professional development. This fund shall be known as the Staff Development Fund.

11.12.1 Any teacher or group of teachers may make application to the Chief Superintendent, or his delegated authority, for funds, such application to include a resume of the proposed project.

11.12.2 It is the responsibility of the Chief Superintendent, or his delegated authority, to rule on each application and inform the applicant of his decision. The decision of the Chief Superintendent, or his delegated authority, shall be final.

11.12.3 An advisory committee of four teachers will be appointed to assist the Chief Superintendent, or his delegated authority, in reviewing and revising the guidelines for the fund. The committee will meet as required.

12. Maternity Leave of Absence

12.1 Women teachers shall be eligible for maternity leave under the following conditions:

12.1.1 The teacher concerned shall apply for maternity leave not less than four months before the date of confinement. The leave shall be effective not less than two months before the date of confinement. However, the Chief Superintendent may decrease the limitation of two months after consultation with the principal of the school in which the teacher is employed. The decision of the Chief Superintendent of Schools shall be final and binding. At the time that leave is requested the teacher shall provide a statement from the attending physician verifying that the teacher is medically fit to continue work and which indicates the anticipated date of confinement.

12.1.2 In general, at least two months shall elapse after the term of pregnancy before the reassignment of the teacher to the staff, subject to the discretion of the Chief Superintendent of Schools.

12.1.3 The Board is under no obligation to reassign the teacher to staff, after maternity leave, except at the beginning of a school year or a semester.

12.1.4 A teacher on maternity leave must give to the Chief Superintendent of Schools at least two months' notice of her intention to return to duties.

12.1.5 Maternity leave shall be without pay or sickness allowances, and periods of absence will not be counted for the granting of increments.

12.1.6 A teacher returning from maternity leave may be required to pass a medical examination before returning to duty.

13. Temporary Leave of Absence — Personal

13.1 Applications for leave for personal reasons can be justified only if they arise from extraordinary situations involving the teacher or his/her family.

13.1.1 Teachers desiring leave of absence for personal reasons and who obtain authority for same through the Chief Superintendent of Schools, or his delegated authorities, shall be allowed up to and including three days in any one school year with the loss of substitutes' pay only, and shall be deducted full salary for days absent for personal reasons in excess of three in any one school year.

Temporary Leave of Absence — Compassionate

13.2 Leave may be granted with respect to critical illness or death of a near relative. For purposes of this Article the term "near relative" shall be defined as the spouse of the teacher, and the grandparents, parents, brothers, sisters, children, and grandchildren (and their respective spouses) of the teacher and of the teacher's spouse and such other persons as the Chief Superintendent of Schools shall in his discretion designate.

13.2.1 In the event of a critical illness of a near relative or other family emergency, a teacher may be granted a maximum of five days leave with pay when, at the discretion of the Chief Superintendent of Schools, circumstances warrant it.

13.2.2 Teachers attending the funeral of a near relative in the city may be allowed three days' leave with pay, and, if outside the city, five days' leave with pay. Where the teacher does not attend the said funeral, reasonable leave may be allowed at the discretion of the Chief Superintendent of Schools.

Adoption

13.3 Leave for adoption purposes shall be granted. The periods of leave shall be at the discretion of the Chief Superintendent of Schools. Leave granted shall be without pay or sickness allowances and periods of absence shall not be counted for the granting of increments. Teachers may be granted, at the discretion of the Chief Superintendent of Schools, a maximum of two days with pay for the purpose of completing the necessary documentation and receiving a child to be adopted.

Graduate Study

13.4 Teachers may be granted, at the discretion of the Chief Superintendent of Schools, temporary leave of absence with pay for graduate study when they are required to leave before the end of June due to enrollment at educational institutions for a program of summer study, provided the Board is reimbursed for the cost of substitute teachers who are employed due to the absence of the applicable teachers. The costs of substitute teachers employed in these situations shall be shared equally by all teachers who received temporary leaves of absence under the terms of this article.

14. Sick Leave With Pay

14.1 During the first year of employment with the Board, or during any subsequent current year, a teacher shall be entitled to draw salary for illness for the number of days provided for in The School Act, that is, to a maximum of 20 days.

14.2 Effective September 1, 1966, a teacher may accumulate the unused portion of the yearly allowance until a maximum of 150 days is reached. Effective September 1, 1968, the maximum will be 160 days. Effective September 1, 1969, the maximum will be 170 days. Effective September 1, 1973, the maximum will be 180 days.

14.3 The days accumulated in 14.2 are exclusive of those allowed in 14.1.

14.4 The Board may grant, at its discretion, additional sick leave with pay.

14.5 A certificate of illness from a qualified medical or dental practitioner is required by the Board to support requests for sick leave with pay when the absence is for a period over three teaching days.

14.6 Teachers who have been ill for a period not exceeding three teaching days may dispense with a doctor's certificate, provided they present to the Board of Education office a teacher's certificate of such illness.

14.7 A teacher who is quarantined by order of the Medical Officer of Health for the City, or by a Provincial authority, may be allowed sick leave with pay if the absences for quarantine are certified to by a duly qualified Medical Officer.

14.8 If deductions are made prior to the accumulation of sick leave, reimbursement, when applicable, shall be paid on the August cheque.

15. Group Insurance Plan

15.1 The group insurance plan refers to life insurance, accidental death and dismemberment, health benefits (hospitalization and major medical) and long term disability insurance as outlined in the applicable group insurance policies.

15.2 Participation in the plan shall be a condition of employment for all teachers commencing employment for a full school year on or after September 1, 1972.

15.3 Participation in the plan shall be available on an optional basis to all teachers employed for less than a full school year if the contract is known to be of a duration of not less than five months at the time of employment.

15.4 The cost sharing of the group insurance plan between the Board and teachers shall be:

	Board	Teacher
Life and accidental death and dismemberment	90%	10%
Health benefit	90%	10%
Long term disability	–	100%

15.5 The Board will administer the plan.

15.6 A joint committee shall be established to review group insurance plans on a regular basis and such committee shall be composed of one Board trustee, two Board management representatives and three representatives named by the Association. The representative to the committee shall be appointed each year. The Committee shall meet within the period of 4 (four) weeks following ratification of this collective agreement, excluding holiday periods.

15.7 The Board agrees that no reduction in the amounts of insurance will occur without the prior approval of the Alberta Teachers' Association.

16. Alberta Health Care Insurance Plan
16.1 The Board shall contribute 100 percent of the premium for participants of this plan.

17. Interpretation and Grievance Procedures
17.1 An Interpretation Committee, consisting of four members appointed by the Association together with one representative of the Board and three representatives appointed by the Chief Superintendent of Schools, shall meet once per month, if necessary. A quorum of this committee shall consist of all members. The Manager of Personnel Services, or his delegated authority, shall act as the Secretary of this Committee.

17.2 Any teacher who believes that a grievance has occurred with respect to the application of the terms of this Agreement shall present, in writing, a statement setting out the nature of the alleged grievance and the articles of the Agreement, which have been allegedly violated, to the Manager, Personnel Services Department, with a copy to the President, Local #38 of the Alberta Teachers' Association. Any such request must be submitted within forty (40) working days after the incident or misunderstanding which resulted in the alleged grievance. In the event that the submission is presented after the forty (40) day period, the Manager, Personnel Services Department may consider the request. If the request is disallowed, the teacher may request consideration by the Interpretation Committee within the limits of Article 17.3. The Interpretation Committee shall decide on hearing applications for interpretation that have been submitted beyond the limitation period when, in the opinion of the majority of that Committee, there are extenuating circumstances to merit such action. No grievance shall be defeated because a teacher has cited no, or an incorrect, article of the Agreement.

17.3 If the grievance has not been settled with fifteen (15) days after the date of submission of the alleged grievance, the teacher may present, within five (5) days thereafter, in writing, a statement of the nature of the grievance to the Secretary of the Interpretation Committee requesting consideration of the grievance.

17.4 When the Interpretation Committee receives notice of the submission of a grievance, it shall be required to give its decision within twenty-one (21) days following the receipt of such notice and shall dispose of each grievance before proceeding to another, except whereby unanimous consent of the Interpretation Committee the hearing of such grievance is adjourned for the purpose of obtaining further information.

17.5 If the Interpretation Committee reaches a unanimous decision as to the disposition of any grievance, that decision shall be final and binding.

17.6 After each meeting of the Interpretation Committee, the Secretary shall forward the Committee's decision to the teacher in writing, also copies to the Chief Superintendent of Schools, to the President of Local #38 of the Alberta Teachers' Association and to the Committee members. When a request has been denied, the reasons for denial are to be made known to the teacher in writing.

17.7 If the Interpretation Committee does not reach a unanimous or any decision, either party may, by written notice served on the other party within ten days after the date on which the Committee voted on the disposition of the grievance or within ten (10) days after the expiration of the said period of 21 days, whichever is the shorter, require the establishment of a Grievance Board as hereinafter provided, and if such notice is not served within the time limit, the grievance shall be deemed to be at an end. The parties may, by mutual agreement, consent to postpone the hearing of the Grievance Board. Such notice shall contain a statement of the nature of the grievance.

17.8 Each party shall appoint one (1) member as its representative on the Greivance Board within seven (7) days of such notice and the two (2) members so appointed shall endeavour to select an independent chairman.

17.9 If the two (2) members fail to select a chairman within five (5) days after the day on which the last of the two (2) members is appointed, they shall request the Minister of the Department of Labour to select a chairman.

17.10 The Grievance Board shall determine its own procedure but shall give full opportunity to all parties to present evidence and to be heard.

17.11 The Grievance Board shall neither change, modify or alter any of the terms of this Agreement, nor shall the Grievance Board make a decision which will be contrary to the terms of this Agreement. All grievances or differences submitted shall present an arbitrable issue under this Agreement, and shall not depend on or involve an issue or contention by either party that is contrary to any provisions of this Agreement or that involves the determination of a subject not covered by, or not arising during the term of this Agreement.

17.12 The Grievance Board shall give its decision not later than fourteen (14) days after the appointment of the chairman except that with the consent of both the Calgary Public School Local of the Association and the Board, such limitation of time may be extended. The findings and decisions of a majority of the members of a Grievance Board shall be the findings and decision of the Grievance Board and shall be binding on the parties. If there is no majority the decision of the chairman shall be the decision of the Grievance Board.

17.13 Each party to the grievance shall bear the expenses of its respective nominee and the two (2) parties shall bear equally the expenses of the chairman.

17.14 Where any references in this Article, Interpretation and Grievance Procedures, are to a period of days, such a period shall be exclusive of Saturdays, Sundays, statutory holidays and summer vacation.

17.15 Notwithstanding anything in the within Agreement, either party to this Agreement may submit, through the interpretation and grievance procedures, any difference respecting the interpretation, application, operation, contravention or alleged contravention thereof.

18. Working Conditions
18.1 Staff deployment is the responsibility of the principal and his/her staff.

18.2 It is understood that teachers are expected to participate in those aspects of student activities which are normal extensions of the classroom program. Also, it is understood that some parameters for extracurricular activities are necessary in order to ensure both the quality of classroom instruction and a viable work load for teachers. The extent of school involvement in extra-curricular activities must be determined by the principal and his/her staff. Teachers who have chosen to undertake a specific extracurricular activity shall be committed to that activity for its duration in that school year, unless an emergent situation prohibits continuance.

18.3 A teacher not in receipt of any administrative allowance will not be assigned duties in excess of thirty (30) hours per week, averaged over the school year. The present policies and practices with respect to instructional time will not be changed to increase the instructional load.

18.4 The teachers recognize the right and responsibility of the Board to formulate policy. The Board agrees that they will not make changes in the present working conditions which are not covered in this Agreement without first having the matter considered by an Advisory Committee consisting of three teachers and three senior administrative personnel.

18.5 In each year there shall be two non-teaching organizational days, the activities of which shall be determined by the staff of each school. A plan of such activities shall be submitted to the area superintendent who may require as a condition of his approval, that the plan be altered or modified prior to each such organizational day. In addition, there shall, in each year, be three non-teaching professional activity days to be determined by the staff of each school in consultation with the area superintendent and in all cases the staff shall submit a report as to the fulfillment of the plan of activities within a reasonable time after each of the five days.

19. Unemployment Insurance Commission Rebate
19.1 The Board and The Association agree that the Unemployment Insurance Commission rebate has been shared, according to appropriate section(s) of the Unemployment Insurance Act, through the increase in the benefits contained in this Agreement, and that no further adjustment will be passed on to the teachers.

20. Secondment
20.1 Teachers seconded from the Calgary Board of Education shall be subject to the following provisions. The teacher shall be entitled to experience increments for each year of the secondment. The teacher shall be listed as a member of the Calgary Board of Education teaching staff. The teacher shall receive his/her salary cheque from the Calgary Board of Education according to the Collective Agreement and shall be subject to its provisions. The rights and privileges of such group plans as specified in the Collective Agreement shall be maintained and continued as for other teachers. All normal deductions (such as pension, income tax, professional fees) shall be maintained as for any other teacher. The teacher shall retain such seniority on the Calgary Board of Education staff as has been established prior to being seconded. The position to which the teacher is assigned immediately after the period of secondment shall be no less favourable than the one the teacher left.

21. General Application
21.1 This Agreement cancels all former Agreements and all provisions appended thereto.

In Witness Whereof the parties hereto have caused this Agreement to be executed by their respective officers, duly authorized hereunto, the day and year first above written.

Appendix "A" to the Agreement

1. Recognition of Non-University Courses for Salary Purposes

1.1 Teachers shall be permitted to retain previously granted credits.

1.2 Credits for Calgary Board of Education In-Service Courses shall be recognized for purposes of transfer to salary categories "B", "C" and "D" on the basis of one course being regarded as the equivalent of one-half of a standard university course.
1.2.1 Credit for transfer to Category "D" shall be limited to the equivalent of one university year.

1.3 Teachers shall be allowed one year of additional education upon the provisions of evidence of an L.T.C.L., A.T.C.L., A.R.C.T, A.T.C.M., L.R.S.M., A.Mus. U.A., A.Mus. U.S., or A.Mus. U.M. music diploma, provided that (a) music shall form part of the teaching or supervisory program of the teacher or be included in assignments beyond the specific class to which the teacher is assigned and (b) the requirements of the diploma are not being counted in any other way for salary purposes.

1.4 In-Service Courses shall mean those courses which are approved as such by the Chief Superintendent of Schools.

REFERENCES

Anderson, M. E., "A Study of Teacher Rating," *The Nova Scotia Teacher,* October, 1962.

Barraclough, T. *Merit Pay Programs for Secondary School Administrators, 1972–73.* Eurgen, Oregon: ERIC Clearinghouse on Educational Management, 1973.

Blount, G. *Collective Bargaining in Canadian Education.* An annotated bibliography. Toronto: Ontario Institute for Studies in Education, 1975.

Bowman, S., "The Negotiation of Collective Agreements With Employees of School Boards," *Ontario Education,* September-October, 1977.

Conte, A. E. and E. R. Mason. *Merit Pay: Problems and Alternatives.* Perspective Series no. 2. Trenton, New Jersey: New Jersey State Department of Education, 1972.

Dulude, A., "Teachers and Collective Agreements: A Puzzle for the Seventies," *Labour Gazette,* February, 1973.

Howsam, R. B., "Merit Pay is Largely a Phoney Issue," *Canadian School Journal,* June-July, 1962.

Lawless, D. S., "School Board-Teacher Negotiations," *Education Canada,*   Winter, 1976.

McLeod, G., "Collective Bargaining Between School Boards and Teachers: A Social-Dramaturgical Interpretation," *Canadian Journal of Education,* Vo. 3, no. 1, 1978.

McDowell, S., "Accountability of Teacher Performance Through Merit Salaries and Other Devices," in T. E. Giles (ed.) *Educational Accountability.* Calgary: Council on School Administration, 1972.

Merit Pay in Teachers' Salary Administration. Series on Problems in Education, No. 5. Edmonton: Alberta Teachers' Association, 1962.

Merit Rating. Bibliographies in Education No. 21. Ottawa: Canadian Teachers' Federation, 1971.

Muir, J. D., "Teachers and Their Right to Bargain: How Far Have They Come and Where are They Going?" *Education Canada,* Spring, 1976.

Rhodes, E. and H. Kaplan. *New Ideas in Educational Compensation.* Washington: Educational Service Bureau, 1972.

Toombs, W. N., "The Use of Power Tactics in Teacher Salary Negotiations," *Education Canada,* December, 1973.

Worth, Walter H., "Can Administrators Rate Teachers?" *The Canadian Administrator,* October, 1961.

Questions for Discussion

1. Compare a number of rating scales for teacher performance to be used for determining salary. Are all the points valid? Are the weightings valid? Are there other points which should be considered?

2. After considering the pros and cons, do you feel that teachers should be merit rated for the purpose of determining salary?

3. To what extent would a merit rating system effect the collective bargaining procedure?

4. If the teachers of an employing board were given the entire right of determination of the allocation of the total negotiated salary amount (with no influence from the administrators, the teachers' association or the employers) would there be any significant differences from the present collective agreements?

5. Do teachers want merit rating for salary purposes?

6. What merit provisions are included in the Calgary School Board collective agreement?

7. It was stated in this chapter that "business and industry have successfully employed merit ratings and merit pay for their employees." Develop a case opposing this statement.

8. Develop a merit rating scale and accompanying merit salary schedule which you feel is fair and just.

Appendices

A

The Caraquet Riots of 1875*

In April of 1871 an education bill was introduced for a non-secretarian school system supported by public funds. The Roman Catholic minority pressed the need for a separate school system in New Brunswick. Twenty-two petitions were sent to Fredericton but the press and public generally supported the principle of non-secretarian schools and on May 5 the bill was passed, this meant that although the Catholics supported their own schools they still had to pay school taxes and when they refused to pay, private property was seized, stock, farm equipment, cows, stoves, books, anything to cover the cost of the taxes.

In Caraquet there were only a few Protestants among a large Catholic population who refused to pay the taxes so the Protestants called a school meeting presided over by the Honourable Robert Young, January 1875 for the purpose of imposing a district school tax.

Spirits were running high and the Catholic people turned out in great numbers to oppose the imposition of the tax. They refused to let the Chairman speak. Several men rushed forward and hustled him out of the building. Another man grabbed the papers from one of the committee and the meeting broke up.

Believing the Protestants would hold another secret meeting, a group of French went to the schoolhouse the next day and they found the school locked against them, they went to Blackhall's house where they were refused the key so they went to Charles Robin's store where they got rum and heated their heads as well as their feet. They went back to Blackhall's office in a boisterous and belliger-

---

*It has not been possible to determine the authorship of this article. Readers wishing a more detailed description of the Caraquet Riots are encouraged to read "The Caraquet Riots of 1875," written by George Stanley in *Acadiensis,* 1972.

ent manner. In the mela that followed papers were torn from the wall, a stove turned over and windows broken. Blackhall was forced to sign a pledge that he would have nothing more to do with school meetings. Rive had been forced to do the same earlier.

The crowd then moved to Robert Young's house, he was not home and Mrs. Young, terrified had locked herself and her children in. The men were carrying clubs and guns. Colson Hubbard, Young's clerk gave some of the leaders provisions and they left.

They then threatened Hubert Blanchard, Martin Hache, Stanislas Legere and Alexander's Store where they extorted $4.00. Now that they had intimidated most of the "Bourbons" as they called those who were paying their taxes, and had persuaded them to change sides, they waited for Robert Young to come home and try and convince him to change.

Mrs. Young had sent her husband a telegram to Fredericton but he had left and was on his way home by way of St. John and Sackville. At Sackville he received the wire January 15th and hurried to Shediac where he hired a carriage and arrived in Chatham Sunday the 17th. Here he received word that his own life was in danger and the Caraquet men were planning to burn his store and destroy all his business records then they were going to all the merchants and make them burn all mortgages and accounts up to date.

Robert Young for some reason did not go home at once. Not until Friday the 22nd, one week after Mrs. Young had been so scared. He found no signs of damage from the riotous situation but there was a lot of tension.

Sunday, January 24th in church the Parish Priest spoke of this disapproval of the excesses of the 14th and 15th and read a letter which he had received that morning ordering him to stop the band of Pirates under pain of having his Presbytery burned to the ground should he fail to do so. The author of the letter remains a mystery, but Colson Buggard, Young's clerk, was seen to hand a letter to the Sexton on the 24th.

This infuriated the people more and at 10 a.m. next morning January 25th, 100 men set out to see Young, there was no sign that they meant violence as Robert Young expected and he had barricaded his doors and windows and assembled some well armed friends to help. He refused to open the door or talk with them. His curt refusal angered them so they went to Andre Albert's house to plan their future action.

Young had already issued warrants for the arrest of the rioters put in the hands of the High Sheriff Robert D. Vail (Mrs. Garry Stratton G. Grandfather). Young ordered him to come to Caraquet with a force of constables to arrest the trouble makers. Vail arrived in Caraquet Tuesday, January 26th. He had four constables, Stephen Cable, Alfred Gammon, Joseph Gammon, and Robert Ramsay. Enroute he picked up William Eddy, and David Eady of New Bandon. At Caraquet they were joined by John Sewell and Richard Sewell from Pokemouche.

Vail went to Youngs telling the men to join him there after having something to eat.

During the morning several arrests were made and they were taken to the Young's home where they were detained till they could send them to Bathurst. Meanwhile Vail being alarmed by Young's story of the situation, had applied to Chatham for additional men, the High Sherriff of Gloucester had no jurisdiction to enroll men in Northumberland County so it was irregular and wrong.

Twenty men from Newcastle and Chatham were assembled and sent to Caraquet on sleighs on the afternoon of January 26th. After difficult journey over almost impassable roads they arrived in Caraquet on the 27th.

It included Sam Wilcox, Peter and Robert Manderson, James Loggie, George Loggie, Dudley Rand, Isaac Clark, Charles Gall, William Reid, James Chapman, John Gifford, Henry Brubridge, Henry Bannister, Wm. Carter, and Wm. Fenton. Vail ordered more arrests on the 27th. One offered strong resistance, it was pretty rough according to Alfred Gammon.

An informer told Vail that some of the rioters were at Andre Albert's house so he sent twenty men to arrest them. Those arrests had alarmed the population especially where they were concerned about the Orangemen from the Miramichi whom they called Young's Army. It was reported they would arrest anyone they could find. The Caraquet people made their way to Andre Albert's house to decide what they would do, some played cards while others talked.

Telesphore Brideau came in and said Young's Army was on its way to make arrests at Saraphin Albert's house and they had rifles so there was no point in resisting. Some left but others remained until Young's Army arrived, then they were afraid and went into the attic to hide.

Blackhill went in and spoke to Albert asking for Charles Parise,

Albert said he did not know where he was while they were talking the room filled with armed men, one saw a woman going to the stove to a pot of boiling water, and presumed she was going to throw it over them, he held his gun to her face and pushed her into another room. Meanwhile Robert Ramsay heard a noise overhead and fired into the hole in the ceiling leading to the attic, with the idea of frightening them. Sewell and Burbridge rushed to the attic and attempted to get into the attic but were pushed back by the Acadians. Some of the constables thrust their bayonettes through the ceiling to pry loose some of the planks when a shot was fired from the attic.

Sewell and Loggie managed to get into the attic, Gifford was hoisting himself in and may have fired a shot from his revolver. Then one of the Acadians fired a shot, Gifford was shot in the head and dropped to the floor below, then the shooting became wild. James Chapman was shooting from below thru the ceiling regardless of his comrades in the attic, then Louis Mailloux, Acadian was hit. In the confusion two Acadians jumped to the floor below and fled to safety. Another one did the same but was hit with a rifle and left lying in the snow. The Acadians then gave up and were led to Young's store, two of the Acadians had wounds. Mailloux died shortly after and Gifford was killed instantly.

January 28th the next day, the prisoners were taken to Bathurst jail, it was bitterly cold and some had frozen hands and feet when they arrived. Thinking there might be more shootings the militia (Newcastle Field Battery) was sent to Chatham on the 28th of January with two nine pound cannons.

They were followed several hours later by a second detachment infantry force made up of four officers and forty-six other ranks of the 73rd Battalion (later known as North Shore Regiment). Both detachments found the going rough and had to dig three high drifts, but arrived safely January 29th.

The gunners remained in Bathurst to guard the prisoners. The infanteers were sent to Caraquet to act as guards and escorts.

On February 3rd all was quiet and the infantry was returned to Chatham. The Bathurst guard remained on duty for six weeks.

At the inquest of Mailloux and Gifford the jury found Mailloux was killed by persons unknown and nine persons were charged with murder for the death of Gifford. As for the rioters, nine were accused of illegal assembly on January 25th, the others were acquitted. The proceedings opened at Bathurst September 7, 1875. As for the murder charge against the nine Acadians, the first man tried was Joseph Chiasson, a verdict of guilty was brought in but the judge was not prepared to pass judgment, he felt there were too many issues at stake and the nine men went back to their cells to wait for the meeting of the court in June, 1876. Many distinguished men raised funds and worked for the nine men, they brought in the fact that there had been many errors on the part of the judge at the trial and that the convictions should be squashed. The prisoners were released and as it was eighteen months since the offence the rioters were also free.

The Acadians were overjoyed and everyone was content to forget the whole thing.

B

Teacher Certification in Canada

The following is a brief summary of teaching certification in Canada. The reader is cautioned to remember that while this summary reflects the position at this time, changes are made by the provinces from time to time. Also the topic of certification is a great deal more detailed and involved than can be reflected in a brief summary. For more details, contact the Registrar of the Department of Education for the respective provinces. It should also be noted that certificates issued under prior regulations usually retain their original validity or are reissued in terms of newer regulations.

British Columbia

Professional Certificate—Four years of university, one of which is basic teacher education; includes completion of an appropriate undergraduate degree or equivalent.

Standard Certificate—Three years of university, one of which is basic teacher education.

Instructor's Diploma—Appropriate trades qualifications and experience plus two to three years' appropriate post-secondary preparation.

Teaching Licence—Two years of university, one of which is basic teacher education.

All four certificates are valid for all grades and for a period of four years. The Professional and Standard Certificates and the Instructor's Diploma are permanent when issued for graduates of provincial universities; others require one year successful teaching. The Teaching Licence cannot be made permanent. Educational requirements are those beyond grade twelve.

234

Alberta

Professional—B.Ed. degree (4 years) or another approved under-graduate degree plus one year teacher education.

Provisional—Journeyman's certificate or equivalent, plus work ex-perience, plus second and third years of B.Ed. program (vocational).

Conditional—Two years' university (restricted to a special program for Indians).

All certificates are interim when issued and are valid for three years. Canadian citizenship is required for permanent certification. The Conditional and Provisional certificates cannot be made permanent; the Professional can be made permanent after two years of success-ful teaching. All certificates are valid for grades 1-12. Early child-hood teachers require a certificate and a five course early childhood specialization.

Saskatchewan

Standard A—Two years of teacher education.

Professional A—Four years of university (B.Ed., B.A. or equivalent) including one year of teacher education.

Standard B—One year of specialized post-secondary training plus one year of teacher education.

Professional B—A degree in an approved area of specialization, plus one year of teacher education.

Vocational—Journeyman's certificate or approved training in a trade, plus one year of teacher education.

Technical—Two years' technical (post-secondary), plus three years' work experience and one year of teacher education.

Probationary—Issued on application of school board to a person who lacks qualifications to teach.

All certificates except Probationary are valid for all grades and are permanent when issued, except for teachers from outside the prov-ince. The Standard B, Professional B, Vocational and Technical are endorsed for subject or area of teaching eligibility. The Probationary specifies particular subjects and a specified grade level in a certain school and is valid for one year. The educational requirements are those beyond senior matriculation.

Manitoba

First Class Certificate—Two years' of teacher education.

Professional Certificate—An acceptable degree plus one year of teacher education, or B.Ed. Degree.

Special Certificate in Business Education—Two years' of teacher education.

Special Certificate in Industrial Arts—Two years' of teacher education.

Special Certificate in Vocational-Industrial Education—Journeyman's certificate after grade eleven or three-year high school vocational course, plus three years practical experience, plus one year of teacher education.

Special Certificate in Physical Education—Two years' acceptable training in physical education.

All certificates are interim when issued and are valid for three years. They are made permanent upon two years' successful teaching and a recommendation from the superintendent of schools or inspector. The First Class Certificate is valid for grades one to nine; the other certificates for grades one to twelve. Except for the Special Certificate for Vocational-Industrial Education, the requirements are those beyond senior matriculation or grade twelve.

Ontario

Interim Elementary School Teacher's Certificate—Approved university degree plus one year of teacher education. Valid for grades one to ten.

Interim Elementary School Teacher's Certificate (bilingual)—Grade thirteen with standing in English and French, plus one year of bilingual teacher education. Valid for grades one to ten in elementary schools where French is the language of instruction.

Interim Primary School Specialist's Certificate—An approved university degree, plus one year of teacher education. Valid for kindergarten to grade three.

Interim High School Assistant's Certificate, Type B—Approved university degree, plus one year of teacher education. Valid for grades seven to thirteen. When made permanent, is called Permanent High School Assistant's Certificate.

Interim High School Assistant's Certificate, Type A—Approved university degree with sixty credits, including specified specialty credits, beyond Ontario grade thirteen, plus one year of teacher education or Type B qualification and a six-week summer seminar. Valid for grades seven to thirteen. When made permanent, is called High School Specialist's Certificate.

Interim Vocational Certificate, Type B—Approved wage-earning experience, plus one year of teacher education or equivalent, beyond grade twelve. Valid for grades nine to twelve in specified subjects. When made permanent, is called Permanent Vocational Certificate.

Interim Vocational Certificate, Type A—Permanent Vocational Certificate and complete grade thirteen, plus two five-week summer courses in education, or, approved university degree in engineering, architecture or nursing, with two years of wage-earning experience in the subject, plus one year of teacher education. Valid for grades nine to twelve. When made permanent, is called Vocational Specialist's Certificate.

Interim Occupational Certificate, Type B (Practical Subjects)—Grade Twelve and approved wage-earning experience involving three occupational or service trade areas, plus one year of teacher education. Valid for the practical subjects in the Secondary School Occupational Program. When made permanent, is called Permanent Occupational Certificate (Practical Subjects).

Interim Occupational Certificate, Type A (Practical Subjects)—Permanent Occupational Certificate (Practical Subjects) and complete grade thirteen plus two five-week summer courses in teacher education. Valid for practical subjects in the Secondary School Occupational Program. When made permanent, is called Occupational Specialist's Certificate (Practical Subjects).

Interim Occupational Certificate, Type B (General Subjects)—Permanent Certificate for an Ontario elementary school, Specialist Certificate in Special Education or Elementary School Teacher's Certificate with a university degree, and five years' successful teaching experience in Ontario. Valid for general subjects in the Secondary School Occupational Program. When made permanent, is called Permanent Occupational Certificate (General Subjects).

Interim Occupational Certificate, Type A (General Subjects)—Permanent High School Assistant's Certificate, Specialist Certificate in Special Education with secondary school option, and two years' successful teaching in general subjects in the Occupational Program. When made permanent, is called Occupational Specialist's Certificate (General Subjects). Valid for general subjects in the Secondary School Occupational Program.

All certificates are valid for five years. They are made permanent upon the completion of two years' of successful teaching in the grades or subjects specified on the certificates.

Quebec

Teaching Permit—Graduation from a CEGEP (a general and vocational college which offers a full spectrum of college-level academic and technical programs), plus a B.Ed. degree (a three-year university course after thirteen years of schooling), *or* an academic degree (Bachelor's, Licentiate, Master's, Doctorate, etc.), plus one year of professional training at a university faculty of education.

Technical-Vocational candidates must have either a Diploma of Collegial Studies, Vocational sector, or a diploma from an institute of technology and at least three years of relevant experience, plus one year (thirty credits) of teacher training.

The Teaching Permit is temporary when issued and is valid for five years. It can be made permanent after two successful years of teaching—the Permit is then called Teaching Diploma. The Teaching Permit and Teaching Diploma are certified for one or more of four teaching levels (kindergarten, elementary, secondary, CEGEP). Specialists' Diplomas are usually pursued only after the basic Teaching Diploma and some experience has been obtained.

New Brunswick

Letter of Standing Four—Five years' work experience and journeyman's status or two years of work experience and technology program, plus a 12 month teacher training program. Valid for Industrial Trades.

Certificate 3 (Elementary, Secondary, Home Economics, Business, Industrial, Music, Art, General)—Certificate 2 (grade twelve plus two years' teacher education), plus five full university courses.

Certificate 4 (Elementary, Secondary, Home Economics, Business, Industrial, Physical Education, Music, Art, General)—An approved four-year university degree, including teacher education, or an approved three-year degree, plus a New Brunswick B.Ed.

Certificate 4 (Industrial Trades)—Certificate 3, plus five university courses in Industrial Education.

Certificate 5 (Elementary, Secondary, Home Economics, Business, Industrial, Physical Education, Music, Art, General)—Certificate 4 plus one year post-graduate degree or four-year undergraduate degree plus New Brunswick B.Ed.

Certificate 6 (Elementary, Secondary, Home Economics, Business, Industrial, Physical Education, Music, Art, General)—Certificate 5 plus Master's degree, Graduate Diploma or higher degree, or Certificate 5 (two degrees) plus five full university graduate courses in one subject in program of studies.

Letter of Standing (for persons educated outside New Brunswick)— Valid teacher's licence, minimum of four years of post-secondary study beyond a program equivalent to New Brunswick grade twelve, and an approved undergraduate degree and teacher education program. This certificate is valid for three years and is changed to the appropriate permanent certification after two years of successful teaching.

The Letter of Standing Four, which is valid for four years, becomes permanent after receiving a degree.

Nova Scotia

Class 2—Senior matriculation, plus one year teacher education; or junior matriculation, plus one year of university, plus one year of teacher education.

Class 3—Junior matriculation, plus two years of university, plus one year of teacher education; or senior matriculation, plus one year of university, plus one year of teacher education; or senior matriculation, plus two years of teacher education.

Class 4—Junior matriculation plus three years of university plus one year of teacher education.

Class 5—Acceptable university degree, plus one year of teacher education.

Class 6—M.A. or M.Sc. in field of study related to elementary and secondary education in Nova Scotia, plus one year of teacher education; or M.Ed. degree, plus one year of teacher education; or four-year honors university course after senior matriculation, plus one year of teacher education; or five-year honors university course after junior matriculation, plus one year of teacher education.

Class 7—Class 6 Certificate plus one year additional study, or Class 5 plus two years of additional study.

Class 8—Class 6 Certificate plus a doctoral degree in a field of study related to elementary or secondary education in Nova Scotia, or a D.Ed. degree.

The Class 3 certificate is the present basic minimum qualification. Special certificates and licenses are issued in the fields of art, business education, guidance, home economics, industrial arts, music, music instrumental, physical education, primary education, teaching of the deaf, vocational education, psychological and testing services, social service related to education, and school library services. All certificates are interim when issued and are valid for three years. They may be made permanent upon completion of two years' successful teaching. There is no provision for permanency of the special certificates in psychological and testing services, social service related to education, and school library services.

Prince Edward Island

Certificate 4—Four years of university, one of which is teacher education, or undergraduate B.Ed. degree.

Certificate 5—Five years of university (one of which is teacher education), or B.A., B.Sc., or other approved degree plus one year of teacher education, or B.A., or B.Sc., plus B.Ed. degree.

Certificate 5-A—University degree, plus one year of teacher education, plus one year of approved study or equivalent.

Certificate 6—University degree, plus one year of teacher education, plus approved Master's degree.

All certificates are valid for grades one to twelve. They are interim when issued and are valid for two years. They may be made permanent upon the completion of two years' of successful teaching.

Newfoundland

Certificate II—Two years of teacher education that includes a course in English and at least two full courses in education, or two years' university study and at least two full courses in education.

Certificate III—Three years teacher education or three years university study and at least three full courses in education.

Certificate IV—Four years of university study including four full courses in education.

Certificate V—Five years university study, an approved degree, including one year of training in education.

Certificate VI—Six years university study, with a Master's degree, or two Bachelor's degrees, including one year of training in education.

Certificate VII—Seven years of university study and a Doctoral degree; or two Masters' degrees; or one Master's degree and two Bachelors' degrees; or one Master's degree and one Bachelor's Degree and an approved Diploma in Education. If none of the degrees is in education, then one year of teacher training or five full courses in education are required.

Permit IV—Four years of university study and a Bachelor's degree in a Special Field.

Permit V—Five years of university study and a Bachelor's degree in a Special Field.

Permit VI—Six years of university study and a Master's degree in a Special Field, or two Bachelors' degrees out of which one must be in a Special Field.

Permit VII—Seven years of university study and a Doctoral degree; or two Masters' degrees; or one Master's degree and two Bachelors' degrees provided at least one of the degrees is in a Special Field.

The initial certificate issued to all beginning teachers is Certificate II. All certificates are interim and may be made permanent upon completion of two years of successful teaching. The Certificates are valid for all grades. The Permits are awarded in the Special Fields of Music, Physical Education, Home Economics, Art, Library Science, Religious Knowledge, or any other fields approved by the Teachers' Certification Committee. The Permits are valid on a year-to-year basis for up to five years, provided the holder successfully completes at least one full course in education prior to the beginning of each year of teaching, and provided there is proof from the school board that the applicant has taught successfully in the Special Field during each year. They may be made permanent upon the successful completion of four full approved education courses (five courses for Permits V, VI and VII).

Yukon Territory

Certificate of Qualification—This certificate has five categories based on two to six years university or teacher education beyond grade twelve. A second requirement is a valid and subsisting teaching certificate or letter of eligibility from a province. The Certificate of Qualification is made permanent after two years of successful teaching.

C

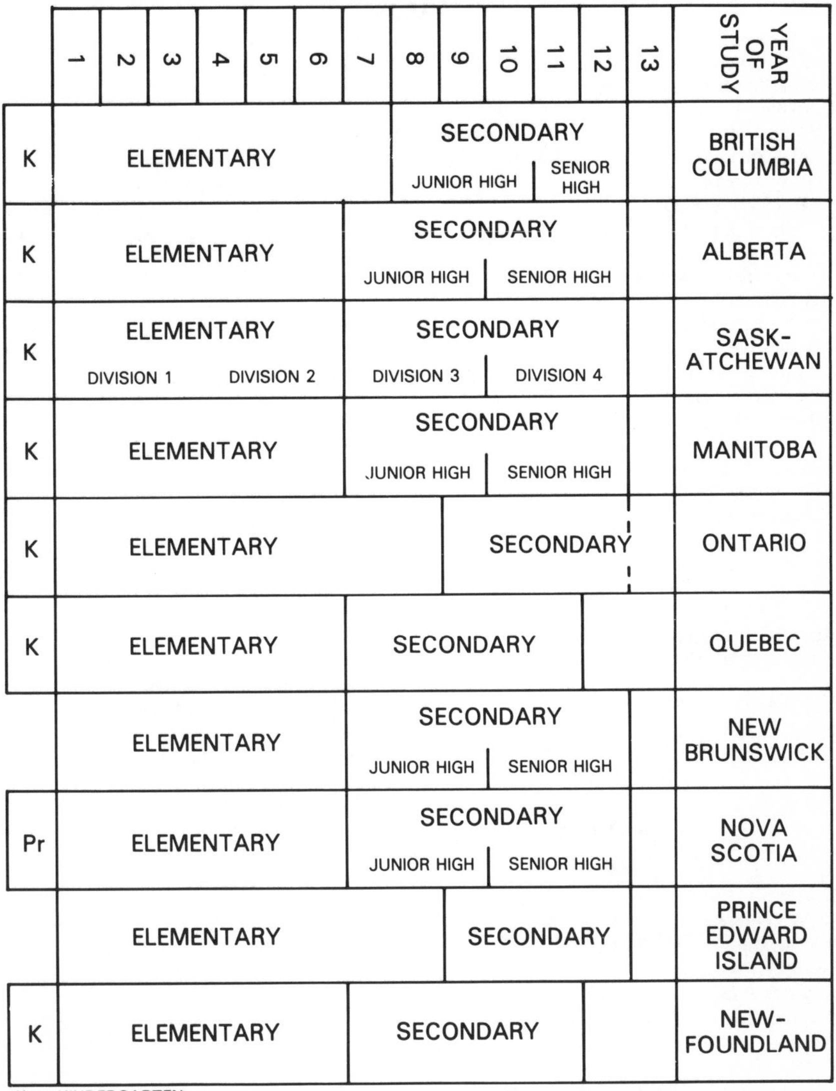

	1	2	3	4	5	6	7	8	9	10	11	12	13	YEAR OF STUDY
K	ELEMENTARY							SECONDARY — JUNIOR HIGH			SENIOR HIGH			BRITISH COLUMBIA
K	ELEMENTARY						SECONDARY — JUNIOR HIGH				SENIOR HIGH			ALBERTA
K	ELEMENTARY (DIVISION 1 — DIVISION 2)						SECONDARY (DIVISION 3 — DIVISION 4)							SASK-ATCHEWAN
K	ELEMENTARY						SECONDARY — JUNIOR HIGH				SENIOR HIGH			MANITOBA
K	ELEMENTARY								SECONDARY					ONTARIO
K	ELEMENTARY							SECONDARY						QUEBEC
	ELEMENTARY						SECONDARY — JUNIOR HIGH				SENIOR HIGH			NEW BRUNSWICK
Pr	ELEMENTARY						SECONDARY — JUNIOR HIGH				SENIOR HIGH			NOVA SCOTIA
	ELEMENTARY								SECONDARY					PRINCE EDWARD ISLAND
K	ELEMENTARY							SECONDARY						NEW-FOUNDLAND

K - KINDERGARTEN
Pr - PRIMARY

FIGURE C-1
COMPARISON OF PROVINCIAL ORGANIZATION OF STUDENTS

243

INDEX